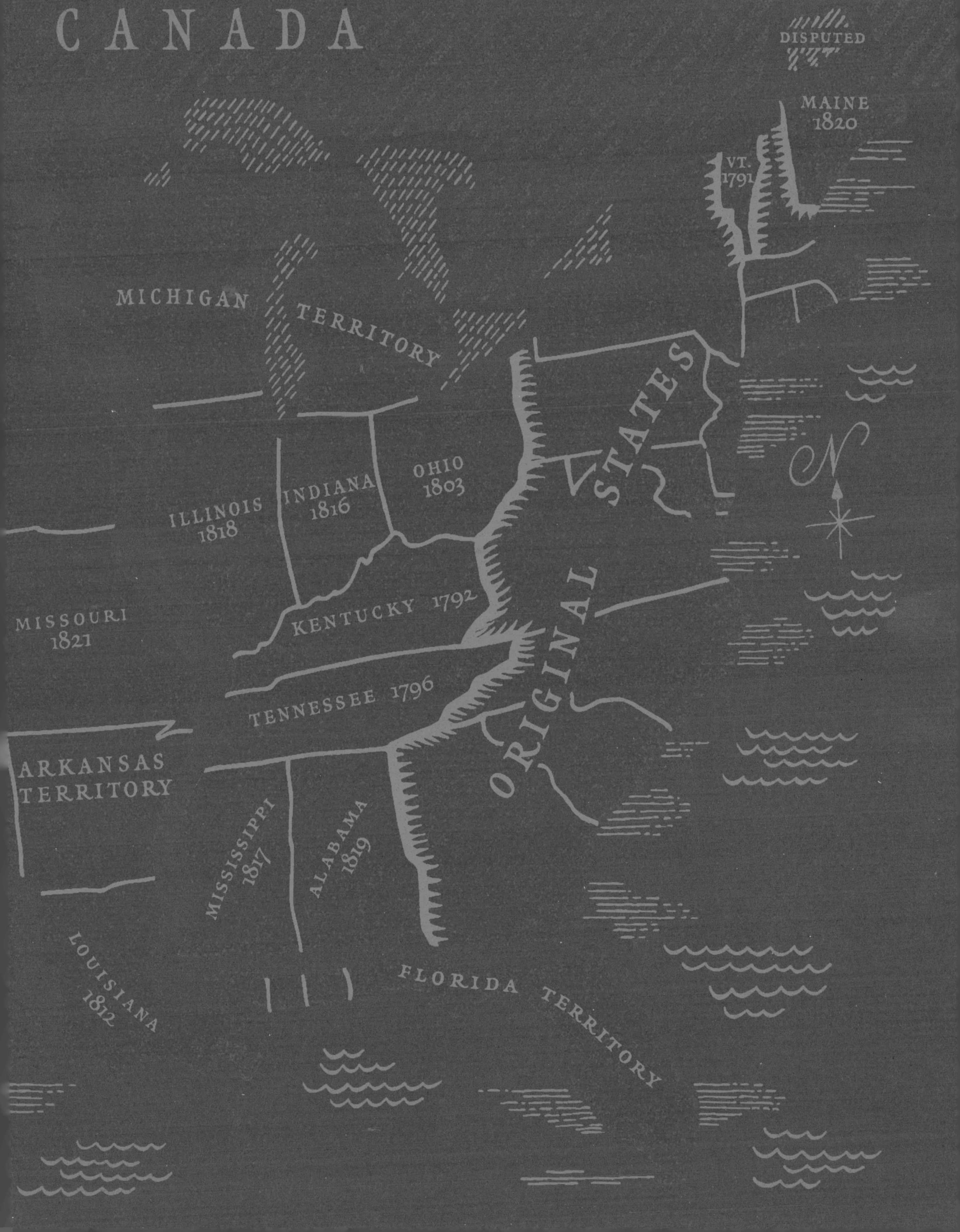

CANADA

DISPUTED

MAINE
1820

VT.
1791

MICHIGAN TERRITORY

OHIO
1803

ILLINOIS
1818

INDIANA
1816

ORIGINAL STATES

N

MISSOURI
1821

KENTUCKY 1792

TENNESSEE 1796

ARKANSAS
TERRITORY

MISSISSIPPI
1817

ALABAMA
1819

LOUISIANA
1812

FLORIDA TERRITORY

THE LIFE HISTORY OF THE UNITED STATES

Volume 3: 1789-1829

THE GROWING YEARS

OTHER BOOKS BY THE EDITORS OF LIFE

LIFE Nature Library

LIFE World Library

LIFE Pictorial Atlas of the World
   with The Editors of Rand McNally

The Epic of Man

The Wonders of Life on Earth
   with Lincoln Barnett

The World We Live In
   with Lincoln Barnett

The World's Great Religions

LIFE's Picture History of Western Man

The LIFE Treasury of American Folklore

America's Arts and Skills

The Second World War
   with Winston S. Churchill

LIFE's Picture History of World War II

Picture Cook Book

LIFE Guide to Paris

THE **LIFE** HISTORY OF THE UNITED STATES

Consulting Editor, Henry F. Graff

Volume 3: 1789-1829

THE GROWING YEARS

by Margaret L. Coit

and the Editors of LIFE

TIME INCORPORATED, NEW YORK

THE AUTHOR, Margaret L. Coit, combines in her work a continuing study of two fields, American history and the English language, both of which subjects she teaches at Fairleigh Dickinson University in New Jersey. This felicitous pairing of interests is seen in her book *John C. Calhoun*, which won many literary honors, including the Pulitzer Prize for biography in 1951. Her other works include a biography, *Mr. Baruch*, and a history, *The Fight for Union*. Born in Connecticut, Professor Coit earned her B.A. at the University of North Carolina, which later awarded her an honorary doctorate.

THE CONSULTING EDITOR for this series, Henry F. Graff, is Chairman of the Department of History at Columbia University.

TIME INC. BOOK DIVISION

EDITOR *Norman P. Ross*
COPY DIRECTOR *William Jay Gold*   ART DIRECTOR *Edward A. Hamilton*
CHIEF OF RESEARCH *Beatrice T. Dobie*

Editorial staff for Volume 3,
THE LIFE HISTORY OF THE UNITED STATES

SERIES EDITOR *Sam Welles*
ASSISTANT EDITOR *Jerry Korn*
DESIGNER *Douglas R. Steinbauer*
STAFF WRITERS *Gerald Simons, John Stanton,*
Harvey Loomis, Jonathan Kastner, Paul Trachtman
CHIEF RESEARCHER *Clara E. Nicolai*
RESEARCHERS *Sheila Osmundsen, Evelyn Hauptman, Malabar Brodeur,*
Natalia Zunino, Patricia Tolles, Barbara J. Bennett, Barbara Moir,
Lilla Lyon Zabriskie, Jacqueline Coates
PICTURE RESEARCHERS *Margaret K. Goldsmith, Theo Pascal*
ART ASSOCIATE *Robert L. Young*
ART ASSISTANTS *James D. Smith, John M. Woods, Douglas B. Graham*
COPY STAFF *Marian Gordon Goldman, Rosalind Stubenberg, Dolores A. Littles*

PUBLISHER *Jerome S. Hardy*
GENERAL MANAGER *John A. Watters*

LIFE MAGAZINE

EDITOR   MANAGING EDITOR   PUBLISHER
Edward K. Thompson   *George P. Hunt*   *C. D. Jackson*

Valuable assistance in the preparation of this volume was given by Roger Butterfield, who served as picture consultant; Doris O'Neil, Chief of the LIFE Picture Library; Donald Bermingham of the TIME-LIFE News Service; and Content Peckham, Chief of the Time Inc. Bureau of Editorial Reference.

THE COVER portrays "Pat Lyon at the Forge," John Neagle's warm study of a Philadelphia blacksmith. The picture, which also appears on page 21, was proudly commissioned by Lyon in 1825, after he had become well-to-do.

CONTENTS

1 THE REPUBLIC LAUNCHED   6
Penn's town in its federal heyday   20

2 THE NEW BATTLEFIELD OF POLITICS   32
A growing force in world markets   42

3 "A WISE AND FRUGAL GOVERNMENT"   54
Monticello: a founder's memorial   64

4 REACHING TO THE WEST   76
A vast, beckoning wilderness   86

5 A SECOND STRUGGLE FOR INDEPENDENCE   96
A small war on far-flung fronts   108

6 SLAVERY: THE GREAT DIVIDE   120
The flush times of King Cotton   134

7 THE END OF A HECTIC ERA   144
The rapid pace of transportation   156

CHRONOLOGY   168
BIBLIOGRAPHY   170
ACKNOWLEDGMENTS AND CREDITS   171
INDEX   172
LIST OF MAPS   173

WE OWE ALLEGIANCE TO NO CROWN.

1. THE REPUBLIC LAUNCHED

MARCH 4, 1789, was the date set for the meeting of the first Congress under the new federal Constitution. On that day guns boomed and church bells sounded in New York City, first capital of the United States of America. But the young republic was only gradually stirring into life. The distances were great and the roads bad, and the members of the first Congress took a long time to get to New York. Not until early April did the House have a quorum present so that it might organize. And only on April 6 could the Senate finally and officially count the ballots cast in February by the presidential electors and announce that George Washington was the unanimous choice as President and John Adams a narrow choice for Vice President.

Washington was named by the electors of only 10 states. New York was involved in an election tangle. Rhode Island and North Carolina had yet to ratify the Constitution. Other states-to-be were still standing in the wings. Kentucky was drawing up its application for statehood. Vermont was still calling itself an independent republic. The federal union's tremendous growing years were about to begin.

At Mount Vernon, waiting for the news he knew would arrive, the first President brooded in what he considered the evening of his years. He wrote to his old comrade of the Revolution, General Henry Knox, that his feelings were "not unlike those of a culprit who is going to the place of his execution."

On April 16 Washington left Mount Vernon, ready to answer his country's

A NEW NATION'S FERVOR infuses this colorful 19th Century banner, which was used in Fourth of July parades in Philadelphia. It honors the nation's seamen and its flag.

George Washington waves to well-wishers as he crosses New York harbor for his inauguration. En route he was serenaded by a choir singing an ode tactlessly set to the tune of "God Save the King." At the inauguration (below) he was obviously disconcerted by all the stir—"agitated and embarrassed," said an observer, "more than he ever was by the leveled cannon."

call but, as he wrote in his diary, "with less hope of answering its expectations." He rode out into the spring. Southward stretched an endless world of tobacco fields, rice fields and vast pine forests. Here, too, were the clay-chinked cabins of the poor. But in the Tidewater areas of the South, nearly every acre was held by landed proprietors of substantial wealth. Sons of this ruling class developed their habits of leadership by managing plantations, but they were not always men of culture. As the disdainful Yankee, Josiah Quincy, Jr., observed, listening to them talk about their cockfights and horse races, "You would think that the grand point of all science was properly to fix a gaff."

Virginia had set the pattern for this way of life. It was an English way. The state still had something of the look of the old England from which it had broken; Washington himself, that most unlikely of rebels, remembered that it had been for the rights of Englishmen that the colonies had fought.

What was true of the South was also true of the North: there was that same look and feel of old England in New England. Washington could still remember the steeples of Boston, as he had seen them in 1775, and the Old World look of Connecticut and Massachusetts: the walled fields, the villages around the greens. He had taken the measure of the Yankees, too, those farmers with much-used muskets and wary eyes, and the rawboned fishermen of Marblehead who had ferried him across the Delaware for a vital triumph at Trenton. Poor men, these hard-scrabbling Yankees often were, but not like the apathetic poor of other nations. Yankees could read the newspapers and the Bible, and they were all zealous in the cause of freedom. Shrewd and inquisitive, they astounded outsiders with their zest for news and argument.

Westward, in the valleys of the Ohio and Cumberland Rivers, was growing a new breed, equally tough and independent, but with a self-confidence amounting to cockiness. Out there, a man was better than his neighbor only if he measured up in the things that counted: virility, physical strength, aggressiveness. Books, culture, family background meant little. These people had conquered the wilderness and felt ready to take on the world. They lived on the edge of danger: in the little settlements along the bluffs of the Cumberland, in the huddled cabins back from the river banks, in the log shanties under the guns of Fort Pitt. Over all hung the ever-present fear of the Indian arrow.

Washington knew this country, too. He had seen the early frontier as a surveyor and a soldier and had appreciated the value of this great area extending from the Alleghenies to the mouth of the Mississippi. Now he knew that settlers were flowing West over the mountains from both North and South.

THIS was a nation of paradoxes. Its white population numbered slightly over three million, but its standing army totaled barely 900, with only a handful of men and a sergeant guarding the rusting muskets at West Point. It was a land whose citizens valued freedom more than most but tolerated slavery; and white redemptioners, or bound men, were still being landed at Atlantic ports to work off their debts in the New World. The Eastern cities were growing fast, but no white man had yet seen the source of the Mississippi. In the canebrakes of Kentucky, settlers were fighting Cherokees. In Connecticut, Noah Webster was trying to standardize an "American language," and in Pennsylvania, a tinkerer named John Fitch was experimenting with a steamboat.

It was an untamed nation, not only in its geography but also in the temper of the time. It was only six years away from its long Revolution, and barely two months from the loosely governed years under the Articles of Confederation. Could these 13 states now become one? Could a revolution be halted halfway? Most important of all, could freedom survive? Throughout history, one experiment in freedom after another had failed. Such questions must have hung heavily in Washington's mind as he rode northward.

THE Old Fox," Washington had been called, but he was more bear than fox. He was six feet tall, with sturdy shoulders, a big nose, reddish hair that was now gray and that look of power and authority large men often have. He had a wonderful quality of silence that in the noisy Constitutional Convention at Philadelphia in 1787 had taken on an eloquence of its own. He was the unlikely combination the people were seeking: a citizen-soldier, a steady, rocklike, responsible man. He was not a genius. There have been better soldiers, more capable executives, more creative statesmen. But he had been once, and was now again, pre-eminently the right man in the right place at the right time.

He had carried the weight of the Revolution on his shoulders, had torn victory out of defeat because he had never known when he was beaten. He could never give in, yet he was no statue. His were passions strung on a hair trigger. When told that the painter Gilbert Stuart had seen signs of a fierce temper controlled only with difficulty, Washington said soberly, "He is right."

He was too honest to evade anything. He was the good soldier who never refused his country's call. Like several later generals, he would bring to the presidential office more prestige than he found in it; unlike some, he would leave the office greater than he had found it, and with an authority that could be handed down to those who came after him.

That he was called the "Father of his Country" was no accident. He had been the patriarchal head of his family clan at 27; the wartime foster father of Lafayette and Hamilton; not only "our great and beloved General," but the father, too overcome to speak, kissing in turn each of his "grieving children" at that emotion-packed farewell to his officers in the Long Room of New York's Fraunces Tavern. Now the fire in him must be doused. The more deeply he felt, the more cautious he must become. He would crack nuts instead of jokes; the volatile Aaron Burr would find him dull.

Washington lacked college training, and felt all the more his need of assistance. But he knew how to utilize the genius of other men. They would be at his side soon—Hamilton and Knox, Jefferson and Adams, Randolph and Jay. But his would be the responsibility for turning into reality Patrick Henry's stirring declaration: "I am not a Virginian, but an American." He could sense the people's needs and transmute them into action, but he would not fawn. Before, he had kept an army from degenerating into a rabble. Now his task was to keep a republic from degenerating into anarchy.

At Gray's Ferry near Philadelphia two triumphal arches had been raised, and as the President-elect crossed the Schuylkill River in his barge, a wreath of laurel was placed upon his head. Every face beamed, every throat roared, and the President-elect was obviously moved. At Trenton, on the spot where he had led his half-frozen men to their incredible victory, was another arch, with 13 columns supporting it, and girls in white sang and strewed flowers in his path. It took him two days to cross New Jersey, making speeches in every hamlet. At last, on April 23, a crew of 13 men rowed his little boat over New York Bay. His journey was done. His task was about to begin.

Frederick Muhlenberg, first Speaker of the House, was the son of the founder of the Lutheran Church in America. Muhlenberg cast the tie-breaking House vote that provided funds to implement the Jay Treaty. A few days later his outraged brother-in-law—whose Republican Party was aligned almost unanimously against the treaty—stabbed him. Muhlenberg lived.

At 12:30 on April 30 the inaugural procession moved from Cherry Street to Federal Hall. There on the balcony, in a suit of American-made brown broadcloth, Washington stood. He was visible up and down the length of Wall Street, standing before a table draped in red. He advanced, placed his hand on his heart and bowed several times to the great crowd. Then he took the oath, as repeated cheers rang out for the President of the United States.

He assumed the presidency with characteristic humility. "On the one hand," he said in his Inaugural Address, "I was summoned by my country, whose voice I can never hear but with veneration and love, from a retreat which I had chosen with the fondest predilection . . . as the asylum of my declining years. . . . On the other hand, the magnitude and difficulty of the trust to which the voice of my country called me . . . could not but overwhelm with despondence one who, inheriting inferior endowments from nature and unpracticed in the duties of civil administration, ought to be particularly conscious of his own deficiencies." Later, bonfires blazed up in the streets along with a great display of fireworks. But the President's first act had been to join the members of Congress in the stately Georgian church of St. Paul's, with its checkerboard marble floor, its cream columns and blue ceilings. There Washington prayed, for himself and for the young republic.

The nation was getting into motion, though there were only about 350 federal employees under Washington—scarcely 100 more than the number of workers and slaves at Mount Vernon. Under the Constitution, the executive branch of the government would include only four department heads. Two were in office—Henry Knox, Secretary of War, and Postmaster General Samuel Osgood, both of Massachusetts, both holdovers from the Confederation. Not until July did Congress officially authorize the organization of the executive branch. Not until September were other department heads named. Alexander Hamilton of New York was appointed Secretary of the Treasury and Thomas Jefferson of Virginia, Secretary of State. But Jefferson was still in Paris as minister to France and would not take office until the following spring. An Attorney General, Edmund Randolph of Virginia, was selected in September —but it would be three years before he would achieve Cabinet rank.

Still, if not all the members of the official family were yet in office, several were on the scene. There were cheerful reunions—with the fat, ruddy-cheeked artillerist Knox, and, even more important, with Hamilton, "young Hamilton," as Washington would always think of him.

A New England town meeting flares into violence as two factions attempt to settle an argument with swords. The town, rather than the county, was the basic government unit in the Northeast, and all residents turned out— as they still do in many small New England communities— to elect public officials and vote on pending issues in a unique display of pure democracy.

As far back as 1780, when he had been stationed with Washington at Morristown, New Jersey, Hamilton had diagnosed "the fundamental defect" of the central government as "a want of power in Congress" and a lack of ability to tax directly. Now, nine years later, these defects were at last remedied, and Hamilton was on hand to play a new role. At 34, enthusiastic and self-assured, he was more handsome than ever, with his chiseled features, his auburn hair subdued by powder, his slight, erect figure always elegantly dressed in the high fashion of the day. But his eyes were hard. "Brilliant" was a word often used to describe him—he had a charm that scintillated and a diamond-like, many-faceted toughness of mind. Ever since the Revolution, his spirit of command had magnetized men into obeying him. Though physically frail, he was a demon for work; if undisturbed, he would labor unceasingly until dawn.

"The evil genius of America," Jefferson would later call him. Why? Although honestly and patriotically determined to help develop the young republic, he did not share Jefferson's conviction that free societies made free men, or that revolutions could alter human nature. Cynical and clear-sighted, even as Washington's wartime aide-de-camp he had known the first law of economics (paper money not backed by gold or silver quickly becomes worthless) and the first law of human nature (a man will do more for love of gain and power than for love of his fellow man). He had no illusions about self-sacrificial patriotism on the part of his compatriots.

In those war years he had conceived the principles of the broad fiscal program he would now try to translate into reality. To stabilize the currency, it was necessary to set up a national bank. The bank would be capitalized by borrowing both abroad and from private investors at home. In this way the nation's wealth would be placed on the side of and in the hands of government, for mutual advantage. Thus a wise government could divert ambition and interest to the public good. These were the guiding policies of Hamilton, one of the real geniuses of the Washington administration.

THE legislative branch of the new regime now began establishing the procedures and precedents so necessary in a continuing government. John Adams, as Vice President, wielded the gavel in the Senate. Frederick A. Muhlenberg of Pennsylvania was elected the first Speaker of the House, a post that would develop in significance with the developing years of the republic.

Among the immediate problems were how to get the new federal machinery under way and how to pay for it. The old Confederation had been crippled by its inadequate power to tax. Appropriately, one of the chief architects of the Constitution—James Madison, now a congressman from Virginia—started the federal revenue system off by introducing the first tariff bill. Signed by the President (also appropriately) on July 4, it covered some 30 items. In March 1791, upon the recommendation of Hamilton in his "Report on the Public Credit," Congress created the first excise—a tax on liquor.

Madison was also the prime mover in making the Constitution complete. There had been concern that it lacked a Bill of Rights. Certain states had withheld ratification until the Federalist leaders had promised to add the desired safeguards. The states had submitted dozens of suggestions; Madison boiled them down to 10, and on September 25, Congress voted to submit these and two others to the states for ratification. By 1791 the first 10 amendments had been adopted. They spelled out in detail the rights of American citizens to jury trial; to free press, speech and religion; to due process of law and so on. They have been known ever since as the Bill of Rights.

Another major measure passed by the first Congress was the Judiciary Act, which organized the third branch of the government. Two days after Washington signed the bill, he named John Jay as first Chief Justice of the United States with five Supreme Court associates. The role of the court was considerably different from what it later became. The first justices did not sit in a marble sanctuary but rode about the country, with two members of the court assigned to each of three circuits—eastern, middle and southern. Jay thought so little of his post that he later resigned to be governor of New York.

The powers of the presidency were only gradually established. Nobody was sure what they were—like everything else in the infant republic, the powers rather vaguely enumerated in the Constitution had to be developed by actual

Fighting cocks square off in a cockpit hemmed in by eager bettors of the early Republic. Cockfighting had quite a large following. Washington reportedly enjoyed the sport, and it is said that he once challenged his fellow Virginian Thomas Jefferson to match birds against a special variety he had imported from New Orleans. It is not known if Jefferson accepted.

practice. Washington, for instance, mindful of the clause requiring him to seek the "Advice and Consent of the Senate," walked into the Senate chamber one day, took Vice President Adams' chair and waited for some "advice and consent" on a pending Indian treaty. The silence was deafening, the embarrassment mutual. Both President and Senate somehow felt their dignity had been violated, and Washington was clearly irritated when the matter was finally referred to a committee. "This defeats every purpose of my coming here!" he said. Finally he stalked out—"sullenly," one senator thought.

The first Secretary of State, Thomas Jefferson was a shambling man careless of his appearance. "A laxity of manner seemed shed about him," a contemporary wrote. Yet in his youth he was so fastidious about his horses that he would not mount one until he passed a white kerchief over it to see if it was clean.

WHAT to call the President was a major cause of dissension. "His Excellency"? "His High Mightiness"? If we were to endow him with such lofty titles, protested one South Carolinian, we should also provide an embroidered robe, a crown and hereditary succession. The House even debated whether the Vice President should be paid his salary by the year; some feared he might choose to stay home on his farm and never show up for work. Sums of six dollars a day for House and Senate members and $12 for the Speaker were voted—and denounced in the newspapers as extravagant. Washington himself was less concerned by what he should be called than with what he should do. Some longed to see the tall, dignified-looking man followed by a train of uniformed flunkies; others thought Congress remiss for supplying him a house and furniture. He had no precedents. Humbly he sought advice, from Hamilton, from Adams. Should he keep open house? Should he visit?

The Senate insisted on the formalities. After receiving the annual message of 1791, a group of senators waited upon Washington. He stood before them, holding his hat throughout, and the senators gathered in a semicircle facing him as Vice President Adams read the address of reply, written by a committee headed by the erudite young senator from New York, Aaron Burr.

What Washington sensed, instinctively and correctly, was that in his own person he must symbolize the majesty and authority of the central government. What counted was not what he did so much as what he was. Most important was the symbol that the people chose to make of him. For this reason he set out in the fall of 1789 for a tour of the eastern states to show himself to the people who had not seen their President upon his ride north to the inauguration. This tour, too, was a triumph—more bonfires, arches and odes, a great outpouring of affection, with crowds flocking to gaze once more on that calm, resolved face.

Secretary of War Henry Knox was an established expert on field artillery but apparently not on fowling pieces. In 1773 while he was on a duckhunting expedition, his gun exploded and he lost two fingers. Ever afterward he wore a colorful handkerchief on the maimed hand when making public appearances.

From the start, Americans were concerned over their nation's finances. The national debt, that most unpleasant legacy of the Revolution, was well over $50 million. Another $25 million was owed by the states. The country's credit was nonexistent, and the cost of government was high. To solve all these problems, funds had to be found—and that was where Alexander Hamilton's plans came in. His first goal was to handle the debt. For until the nation began paying off its foreign debts—owed mainly to France, Spain and certain Netherlands bankers—it could never get the future credit it needed. Paying the debts and re-establishing credit, said Hamilton, were "the price of liberty." The domestic debt consisted largely of money owed to veterans of the Revolution and to small merchants who had helped support the war. Both groups had received government certificates promising to pay at a future date; the certificates had so lessened in value that thousands of holders had sold them to speculators for as little as 12 cents on the dollar. Now Hamilton proposed to make good the government's obligations—but only if the debt could be refunded at a lower interest rate. Furthermore, he wanted the nation to assume the $25 million in state debts; otherwise, he feared, there would be a ruinous competition between the state and federal governments to collect taxes.

The trouble was that the Northern states owed most of the debts, which Southern states would have to help pay. Furthermore, the speculators would benefit from the redemption of the certificates more than the hard-pressed Revolutionary veterans. Jefferson also believed it was Hamilton's purpose to get the wealth of the country on the side of government (as indeed it was; capitalists, he felt, would spend boldly and usefully), and the Virginian spoke bitterly of the assumption bill as a plum for "the stock-jobbing herd." Congress, spurred on by Jefferson's friend Madison, rejected Hamilton's plan; the House voted it down five times. But Hamilton, with that tenacity which characterized him, pressed all the harder.

Anxiously, he approached Jefferson, walked him up and down for half an hour. Some states were talking of secession unless the debt-assumption bill was passed, he said. The Union was in danger—and in such critical times "the members of the administration ought to act in concert." Jefferson suggested a dinner; he was sure reasonable men could arrange a compromise to save the Union. Dinner was served and a bargain made which Jefferson later regretted greatly. In return for two Southern votes needed to pass Hamilton's funding plan, the Hamiltonians would provide the few Northern votes necessary to locate the national capital on the banks of the Potomac, right next to Jefferson's own dear Virginia. Moreover, the debt-assumption bill would be rewritten to provide special subsidies to the states that had already paid off their debts; Virginia would be one of the chief beneficiaries.

Jefferson complained long after that he had been "ignorantly and innocently" misled by Hamilton on this log-rolling deal. But his "innocence" was typical of this most astute political craftsman who was to appear on the scene until Lincoln's time. For Jefferson had bought a great honor for his region at little cost—and to his friend James Monroe he wrote frankly that he considered some compromise necessary on the Hamilton plan to save America from the calamity of "the total extinction of our credit in Europe."

H AMILTON'S other major project, the establishment of the Bank of the United States, was also achieved with difficulty. Modeled after the Bank of England, it would be a part-private, part-public institution—a repository for federal funds, a source of federal loans and, not least, a major stimulus for American manufactures. Unlike the British bank, all of whose directors were chosen by stockholders, one fifth of the board of the American bank was to consist of government officials and one fifth of the stock was to be owned by the government. An 8 per cent dividend was anticipated.

Hamilton's bill was passed by Congress after relatively little debate, but in Washington's Cabinet it created a considerable disturbance. Before signing the measure, Washington sought the opinions of Randolph and Jefferson —and he even asked James Madison, whom he knew to oppose the bill, to draft a possible veto message.

All three of these Virginians opposed the bank on constitutional grounds. As Jefferson's written opinion sternly noted, there was nothing in the Constitution about the establishment of a national bank. Advancing the doctrine

Secretary of the Treasury Alexander Hamilton valued power more highly than philosophy. Jefferson once told Hamilton he considered Bacon, Newton and Locke the three greatest men the world had ever produced. Clearly surprised, Hamilton shot back: "The greatest man that ever lived was Julius Caesar."

Attorney General Edmund Randolph was so fickle two of his cousins, John Randolph and Thomas Jefferson, separately called him a "chameleon." "When he is with me," Jefferson said, "he is a whig. When with Hamilton he is a tory. When with the President, he is [what] he thinks will please him."

Mrs. John Adams (above) enjoyed Shakespeare, Handel and ballet— though the flimsy dancing clothes shocked her. But Alexander Hamilton felt that his wife (below) had neglected her intellect. Before their marriage he wrote her: "You excel most of your sex in all the amiable qualities, endeavor to excel them equally in the splendid ones." She tried for a while, but soon gave up.

that came to be known as "strict-constructionist," Jefferson asserted that the federal government had no right to take any action not specifically provided for in the Constitution and that the bank bill should therefore be vetoed by the President. Any other course, the Virginian claimed, would give the federal government a "boundless field of power." Hamilton countered with his own brand of constitutional interpretation, the "loose-constructionist" view. Where the Constitution did not set specific limits, he said, the national government had authority to act. He argued that if Americans intended to set up a government at all, they could not possibly object to having it provide the "necessary and proper" means to advance the public good.

Jefferson sensed instantly the implications of this doctrine of "implied powers." If the Constitution could be interpreted to mean what it did not actually say, then all sorts of powers could be invoked by the central government. But his objections to the proposed bank went even further. He was against it for one of the very reasons Hamilton was for it—that the bank could rear itself into a mammoth of special privilege, with its greatest advantages going to the men with the greatest wealth. It promised even further benefits—on top of those already provided by the funding-assumption act— to the North, where most of the wealth was concentrated, at the expense of the agrarian South.

Washington did not wholly agree with either Jefferson or Hamilton. But on February 25, 1791, he did sign the bill, apparently out of reluctance to use the veto, plus a growing conviction that a strong federal government was essential. As for the bank, its achievements during the 20-year life of its charter were all that Hamilton could have dreamed. It made the government more highly centralized and, just as Jefferson had feared, more closely linked to business interests in the Northeast than to landed property holders in the South and elsewhere. But, most important of all, for many years it gave the United States a sound dollar and a more prosperous economy than many thoughtful men had believed possible in the chaotic every-state-for-itself days of the old Confederation.

IN 1790, Philadelphia became the second American capital. It remained so until 1800, when the partially constructed government buildings in Washington were at last near enough completion to justify a move there. Philadelphia was the largest, gayest and most cosmopolitan city of the period (*see pages 20-31*), but some grim events marked its decade as the capital.

Late in 1791 came news that General Arthur St. Clair, sent to control the Indians in Ohio and Indiana by constructing a series of forts, had been routed near the Wabash by an inferior force of Indians after a woefully mismanaged campaign. Washington was infuriated. There were 900 casualties among St. Clair's 1,400 men. Americans in the region were convinced that the British were inciting the Indians to massacre the settlers. At last, in 1794 General "Mad Anthony" Wayne, a hero of the Revolution, struck hard at a war party of Indians who had gathered around a new British fort that had been built on United States soil. In the Battle of Fallen Timbers near what is now Toledo, Wayne decisively trounced the Indians and, for the moment, effectively pacified the frontier.

Yellow fever, disastrous in those days, repeatedly struck Philadelphia, but never in so ghastly a fashion as in the outbreak of 1793. All business stopped;

whole families died; hungry, orphaned children roamed the streets. Some stagecoaches and wagons out of Philadelphia were shot at or burned by people in the countryside who feared infection. At one point 17,000 people—about one third of the population—were refugees from the city. When at last the advent of cool weather brought the epidemic to an end, between 4,000 and 5,000 Philadelphians were dead of the disease.

ALTHOUGH Hamilton was probably the foremost figure of Washington's official family, the place of honor at the President's right was reserved for the Secretary of State Thomas Jefferson. At 47, he was the oldest of the President's advisers. He was rawboned and redheaded, and he startled his neighbors by stalking forth in the red breeches and waistcoat of revolutionary France. From the moment he assumed office in March 1790, to face a towering stack of important documents and a three-week nervous headache, he and Hamilton, by his own account, were "pitted against each other every day in the cabinet like two fighting-cocks." Jefferson saw Hamilton's philosophy as opposing everything in which he most deeply believed. Actually, each felt that the virtue and talent of a "natural aristocracy" should rule; but Hamilton, unlike Jefferson, felt that these qualities were to be found mainly in the rich, and that inequality was the natural result of liberty. Hamilton favored the bankers and merchants, Jefferson the farmers and plantation owners. Hamilton, almost alone in his time, was aware of the implications of the Industrial Revolution and looked to an industrial America. Jefferson shunned the idea. The Virginian favored the broadest possible extension of democracy; Hamilton looked to a strong government that would put down mob rule and divert man's natural selfishness to the public good.

Hamilton may well have termed the Constitution, as written, "a shilly-shally thing," but he felt that the implied powers provided what was necessary and proper. Certainly, if the government had the power to build warships it had the power to raise the money to build them. Jefferson, on the other hand, saw government itself as the enemy and corrupter of the people and favored only the most limited police powers. Hamilton, himself a man of overpowering ambition, was convinced that Jefferson's only desire was to be President. Moreover, the Secretary of the Treasury felt that the Secretary of State had a "womanish attachment" to France and French ideals.

Jefferson knew France, it is true, and he had just seen the start of the French Revolution. To him and other Americans it had seemed a shining beginning, and news of the French Republic's victories against invading armies intent on restoring the king brought outbursts of toasts and cannonades in America. Liberty poles were raised and oxen roasted. All over the United States men put on cockades and called each other "citizen," sang French marching songs and toasted the French Republic and the Rights of Man.

News that France had beheaded its king jolted many people out of their delirium. And when the movement steadily became more brutal and dictatorial, even Jefferson had little good to say of it. Washington left Mount Vernon and called the Cabinet into session. We had been allies of royal France. Were we bound to republican France? Should we declare neutrality? Should we receive the new French minister? But the minister did not await an invitation.

On April 8, 1793, a 36-gun French frigate entered Charleston harbor. Down the gangplank walked Citizen Edmond Genêt, 30 years old, on fire with his

Life was a series of reverses for General Arthur St. Clair (above). He failed in college, failed in an effort to be a doctor, in the Revolution lost the "impregnable" Fort Ticonderoga to the British, and finally, in 1791, was defeated in the Northwest by Indians. The tough "Mad Anthony" Wayne (below), called in to do the job, bested the Indians at Fallen Timbers in 1794.

mission, and about as safe to have around as a lighted time bomb. "Never in my opinion," wrote Jefferson, "was so calamitous an appointment. . . . He renders my position immensely difficult." As Genêt moved on Philadelphia, in one long parade of ovations, civic feasts and passionate avowals of how much France loved America and America loved France, a parade of a different sort began marching into the office of the Secretary of State—a parade of complaints. Genêt, this one-man expeditionary force, had turned every French consulate into a court of admiralty. He had bought armed vessels to hunt down British merchantmen. He had agents busy stirring up forays against Spain in the South and West, and Jefferson was even informed that whole armies were gathering to lay siege to New Orleans and the Floridas. A protest soon arrived from the British minister that privateers were being fitted out in Charleston and that American ships, loaded with guns, were already on their way to France. A French frigate equipped by Genêt actually seized a British merchantman in American waters.

The danger to the United States was obvious. Neutrality had been declared by the time of Citizen Genêt's arrival in Philadelphia, but could it be maintained? In the capital city, the French minister was greeted by thousands of cheering Americans. In chilly contrast was his formal reception by Washington. The young Frenchman proceeded to instruct the President on his duty, and to make the time-hallowed request of a foreign envoy—for money. After all, the United States still owed France more than two million dollars which could be credited toward purchases. He suggested that a commercial treaty be drawn up immediately. Jefferson pointed out that the Senate was not in session, and the Senate was required to ratify a treaty. Hamilton added that Great Britain would say we were violating neutrality—and that we had no money anyway. Angered, Genêt shot back that he would credit part of the war debt due from America to anyone who would sell him goods.

Washington held firm. So did Jefferson, sternly rebuking the young Frenchman for communicating directly with the President by letter. "His conduct has been that of a madman," wrote James Madison. Genêt was finally recalled by his government, at America's request, and a new French minister arrived. But the Revolution had moved so quickly that it was learned a guillotine now awaited Citizen Genêt. He had to seek sanctuary in the country he had tried to drag into conflict. Retiring from history, he found some consolation by marrying the daughter of Governor Clinton of New York and siring generations of good Americans.

AFTER the antics of Citizen Genêt, there came a revolutionary challenge to law and order at home. In retrospect, the Whiskey Rebellion of 1794 seems a minor incident of history, but it was the first serious threat to the authority of the young federal government. The first excise, the 1791 tax on whiskey, had created an uproar among the farmers of western Pennsylvania. The economy of the upper Monongahela was virtually based on distilled spirits. Since farmers raised more grain than they could eat or transport, they found it necessary to convert the surpluses into a product that was handy to carry. That product was rye whiskey, which was interchangeable with money all through the region. The tax—which ranged, at various times, and for various qualities of whiskey, from seven to 25 cents per gallon—was a savage blow. At least one federal official who tried to collect it was tarred

Demonstrating against the treaty with Britain, angry citizens burn an effigy of John Jay, who negotiated it. Reactions were violent everywhere. In Charleston, copies of the treaty were burned and a Jay effigy was hanged. In New York, Hamilton defended the pact in public and was stoned. In Philadelphia, another effigy was filled with powder and blown to bits.

and feathered. Farmers who told where stills were located (stills, too, were taxed) had their barns burned. Court officials in the area were terrorized, and there was even a threat of an armed attack on Pittsburgh.

The governor of Pennsylvania was too frightened to take action. But Washington, urged on by Hamilton, was determined to stamp out insurrection. He got a Supreme Court justice to declare that the courts were unable to enforce the law in the strife-torn area; then he called up the militia. The response was staggering. The United States wound up with a volunteer army of 15,000—more than Washington had led for most of the Revolution. Soldiers marched from Trenton, Philadelphia and Baltimore. Daniel Morgan, hero of Cowpens, led the troops from Virginia. Youngsters who had missed the Revolution thrilled to the hard six-week march in the rain and mud over the jagged slopes of the Alleghenies to encampments white with tents by day and red with campfires by night.

The show of strength terrified the insurrectionists, and the soldiers actually had to scour the countryside for them. At Parkinson's Ferry the militia caught the suspects, hauling them from their beds and marching them off half-dressed. Actually only two men were found guilty of treason, and Washington later pardoned those. But the troops came home proud as peacocks in their uniforms and were toasted as heroes, not quite knowing that they had been part of a great experiment. The first challenge had been met: men of one state would, if necessary, invade the territory of another to preserve the authority of the federal government.

IN 1794, there occurred an event that history was to view as one of the most important acts of Washington's Administration and certainly the most courageous. It was also at the time the most vilified, and it ended the legend of his political invincibility. The "crime" for which he was attacked was the Jay Treaty of 1794. The treaty was an attempt to solve the nation's chief foreign policy problem of the time: how to live in peace with a Britain that Americans wanted to fight but were in no condition to fight. Certainly American grievances were real. The British still held their military posts in the Northwest Territory, monopolizing the fur trade and arousing the Indians against the pioneers. As part of its war with France, Britain was halting and searching American ships, seizing their cargoes and forcing American sailors to serve in the British navy. Britain was trying to stop not merely America's trade with France itself but with overseas French possessions; in one affair, a number of United States ships in the harbor of Martinique were boarded, set adrift or sunk, and their crews imprisoned.

Yet war was unthinkable. Obviously negotiations were in order, particularly with the more powerful and annoying of the combatants. At Washington's request, Chief Justice John Jay sailed for England as a special envoy. Jay's diplomatic experience in Europe during the Revolution, and his effective service as the nation's Secretary for Foreign Affairs under the Articles of Confederation, eminently qualified him for the assignment. But he faced a thankless task, since he had little leverage with which to pry concessions from Britain.

After some months of bargaining, Jay signed a treaty on November 19. It settled two real grievances: Britain agreed to pay for certain goods seized from American ships and promised to withdraw from their Northwest posts by June 1796. The treaty also made some improvements in Anglo-American trading

Insurgents mob a tax collector in the Whiskey Rebellion. Drink was the cause of the uprising but also helped keep it from growing. In 1794 more than 2,000 rebels were set to attack the federal garrison in Pittsburgh—but as they marched through the streets, the townsmen plied them with whiskey by the hundreds of gallons. They got to their destination in no condition to fight.

Winner in the government-sponsored competition for a presidential residence was this Georgian design by James Hoban, who later supervised the building's construction. Congress voted to give a prize award of either $500 or a gold medal for the design. Hoban, who had to feed a wife and his 10 children, chose the $500.

One of the many entrants in the White House design competition was a mysterious Mr. A. Z. For years the plan (above) was attributed to builder Abraham Faws. Then the truth came out. Believing a gentleman should sometimes remain anonymous, Thomas Jefferson had kept his authorship secret.

conditions. But on a long list of other problems the treaty was silent. It did not guarantee against the impressment of American seamen, nor end Britain's interference with American shipping. It said nothing about British support of the Indians or about British payments for slaves removed during the Revolution. And it did guarantee payment of large pre-Revolutionary debts owed to Englishmen by American citizens (finally settled for $2,664,000 in 1802).

When these disagreeable terms were made public in June 1795, there was a storm of protest. Jay was condemned as a traitor who had betrayed liberty for gold. The words "Damn John Jay. Damn everyone who won't damn John Jay!" were painted on the wall of a house in Boston. Jeffersonians claimed that the treaty was signed at the expense of France. Southerners were furious at the lack of any British restitution for the stolen slaves. Westerners objected to the omission of more specific terms dealing with the Indian troubles. Even Hamilton, at whose urging the treaty had been negotiated because his revenue system required it for success, reportedly condemned Jay as "an old woman" for agreeing to its terms. In France a toast was drunk to "The Republic of America: May she never mistake Jaybirds for eagles."

Washington, too, disliked the treaty. But it was obviously the best that could be had, and the President finally submitted it for ratification after holding it up for months. For two weeks the Senate engaged in heated debate. At last it reluctantly accepted the treaty by the necessary two thirds vote. Then the House of Representatives, where the opposition was stronger, tried to make the treaty ineffective by refusing to appropriate the money needed to carry out its provisions. The House also asked to see all the papers relating to the treaty; Washington's refusal to show such documents—on the ground that treaty matters were the sole prerogative of the Senate—set a vital precedent. Not until April 30, 1796—nearly a year after the Senate had ratified Jay's Treaty—did the House finally appropriate the money.

Washington had put aside local interests on this entire question. As President, he had looked on America as a whole and disregarded the mood of the moment to think of the future. But he was no longer the popular hero he had been before. He was attacked venomously, and the attacks were, to a great degree, partisan. More and more, it was becoming clear that a great split existed among the nation's political leaders, with the Federalists of Washington and Hamilton arrayed against the Republicans led by Thomas Jefferson. And the Republicans—anti-British, pro-French, against a strong central government and in favor of democracy—were gaining strength steadily. At the same time, the assaults on Washington mounted. The traditional celebrations of his birthday in towns across the land tapered off or became occasions of controversy, and the House in 1796 even failed to offer its usual birthday tribute.

To add to Federalist troubles, Alexander Hamilton got himself involved in a mess. Early in Washington's administration, when the Secretary of the Treasury was issuing his reports on public credit and other fiscal matters, Jefferson's followers became convinced that it might be possible to pin evidence of wrongdoing on him. Then, in December 1792, James Monroe was told of financial irregularities in the Treasury Department, which, it was said, could "hang the Secretary." Hamilton, who had made the Treasury so airtight that it took four signatures for him to get his own salary, was appalled.

The fact is that he did have a guilty secret—and his accuser knew all about it. It involved not the Treasury but the secretary's personal life. Although Hamilton was the most tender and devoted of husbands and fathers at home, he indulged warmer passions outside. A year earlier he had been trapped into paying attentions to a Mrs. James Reynolds—and soon after that, into paying blackmail to her husband, who had arranged the trap. Then Reynolds, who had a long background of illegal activities, was arrested for trying to fleece a former soldier. When Hamilton refused to come to his rescue, Reynolds told the secretary's political enemies that he could supply evidence of Hamilton's criminal activities in the Treasury Department. This was the information that had come to Monroe.

To avoid a congressional investigation, Hamilton was obliged to tell Monroe and two others the whole sordid story of his affair with Mrs. Reynolds. Monroe and his two political colleagues agreed to keep the secret.

But by 1797, at the height of the Federalist-Republican rancor, some of the racier details leaked into the Republican press. Hamilton, convinced that Monroe was responsible, first threatened the Virginian with a duel. When friends convinced him that a duel would solve nothing, he decided with characteristic courage to bare his private shame. He issued a pamphlet admitting his affair with Mrs. Reynolds. The story created a sensation. Hamilton's wife stood firmly by him, but Republicans rejoiced in his discomfiture. Most important, his political career fell into shadow. If Hamilton had any hopes of someday running for the presidency, this episode dashed them forever.

Noah Webster is famous for his dictionary, but another successful work was a speller (below). It contained many words, but omitted "God"— because, he said, "nothing has greater tendency to lessen the reverence for the Supreme Being than a careless repetition of his name upon every trifling occasion."

THE eight years of Washington's administration had passed. He had refused to run again; instead his Vice President, John Adams, was elected to the office. Washington's work was done. He had played his part of leader with skill and reluctance. He had neither turned the young republic into a dictatorship nor let it tear itself apart. The nation still had its troubles. But taxes were hardly known, and in virtually every home there was evidence of solid prosperity. Washington despised politics, but he had learned the politician's chief stock in trade of "appearing to accommodate and yet carrying his point," as the acute Abigail Adams had observed. Still he shrank from becoming a party chieftain, and he was too thin-skinned for partisan abuse.

Before leaving the presidency, Washington left a last testament in which he paid his final respects to partisan politics and the political rancor that was in the air. In his Farewell Address, which he sent to the newspapers, he warned against permitting political parties and the dissension they stirred up to weaken the unity so necessary for the nation's survival. He cautioned also against permanent alliances with other countries and instead recommended "temporary alliances for extraordinary emergencies." (He did not use the phrase "entangling alliances" often credited to him; Jefferson later did so in his First Inaugural Address.)

The Farewell Address only brought more abuse down on Washington's head. He had forced the nation into a treaty with Britain, people said, yet now was afraid of a treaty with France. "If ever a nation was debauched by a man," a newspaper said, "the American nation has been debauched by Washington." "All self-respect is forgotten!" cried another.

Haggard and drained, farmer Washington prepared to leave Philadelphia for Mount Vernon. He did not look back. A Republican journal, pleased to see him go, advised its readers: "Lettest thy servant depart in peace."

Groan, to figh
Grown. increafed
  Hail, to falute, or frozen
    drops of rain
  Hale, found, healthy
Hart, a beaft
Heart, the feat of life
  Hare, an animal
  Hair, of the head
Here, in this place
Hear, to hearken
  Hew, to cut
  Hue, to colour
Him, that man
Hymn, a facred fong
  Hire, wages
  High er, more high
Heel, of the foot
Heal, to cure
  I, myfelf
  Eye, organ of fight
Isle, an Ifland
Ile, of a church
  In, within
  Inn, a tavern

Penn's town in its federal heyday

BEFORE the Revolution, William Penn's "greene countrie towne" had grown into the most populous and prosperous of American cities. But even greater expansion was started by a political windfall in 1790. The Residence Act, which ordained that the nation's permanent capital would be built on the Potomac, snatched the federal government from New York and awarded it temporarily to Philadelphia, already the home of Pennsylvania's state government. With the arrival of President Washington and his glittering "Republican court," the Quaker city rose to a cosmopolitan brilliance.

In the next 10 years, waves of immigrants swelled the population by 50 per cent to 81,000, feeding skilled craftsmen into the booming economy and spilling farmers into the rich hinterlands to return more produce to Philadelphia markets *(below)*. Affluence kept the city progressive, humanitarian and boiling with intellectual activity. Wealthy Philadelphians encouraged gifted scientists and established American painting with their lavish patronage. Thus Philadelphia became in fact, as it had once been described in high-flown rhetoric, the "mistress of our world, the seat of art, of science and of fame."

IN BUSY MARKETS, Philadelphians buy fresh foods brought to town in Conestoga wagons. In the background is "Cooke's Folly," so named because it struck townspeople as pretentious.

AT THE FORGE, Pat Lyon *(opposite)* labors in sight of Walnut Street Jail, where he was once held on false charges. Exonerated, he made sure the jail appeared in his triumphal portrait.

PENN'S TREATY ELM, in whose shade the Quaker founder reputedly made peace with the Indians, frames a long arc of wharves on the Delaware River. The country's largest port,

Philadelphia recovered quickly from the commercial stagnation of the Revolution. Its foreign trade quadrupled between 1791 and 1796, and more than 1,400 ships docked here in 1797.

The firm foundations of progress and civic pride

PHILADELPHIA'S flowering in the decade that followed Franklin's death in 1790 was due in no small degree to institutions Ben himself had helped to start: America's first public library; the American Philosophical Society, the country's oldest scientific body; a school that grew into the University of Pennsylvania; the intrepid Union Fire Company. Combining business acumen with a Quaker sense of responsibility, the town's citizens went on to found a college of medicine, a free dispensary, a commercial bank, a daily newspaper—each the first of its kind in America. Having laid this groundwork, Philadelphia in the '90s burst its city limits, paved many streets, appointed public parks, built a turnpike to Lancaster, started construction of a bridge across the Schuylkill and set up a unique municipal water system.

INDEPENDENCE HALL, a constant reminder of Philadelphia's role as the birthplace of freedom, is visited by a group of Indians (*right*). The present clock steeple was erected in 1828.

A PERAMBULATING OYSTERMAN, whose cry "Ah yer oys-ta-oh!" preceded him by blocks, sells his wares to strollers. Behind him is the Chestnut Street Theatre, whose opening in 1794 made Philadelphia the nation's capital of drama. When a famous actor was billed here, crowds would wait all day to get in and sometimes ruined their clothes in the rush for seats.

The cosmopolitan world of ordinary folk

EVERYDAY life in Philadelphia was characterized by a distinctive urbanity. Citizens of many national origins rubbed elbows in a tolerant society where money opened doors formerly closed to all save those of gentle birth. Despite a number of yellow-fever epidemics, the people went on acquiring, spending, expanding. They worked in more and more specialized trades, some of which banded into protective unions. They began doffing breeches and buckled shoes in favor of pants and boots. They drank lager beer, ate that new delight "ice cream," took up dance fads like the "pigeon-wing," and improved their minds at the theater and their prospects in flirtations by lamplight. Yet they found time to attend their churches, which were so numerous that one foreign visitor described Philadelphia as "almost . . . an Imperial or Popish city," with "always something to be chimed."

A QUAKER FAMILY arrives at the Arch Street Meeting House. Quakers dressed sedately, but the women—"distinguished by fine figures and small feet"—made their frocks of rich fabrics.

Philadelphia Anabaptists watch as their religious leader immerses a believer. The sect, of Germanic origin, included the Mennonites.

A great tinkerer and genius of the arts and sciences

THE artists, scientists and students who flocked to Philadelphia in its golden decade soon found at the center of things a long-nosed, birdlike man with inexhaustible energy and enthusiasm. He was the painter Charles Willson Peale, whom John Adams described as "a tender, soft, affectionate creature" who "has vanity, loves finery, wears a sword, gold lace...."

A captain in the Revolution, a friend to Jefferson and Lafayette, Peale was astoundingly versatile. He made boots, repaired watches, developed new techniques of taxidermy, invented a corn planter and fashioned dental plates for George Washington. In the sciences, his supreme achievement was his discovery of a mastodon (below), whose skeleton attracted thousands to his natural history museum (opposite). In the arts, he contributed a superb gallery of portraits of the great men of America's youth. Under his leadership, 71 eminent Philadelphians founded the Pennsylvania Academy of the Fine Arts, which still keeps their pledge "to unfold, enlighten and invigorate" the talents of their countrymen.

EXHUMING A MASTODON, the first to be shown complete, Peale (at the edge of the pit) directs workmen in his picture of his greatest coup. For rights to dig, he paid $300 and a rifle.

SELF-PORTRAIT AT 81 shows Peale (opposite), still vigorous and upright, presenting his collection of stuffed birds and mastodon bones, on display in the Long Room of Independence Hall.

IN A RESIDENTIAL AREA, a troop of militia gallops down High Street, later renamed Market Street after the stalls that lined it near the Delaware. Washington lived three blocks away.

IN A SHOP DISTRICT, loungers *(below)* near the building at left, which housed butchers, watch passersby at the intersection of Second and High Streets, in the heart of the old city.

An orderly pattern of busy streets and elegant buildings

BUILT to a checkerboard town plan, Philadelphia stretched its grid of tree-lined avenues between two rivers with a regularity which one critical foreign visitor called "a mathematical infringement on the rights of individual eccentricity." But the city was slowly gaining in architectural variety. Buildings in the classical new Federal style arose beside more elaborate Georgian structures and among the "brave brick houses" of early Quakers. Some Federal show places, such as Alexander Hamilton's Bank of the United States (right), ran to giant size and colonnaded marble façades. One mansion was so lavish that aspiring young architect Charles Bulfinch was moved to moralize: "Elegance of construction . . . and the utmost magnificence of decoration make it a palace . . . too rich for any man in this country."

"A TRULY GRECIAN EDIFICE," built to house the Bank of the U.S., still stands on South Third Street. Its high costs caused "an injurious deviation" from marble to brick for its sides.

MOURNING WASHINGTON, who had died in Virginia 12 days before, Philadelphians (below) in doleful procession escort an empty casket through the city streets on December 26, 1799.

Philadelphia on the Fourth

In 1800 the federal government moved from the Delaware's banks to its permanent home on the Potomac. Yet Philadelphia continued its phenomenal growth. In 1819, when J. L. Krimmel painted these Fourth of July festivities in the nation's birthplace, most of the city's 130,000 people turned out to

celebrate with the usual banquets, fireworks and patriotic addresses. Many who watched the soldiers parade past the domed marble waterworks *(background)* could remember the controversy that structure had provoked as it materialized from Benjamin Latrobe's drawing board around 1800. Fewer could remember back to 1790, when the Fourth, falling on Sunday, was soberly observed with religious ceremony. But in 1819 only a handful were left who could recall the actual event. The Fourth, by then overlaid with almost a half century of history, had passed from personal experience into national tradition.

31

2. THE NEW BATTLEFIELD OF POLITICS

JOHN ADAMS was his own worst enemy. No President ever stood more in his own shadow—a weighty shadow indeed, for in every sense John Adams was a weighty man. He was also a profound and original thinker, a courageous patriot and one of those tragic examples in American history of a great man who did not make a great President. Many lesser men in the presidential office have accomplished more, perhaps because they realized, as Adams never did, that it is only what a man earns as a politician that pays for his right to be a statesman.

In many ways, Adams would seem to have been made for his job. He had sharpened his fine mind at Harvard, shown his moral fiber by serving as defense attorney for the hated British redcoats who were tried for the Boston Massacre, spoken eloquently and worked tirelessly in the Continental Congress. He had learned foreign affairs at first hand as an American envoy in France, Holland and Britain, and had gained a first-hand knowledge of domestic affairs as Vice President during the first eight years of the republic. He had married a remarkable woman, Abigail Smith, whose charm did not disguise her force of character. He had sired a remarkable son, John Quincy, through whom the impressive Adams line would continue.

Alexander Hamilton, who was John Adams' chief opponent in his own Federalist party, said with some truth that Adams had "disgusting egotism" and an "ungovernable indiscretion of . . . temper." But the more generous

THE MEMORABILIA OF A STATESMAN remain on the desk of John Adams in his home in Massachusetts: his quills, his book of correspondence, a letter to Thomas Jefferson.

Thomas Jefferson, his chief opponent among the Republicans (who were to develop into the modern Democrats), wisely observed in 1787 after years of regular communication with him that Adams was "as disinterested as the being who made him," and "so amiable, that I pronounce you will love him if ever you become acquainted with him."

This forthright pepperpot of a man wrote some of the best letters of his time. A puritan who believed that "men are never good but through necessity," he yet enjoyed all five of his senses. Eminently practical, very sure of himself, Adams had high intentions and unyielding integrity. He also had too much individuality and independence to work effectively with others. Another great handicap throughout his administration was his frequent absence from the seat of government. He liked to live and work amidst a pleasant clutter of books and papers in his comfortable house at Quincy, Massachusetts. George Washington, although he had an equally deep devotion for Mount Vernon, had been away from the capital only 181 days in eight years as President—and often then only because he was on official tours. In four years Adams was away 385 days, sometimes for months at a time. And he was hard to reach, more than 400 miles from Washington in an era when every kind of transportation was slow and difficult.

The "Old House," John Adams' mansion in Quincy, Massachusetts, is now a national shrine. Adams himself sometimes called it Montezillo, which he whimsically explained by saying "Mr. Jefferson lives at Monticello the lofty Mountain. I live at 'Montezillo' a little Hill." Adams was also the first occupant of the White House, for which he wrote the blessing below.

I Pray Heaven To Bestow THE BEST OF BLESSINGS ON This House And All that shall hereafter Inhabit it May none but Honest and Wise Men ever rule under This Roof.

IN the election of 1796, Adams had barely managed to best Jefferson, 71 electoral votes to 68. Many citizens were still angry over the Jay Treaty and blamed the Federalists for it. When he took office the new President assumed not merely the burdens Washington left behind, but also a unique additional load: for the only time in American history, the Vice President was the President's recent opponent in the campaign. In office, Jefferson, who could handle men and political situations with a shrewdness Adams seldom showed, was to combine various forces hostile to Adams and his policies, thus furthering his own succession to the presidency.

Adams' immediate problem was with France, which was now pursuing a hostile course toward America. The French had been infuriated by the Jay Treaty, which allowed the British to confiscate French goods found on American vessels and accordingly—in French eyes—made the United States simply a tool of England. They were also angered by the recall of Minister James Monroe, a notable Francophile. By the time Adams assumed office in March 1797, France had seized some 300 American ships and had ordered Monroe's Federalist successor, Charles Cotesworth Pinckney, to leave French soil. The new President summoned a special session of Congress, but even before it met word came that the French government had proclaimed that all neutral ships bound for British ports would be subject to seizure. Many Federalists were eager to wage war against France. But Adams favored peace and greater preparedness, knowing America was not ready to defend itself against an invasion that France might attempt. He decided to send a bipartisan mission to Paris, in the hope of improving relations and ending the French seizures of American vessels.

Pinckney, John Marshall and a leading Republican, Elbridge Gerry of Massachusetts, arrived in France in October. They were unofficially received by Foreign Minister Talleyrand, but he found excuses for postponing any official negotiations for a treaty of commerce and friendship. Subsequently, however, the American delegation was visited by three aides of Talleyrand named

Hottinguer, Bellamy and Hauteval, who proposed an American loan to France—and a bribe of nearly a quarter of a million dollars for Talleyrand's own pocket. Appalled and angry, the three American emissaries reported the affair to Adams, describing the agents as X, Y and Z. When one of the French agents pressed for an answer, he was told by one of the Americans, "It is No! No! Not a sixpence!"

Without disclosing these unpleasant facts, the President told Congress in March 1798 that the mission had failed, and that America must prepare for war: coastal fortifications must be strengthened and foundries established. Some members of both parties cried out in protest, with the Republicans in particular raging that they would not fight alongside England against the country's noble ally of the Revolutionary War. In April, Adams gave Congress all the correspondence in the "XYZ Affair," and the tide turned overnight. Adams was suddenly abreast a roaring torrent of popularity. Crowds in the theaters shouted for the "President's March," and cries for French songs were hissed and howled down. A new version of Yankee Doodle was struck up:

> Bold Adams did in '76
> Our Independence sign, sir,
> And he will not give up a jot,
> Tho' all the world combine, sir.

On the night of May 7, 1798, a crowd of 1,200 young men cheered Adams at his home, wearing in their hats the black cockade, or badge, associated with the American Revolution and liberty. The Federalists adopted a new slogan, "Millions for defence, but not one cent for tribute." An undeclared naval war was begun against France. Stephen Decatur Sr., having disguised his armed sloop *Delaware* as a merchantman, brought in a French prize and joined Adams as the hero of the hour. Early in 1799 salutes boomed out for the "wooden walls of America" after the American ship *Constellation* forced the French ship *L'Insurgente* to strike the tricolor.

Meanwhile, Congress had indeed voted millions for defense, by one of its measures creating the nation's first Navy Department. Washington was designated as the commanding general of a greatly enlarged army, with Hamilton as the second-ranking general. Washington did little in his new assignment, but his former Secretary of the Treasury gleefully prepared for combat. Congress, still without actually declaring war, also voided America's treaties with France. During the next few years American vessels, mostly privateers, proceeded to capture about 80 French ships. But to the dismay of Hamilton and some other Federalist leaders who were on fire for a fight, the President steadily declined to ask Congress to make the war official. Adams also resisted pressure to use the army, either against France itself or for seizing the New World territories of France's ally Spain.

D URING all this excitement, Elbridge Gerry—who once said, "The whole business of life [is] what is best to be done for our country"—had remained in Paris to see if any acceptable means of settlement could be reached. Nearly a year after the XYZ Affair, Gerry returned to America and reported certain findings to Adams at Quincy. He was convinced that an American mission would now be courteously received.

Persuaded that Gerry was right, the President now took the initiative,

The anti-French feeling aroused by the XYZ Affair is displayed in this cartoon showing the five-headed French directory demanding money at knife-point from the U.S. commissioners. Pro-French Republicans were badly upset by this affair. "Trimmers dropt off from the party like windfalls from an apple tree in September," wrote Federalist Fisher Ames in delight.

against the wishes of the Secretary of State, Timothy Pickering, and of Hamilton, who still dreamed of winning martial glory. Adams officially reopened negotiations, naming a three-man commission consisting of William Vans Murray, Chief Justice Oliver Ellsworth and Governor William R. Davie of North Carolina. On March 8, 1800, the three men presented their credentials to Napoleon Bonaparte, who had just become the sole ruler of France, and after long-drawn-out parleys the Treaty of Morfontaine was signed on the night of September 30-October 1, ushering in a period of peace with France that has never been broken.

By his selfless and singlehanded action Adams had prevented war, though in so doing he had badly divided his own party, many of whose members were eager to fight. He may also have seriously hampered his own chances in the next presidential election, although it is possible that his policies helped him more than they hurt. In any event he did not worry. In later years Adams would write: "I will defend my missions to France, as long as I have an eye to direct my hand, or a finger to hold my pen. They were the most disinterested and meritorious actions of my life. I reflect upon them with so much satisfaction, that I desire no other inscription over my gravestone than: 'Here lies John Adams, who took upon himself the responsibility of the peace with France in the year 1800.'"

Judge Samuel Chase, notorious for his Sedition Act trials, actually had a fine legal mind which attracted many admirers, including Washington and John Marshall. But Chase's violent temperament won him even more enemies. Alexander Hamilton once addressed him in an open letter thus: "It is your lot to have the peculiar privilege of being universally despised."

UNFORTUNATELY, during the same years when he was showing such large vision abroad, the President was showing pettiness and worse at home. He had some justification. Even at the high point of his popularity Adams had been the subject of fierce political criticism; the violent attacks made on Washington during the closing years of his administration were made on his successor in even more vitriolic fashion. The clamor against Adams and his fellow Federalists came not only from native Americans such as Franklin's grandson Benjamin Bache (editor of the chief Republican newspaper, the Philadelphia *Aurora*) but also from many recent refugees from Europe. These included Frenchmen who had fled their country's revolution, English radicals who found the times too oppressive in England, and Irish nationalists, vanquished in their struggle for Ireland's freedom, who wanted to vent their Anglophobia just when the Federalists were being strongly Anglophile. Most of these new arrivals were strongly pro-Republican. Many of them, moreover, were highly articulate.

When the Federalists controlling Congress decided it was time to muzzle these critics, Adams did nothing to restrain them. In June and July of 1798 they voted four highly restrictive measures known collectively as the Alien and Sedition Acts—and each hammered one more nail into the Federalist coffin. The first, a new Naturalization Act, increased the period of American residence required for citizenship from five to 14 years, and required every alien who entered America to register and to give five years' notice of his intention of becoming a citizen.

Next came the Alien Act, which permitted the President to expel at any time all aliens whom he thought "dangerous to the peace and safety of the United States" or who he had "reasonable grounds to suspect are concerned in any treasonable or secret machinations against the government." If the alien refused to leave, the President could put him in jail for a period up to three years. The third law was the Alien Enemies Act, which empowered the

President in wartime to restrain, imprison or banish at his pleasure any alien who was a subject of an enemy power.

Last came the Sedition Act, clearly aimed at the Republican opposition. It provided fines up to $2,000 and imprisonment up to two years for any person who should "write, print, utter, or publish . . . any false, scandalous and malicious writing or writings against the government of the United States," the members of Congress or the President. It also specified fines up to $5,000 and jail sentences up to five years for all citizens or aliens who illegally combined or conspired "to procure any insurrection, riot, unlawful assembly, or combination," or who tried "to impede the operation of any law of the United States, or to intimidate or prevent any person holding a place or office . . . from undertaking, performing, or executing his trust or duty."

WITH these measures America had embarked on its first major anti-alien scare, and it was a big one. Hundreds of foreign residents fled the country. But as a matter of fact, the three Alien Acts were never really enforced. They were used primarily as threats.

What caused the greatest stir, and the most bitter resentment, was the harshly partisan use of the Sedition Act. Jefferson and his Republicans realized that if simply attacking the President were now a crime, then the entire question of free speech and free press under the Bill of Rights was at stake. The Republicans denounced the Act as not merely despotic but as clearly unconstitutional. The Federalists countered that nobody could expect complete liberty of action. As one Federalist put it, he had liberty to drive a horse, but did that mean he could run down everyone he met? The trouble was that these bills did obviously give the Federalists power to run almost anyone down. Twenty-four Republican editors were rounded up and arrested soon after the Sedition Act was passed. Among them were Bache, the English newspaper editor Thomas Cooper (who drew a six-month jail term) and James T. Callender of the Richmond *Examiner* (sentenced to nine months' imprisonment). Many of the trials were grotesque parodies of justice, notably those conducted in the circuit courts by United States Supreme Court Justice Samuel Chase, who convicted both Cooper and Callender. When told Callender had once been arrested as a vagrant, Chase trumpeted: "It is a pity that they had not hanged the rascal."

Dozens of others were also prosecuted under the act, notably the Irish-born Congressman Matthew Lyon of Vermont, who had vigorously opposed the sedition measure on the floor of the House and had infuriated the Federalists by his sharp-tongued resistance to their program. Lyon had arrived in America in 1765 as a "bound boy" of 15. After working out his time, he married a niece of Ethan Allen, fought in the Revolution and prospered mightily. Within a few years he owned his own ironworks, sawmill, papermill and printing press, and was publishing a newspaper.

Lyon was tried and convicted on three counts of libel, one involving a letter he had published which suggested that the President should be sent "to a mad house." Instead Lyon himself was sent to a filthy jail in Vermont, with nothing but "iron bars to keep the cold out." The cell was described as "the common receptacle for horse-thieves . . . or any kind of felons." Lyon was triumphantly re-elected to Congress while imprisoned.

On hearing of Lyon's imprisonment, Jefferson wrote: "I know not which

Matthew Lyon, jailed in 1798 under the Sedition Act, was involved in a brawl in Congress earlier that year which reflected the tense interparty feeling of the day. This contemporary drawing depicts the scene. Federalist Roger Griswold of Connecticut, goaded by insults from Republican Lyon, attacks with a cane while Lyon replies enthusiastically with the fire tongs.

THE PROVIDENTIAL DETECTION

Thomas Jefferson's French sympathies are derided in an 1800 cartoon in which the Federalist eagle rescues the U.S. Constitution before Jefferson can burn it on "The Altar to Gallic Despotism." The French were believed to favor free love, and Yale's president warned that Jeffersonianism would surely make "our wives and daughters the victims of legal prostitution."

mortifies me most, that I should fear to write what I think, or my country bear such a state of things." Jefferson felt that the Federalists were headed for trouble, especially since they had also alienated two other groups. Southern slaveholders were being taxed 50 cents on every slave, and property owners were compelled to pay a federal levy on each piece of real estate. In Pennsylvania attempts to collect the property tax were bringing protests. One woman set the dogs on a collector and then dumped scalding water on his head. "Jefferson and Liberty" were cheered, "Adams and the Constitution" were damned. And late in 1798 came a challenge from the states of Kentucky and Virginia which went to the heart of the entire constitutional question.

As a philosopher, Jefferson was fully prepared to draw up a detailed and public denunciation of the whole Federalist position. But as a practical man the Vice President had no desire to expose himself either too much or too soon. Therefore, when the Kentucky legislature passed a series of resolutions that November calling the Alien and Sedition Acts unconstitutional, almost nobody knew that they had been written anonymously by Jefferson. His draft pointed out that the states had delegated certain specified powers to the national government and that "whensoever the general Government assumes undelegated powers, its acts are unauthoritative, void, and of no force." The states had united by compact to set up a government, and since there was no common judge of their actions each state had "an equal right to judge for itself." At the same time Madison put together a set of similar but somewhat milder resolutions adopted by the legislature of Virginia, claiming that the states "have the right and are in duty bound to interpose for arresting the progress of the evil [in order to maintain] the authorities, rights, and liberties appertaining to them." The Virginia resolutions also stressed that Congress had no power to interfere with freedom of speech or of the press.

During 1799 several northern states still controlled by the Federalists attacked the stand of Kentucky and Virginia, and declared that federal judges were the sole arbiters of constitutionality. That same year the Kentucky legislature passed a second set of resolutions, reiterating that the individual states had the right to judge any infraction of the Constitution and insisting "that a nullification . . . of all unauthorized acts done under color of that instrument, is the rightful remedy."

THE doctrine of state nullification, or interposition, against federal law was now clearly stated for the first time. Alexander Hamilton saw the full implication of the new and vigorously expressed states' rights position. It could, he said, "destroy the Constitution of the United States."

But as the war fever died down after the signing of the treaty with France so did the excitement over aliens and "seditious" criticism of the government. The Alien and Sedition Laws were still on the books, but Congress did not again make use of them. A few years later all of the discriminatory legislation was repealed or allowed to lapse.

During the controversy, however, the states did effectively consolidate one useful bastion for themselves against the central government. They achieved this by ratifying the 11th Amendment in 1798 after a four-year effort. Congress had proposed the amendment in answer to protests in Georgia and elsewhere over the Supreme Court's ruling of 1793 in *Chisholm vs. Georgia.* In this case the state was sued for a debt it allegedly owed a British creditor. The

Constitution specifically provided for suits "between a State, or the Citizens thereof, and Foreign States, Citizens or Subjects." Georgia, claiming that a state could be sued only with its own consent, denied the Supreme Court's jurisdiction and refused to appear. When the court decided 4-1 in favor of Chisholm, the Georgia legislature voted that any federal official trying to carry out the court's decision would thereby commit a felony and could be hanged "without benefit of clergy." In effect, the 11th Amendment declared that a state could be sued by a citizen of another state only in its own courts and with its prior consent.

As if symbolic of the waning strength of the Federalists, the death of George Washington at the age of 67 occurred in the last month of 1799. As one historian later commented: "His century was over, and he with it." The mourning was genuine and prolonged, and all the harsh criticisms of his last years in the presidency were forgotten. Republican Congressman Henry Lee of Virginia wrote the immortal words: "First in war, first in peace, first in the hearts of his countrymen." For the Federalists it was as if the ridgepole that held the party tent together had been struck down, even though Washington had always avoided formal party identification.

For the Republicans the hero's passing meant greater freedom of political action, since they no longer faced the opposition of the country's first citizen. Jefferson could now step up the pace with which he was weaving together into one potent unit the South's farmers and planters, the Northeast's city laborers and the great bulk of the settlers along the expanding Western frontier. These varied groups had one common interest: they all had some cause to dislike the Federalists and to favor the anti-British, low-tax, pro-agrarian policies of the Republicans. The 10-year Federalist domination of the national government was coming to a close.

In June 1800 the national capital was moved permanently to the new city named for the first President—though to call Washington a city was at that point something of an exercise in optimism. Although some houses had been built as early as 1796, over a large area there was nothing to see but the temporary huts of the laborers. Part of the Capitol had been erected and some $97,000 spent on the still-unfinished President's House. The French planner Pierre L'Enfant's dream of the ideal city was still very much of a dream. The sardonic Federalist Gouverneur Morris of New York noted: "We want nothing here but houses, cellars, kitchens, well-informed men, amiable women and other trifles of this kind to make our city perfect. . . . It is the very best city in the world for a future residence."

To the housewifely eye of Abigail Adams, all of Washington seemed to be in the woods. The new city boasted only one good tavern near the Capitol and a few frowzy boardinghouses for congressmen. The First Lady hung her wash to dry in the barnlike East Room of the President's House and felt as if she had come into a new country.

If the Adamses found their personal surroundings cheerless, they found the political atmosphere even more so. Looming up was the first truly fierce federal election. What the founding fathers had hoped would be mere temporary factions seemed now to have become permanent parties. Organized Federalists and Republicans were openly contending for the presidency. It was becoming more and more obvious to everyone in public life, including Adams,

TIMOTHY PICKERING
SECRETARY OF STATE

OLIVER WOLCOTT
SECRETARY OF THE TREASURY

JAMES McHENRY
SECRETARY OF WAR

All three of these Cabinet ministers were disloyal to President Adams but Pickering was the worst: he intrigued against Adams' army appointments and tried to block the peace with France. Following the death of his mentor, Alexander Hamilton, Pickering led the dying Federalist party, remaining active and vigorous until his last years (at 75 he won a plowing contest).

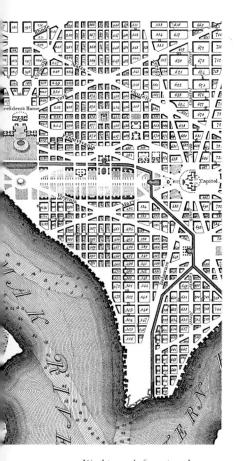

Washington's first city plan was drawn by French soldier-architect Pierre L'Enfant (below). After a century of neglect, his ideas were reappraised and adopted in 1901 for future city planning. His body was subsequently removed from its unmarked grave and interred in Arlington National Cemetery.

that this partisan division was to be the basis for all political contention from then on. Adams could accept that. What was more difficult to endure was the disruptive presence of an extremist element in his own party, under the leadership of Alexander Hamilton.

Probably his clash with Hamilton was inevitable. It was understandably galling to the older man to know that people looked to Hamilton as the real party chief. Ostensibly, the Little Lion was in retirement, practicing law in New York and, as always, working at top speed. Talleyrand, on a visit to America a few years before, had passed Hamilton's law office on his way to a party in the evening and saw him in the candlelight bending over his desk. "I have just come," Talleyrand told the gathering, "from viewing a man who had made the fortune of his country, but now is working all night in order to support his family."

Hamilton had been relatively content during the years 1798 and 1799, when he was laboring to build an army which he himself hoped to lead into battle against France or into the conquest of Spanish-held lands in Latin America. As long as the undeclared naval war between the United States and France continued, with the possibility that it would erupt into all-out hostilities, Hamilton was happy politically because the Francophile Republicans were on the defensive and happy personally because he might soon be the field commander of a triumphant army.

Adams' move to make peace with France had angered Hamilton—not only because it ruined a Federalist campaign issue for 1800 but also because it ended his own chance to gain a general's laurels. Hamilton now disavowed Adams. "For my individual part, my mind is made up," wrote Hamilton, "I will never more be responsible for him."

How responsible he had already been, Adams was just beginning to realize. Hamilton in truth had been (though still only in his early 40s) the federal government's first elder statesman of high rank. He had remained an unofficial member of Washington's Cabinet even when officially out of it. Now Adams learned that though he himself had never sought Hamilton's advice, every member of his Cabinet had privately and regularly done so. Worse still, his Cabinet had followed Hamilton's thinking on almost every vital question. An explosion was inevitable.

Convinced that his own Cabinet was conspiring against him, and that it was even trying to keep him from getting the renomination, in May 1800 the President fired Secretary of State Pickering and demanded and got the resignation of Secretary of War McHenry. Both men had tried to thwart the President's plans for peace with France. Not knowing how deeply his Secretary of the Treasury, Oliver Wolcott, was also involved with Hamilton, Adams let him retain his post—and from this key position Wolcott kept the others intimately informed on what the administration was doing.

The two great Federalist leaders now fell out with each other once and for all. Adams angrily charged Hamilton with helping the Republican party in New York by approving weak Federalist candidates for the state legislature. More charges and countercharges followed. Finally, in October, Hamilton wrote an impetuous and ill-judged *Letter from Alexander Hamilton Concerning the Public Conduct and Character of John Adams, Esquire, President of the United States*. It was intended only for the eyes of key Federalists. Hamilton accused Adams of "violent rage" and "distempered jealousy," and even questioned "the solidity of his understanding." Inevitably, a Republican got hold of a copy of the letter. He was Aaron Burr, candidate for Vice President, and he joyously saw to it that it was published. This letter, bringing the Adams-Hamilton dispute into the open in all its ferocity, exploded squarely in the midst of the Federalist party, and wrecked it. Adams said of the letter that "if the single purpose had been to defeat the President," no better way could have been chosen, and that he was a sacrifice "to the unbridled ambition of Alexander Hamilton."

In the election of 1800 Jefferson and Burr each received 73 electoral votes, while Adams and his running mate, Charles Cotesworth Pinckney of South Carolina, respectively got 65 and 64. These results exposed an unforeseen weakness in the machinery the founders had created for choosing a President. Under the Constitution as it then read, the nation's top office went to the man with the highest electoral vote, and the vice presidency to the man with the second highest total. Each elector had duly cast two ballots, but without indicating which was for the top office and which was for the second. Before the election of 1804, the 12th Amendment would be adopted to prevent such a dilemma from ever recurring; it would specify that separate ballots must be cast for President and Vice President.

But this subsequent hindsight was of no help in solving the problem posed in 1800. The electoral tie between the two Republicans went to the Federalist-dominated House of Representatives, where each of the 16 states would cast one vote, and a clear majority of nine was needed to win.

Some Federalists scented the heady prospect of beating out the agrarian Jefferson by sneaking the much more mercantile-minded Burr into the presidency. In January 1801, the Washington *Federalist* editorialized that Burr was "a friend of the commercial interests . . . the firm and decided friend of the *navy*. . . . The *Eastern* States have had a President and Vice President; So have the *Southern*. It is proper that the *middle* states should also be respected. . . . Mr. Burr can be raised to the Presidency without any *insult* to the feelings of the Federalists, the friends of Government." But the newspaper had not reckoned with the feelings of one Federalist named Alexander Hamilton, to whom Burr was "the most unfit and dangerous man of the community"—"no agreement with him could be relied upon." Hamilton also said: "If there be a man in the world I ought to hate, it is Jefferson. With Burr I have always been personally well. But the public good must be paramount to every private consideration."

Yet to do Burr justice, he had not intrigued to be elected President. When the Federalists made overtures to him, Burr refused (as Jefferson later put it) in an "honorable and decisive way."

ON the first ballot, neither had the necessary nine votes; Jefferson was backed by eight states and Burr by six, with two undecided. The deadlock continued through seven days and 35 tense ballots. Jefferson wrote his daughter that "Hamilton is using his uttermost influence to procure my election rather than Colonel Burr's." It was Hamilton's friend from Delaware, James H. Bayard, who at last persuaded some Federalists to abstain from voting for Burr. Thus, in the final ballot, the Virginian was named by 10 states, and riders bore the tidings across the Republic.

Vice President Aaron Burr, shown in 1834, was an astute politician. First boss of New York's Tammany Hall, he found a loophole in state voting laws: groups of good Republicans met the property requirement by buying small plots together. Thus New York—and the nation—went Republican in 1800.

New Yorker Gouverneur Morris left in his writings a vivid record of the era ending in 1800. Very active in the republic's early affairs, his enthusiasm was later dimmed by Jefferson's republicanism. "Give the votes to the people who have no property," he maintained, "and they will sell them to the rich."

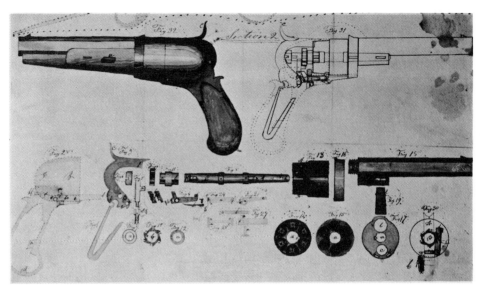

A diagram of the Colt revolver shows interchangeable parts that made possible the first assembly line.

A growing force in world markets

T HE War for Independence over, America's chances of becoming an industrial power seemed scarcely worth a Rhode Island bank note—and Rhode Island, as everyone knew, led all states in the carefree printing of worthless currency. The money situation could be remedied; in every state the currency was eventually stabilized. But there were other symptoms of economic illness that were far less amenable to treatment.

Domestic manufacture in the new United States was almost nil. Among a largely agrarian population skilled manpower was in short supply. Though shipping was the nation's lifeblood, its merchant fleet of 2,000 had been decimated in the war. Worse, the British now restricted America's trade with England and with the convenient West Indies.

In this desperate situation New England shippers struck out for the far corners of the earth. In a typical voyage, the square-rigged *Astrea* sailed from Salem on February 17, 1789, bound for China with a cargo that included New England butter and Philadelphia beer, Nantucket candles and mountain-country ginseng, an herb the Chinese credit with curative powers. The new trade helped revitalize the nation. Port cities like Salem, New York and Boston *(opposite)* benefited hugely. The fleet brought back hard money that capitalized new industry. Factory towns sprang up, and Americans began to experiment with the techniques of mass production *(above)*. Soon the groundwork had been laid for the greatest industrial expansion the world had seen.

A THRIVING PORT, Boston's waterfront teems with shipping and seamen. In the 10 years that ended in 1840, ship arrivals here leaped from around 4,000 a year to 6,000.

America's first boom town

AN early beneficiary of expanding trade was the town of Salem, a small Massachusetts fishing community whose merchants launched a series of commercial ventures that were masterpieces of improvisation. Ships' masters were told to stop wherever convenient, to buy anything reasonable, sell what they could—the ship itself, if the offer was right. One captain, John Prince, sent to buy tea in Canton, returned instead with a cargo of goats' hair, madder dye, opium, Turkish carpets and dried figs. Another, Jonathan Carnes, sailed to Sumatra in 1795, filled his holds with pepper bought cheap from the natives, and cleared a 700 per cent profit. Mansions rose in Salem. But in the 1830s, as ships grew larger, Salem's shallow harbor lost its traffic and the boom ended.

Adorned by huge banners, the ship "Fame" is launched in Salem in 1802. Launchings were exciting events, and townspeople sometimes

MERCHANTS' HOMES on Essex Street in 1830 reflect the solid grace of Federal architecture. By then Salem had a population of 22,000, making it the country's 10th city. It was so famous abroad that one oriental merchant firmly believed it was a nation.

FIRST MILLIONAIRE in the U.S., Elias Derby sits at a window facing the sea that brought him his wealth. Merchants who got their start in his employ were the apples of his eyes (one of which was brown, the other blue). He called his protégés "my boys."

paid for choice vantage points. In 1806, probably Salem's peak year for foreign trade, local merchants owned 73 ships, 11 barks, 48 brigs.

The exotic hub of the China trade

A seagoing paramour enlivens the China stay of a Yankee sailor.

Until 1840 China restricted foreign traders to the port of Canton, and this busy city became the Orient's most cosmopolitan community. Ships called there from all over the world, but particularly from the U.S., which was making a determined bid to capture the bulk of the China trade. American firms established offices in Canton, and the Cantonese developed a special fondness for Yankees. One wealthy merchant named Houqua tore up a $72,000 promissory note of a Bostonian he liked, and also bought a half-million dollars' worth of stock in New England factories. The China trade, mutually profitable, seemed destined to go on forever. But by 1815 it began to dwindle as U.S. commerce with Europe increased and Americans found domestic opportunities for investment. By the Civil War it was a thing of the past.

A CANTON "HONG," or warehouse, hums with activity as Chinese workers (left) tramp tea into chests while the proprietor (foreground) keeps track on an abacus. Hongs also provided lodging for foreign traders like the two men shown wearing top hats.

FOREIGN BANNERS, including the American (third from the left), fly over hongs on the colorful Canton wharf. Chinese referred to America as the "Flowery Flag Kingdom." This painting, like the others on these pages, was done on glass by a Chinese artist.

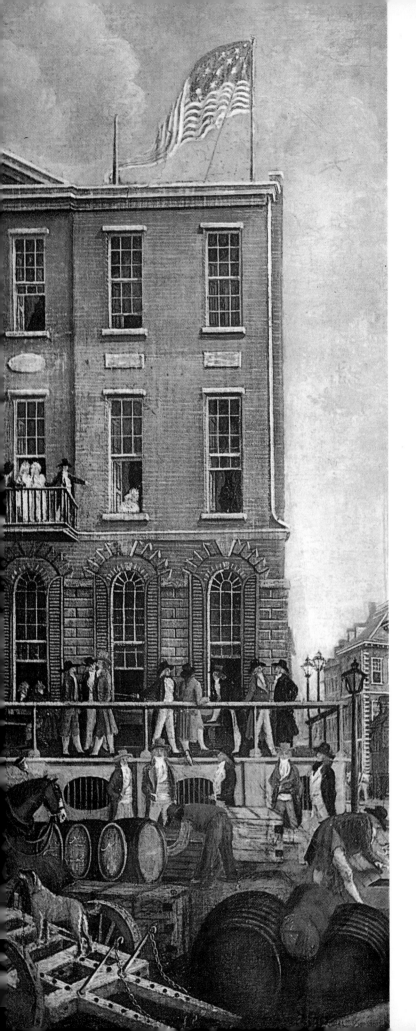

New York's rise: "a multitude absorbed" in making money

CENTER OF COMMERCE, the Tontine Coffee House dominates busy Wall Street in New York. Merchants lounge on the porch of the building, which housed the city's Stock Exchange.

AFTER the Revolution Philadelphia was America's largest port, but soon New York was challenging it. In 1807 an English traveler wrote of the Manhattan waterfront: "Every thought, word, look, and action of the multitude seemed to be absorbed by commerce." Eleven years later New York shipowners inaugurated regularly scheduled packet service across the Atlantic, carrying passengers and cargo. Though only eight persons made the first trip, within five years passengers were paying premiums above the $175 passage to get aboard, and by 1845 the original vessel had been joined by 52 others making 13 round trips monthly. The ships brought fine textiles from Europe and carried back such products as cotton, flour, tobacco and naval stores. After 1830 the city was the nation's largest port. By 1840 it accounted for more tonnage than any city except London.

SHIPS AND WAREHOUSES line busy South Street along New York's East River. In the pre-Civil War era, most ocean transport docked here rather than on the Hudson as at present.

South Street's 50 piers extended for three miles—a stretch called Packet Row. The value of the merchandise handled here rose from $84 million in the year 1825 to $146 million in 1836.

THE FIRST COTTON MILL in America, started by Samuel Slater at Pawtucket, draws its power from the falls of the Blackstone River. The factory, formerly a clothier's shop, manufactured yarn that was distributed to home weavers who turned it into cloth. In only two years Slater and his partners were selling their product in Salem, New York, Baltimore and Philadelphia.

"LOWELL GIRLS," as they were called, operate looms in one of the town's mills. The girls, most of whom came from local farm families, were well paid for their work, and were very closely chaperoned.

From a copied invention, the beginnings of industry

AMERICA'S first major manufacturing industry, textiles, was a product not of American ingenuity but of a Briton's feat of memory. Richard Arkwright had launched a textile revolution in England by inventing complicated spinning frame machinery, whose secrets his government guarded zealously. But a young apprentice named Samuel Slater memorized the operation, then set out for America. In 1789 he persuaded financier Moses Brown to capitalize America's first cotton spinning mill at Pawtucket, Rhode Island. Soon Slater added new mills, and many of his workers struck out on their own as well. Copying again from the British, Slater introduced child labor and provided it with schooling.

In 1810 Francis Lowell, his memory the equal of Slater's, visited England and on his return founded at Waltham, Massachusetts, the first American mill that carded, spun thread and wove cloth under one roof. After his death, his financial backers—a group of merchants who called themselves the Boston Associates—transformed the farming village of East Chelmsford, Massachusetts, into the nation's first factory town and named it Lowell. In 1840 the town had six corporations operating nine mills with 4,000 looms and more than 100,000 spindles. Lowell's industrial expansion in the 1830s has been described as "the most remarkable decade of progress" for a one-industry town in American manufacturing history.

Lowell in 1833 presents an appearance of tidy prosperity on the banks of the Merrimack, where 11 years before had been only farm fields.

. . . and all "Made in America"

An abundance of domestic products provides a glittering spectacle at the 1845 trade fair held at New York's Niblo's Garden. The fairs, inaugurated in 1828, were sponsored annually by the American Institute of New York to spur U.S. industry. They offered a mounting variety of American-made manufactures, in-

cluding such new inventions as Morse's telegraph, McCormick's reaper, Singer's sewing machine, Bell's telephone and the Remington typewriter. As time passed, the fairs reflected America's increasing commercial independence. During the early 1800s, there were Societies for the Encouragement of Domestic Man-ufactures throughout the country, and newspaper advertise-ments felt it necessary to admonish women to resist foreign-made luxuries in favor of simple American products. But by mid-century, U.S. goods were on a par with the best imports, and New York boasted 4,000 shops able to cater to all tastes.

53

3. "A WISE AND FRUGAL GOVERNMENT"

THE day he became President, Thomas Jefferson quietly stepped out of Conrad's boarding house and, at the center of a little cluster of Republican congressmen, strolled through the crowds to the Capitol. He climbed the steps of the north wing to the Senate chamber. There he took the oath from his distant kinsman and implacable political opponent, Chief Justice John Marshall, and stood before the members of Congress—a long, rangy farmer-philosopher, now in his 58th year, plainly dressed and a little bent, but still rugged and strong-willed.

As he began his inaugural address, many in the audience may have missed his words; on public occasions Jefferson's voice was almost inaudible. It did not matter. The nation would read what he had to say. Jefferson, as usual, was worth reading and on this occasion, after the virulence so abundantly demonstrated by both sides during the election, he consciously strove to show he would serve the whole country.

"We are all Republicans, we are all Federalists," he said. "If there be any among us who would wish to dissolve this Union or to change its republican form, let them stand undisturbed as monuments of the safety with which error of opinion may be tolerated where reason is left free to combat it. Kindly separated by nature and a wide ocean from the exterminating havoc of one quarter of the globe . . . possessing a chosen country, with room enough for our descendants to the hundredth and thousandth generation . . . with all

A MANY-SIDED GENIUS gazes out of this portrait of Thomas Jefferson made by Rembrandt Peale in 1800. His is still considered one of the sharpest minds America has known.

"Mad Tom in a Rage," a Federalist cartoon of 1802, depicts Jefferson and the devil tugging at the pillar of government, as the American Eagle wards them off. When Jefferson became President, some New England ladies buried their Bibles, afraid that government agents would seize and burn them.

these blessings, what more is necessary to make us a happy and a prosperous people?" Answering his own rhetorical question, Jefferson said that America needed only "a wise and frugal government, which shall restrain men from injuring one another, shall leave them otherwise free to regulate their own pursuits of industry and improvement, and shall not take from the mouth of labor the bread it has earned. This is the sum of good government, and this is necessary to close the circle of our felicities."

His utterance was more a statement of faith than of policy, the faith of a statesman who truly loved his fellow men and accepted them, who saw them as equal—not in status or ability perhaps, but in their rights. In his view man was not made to be the tool of business or government, but rather they were made to serve him. The greatest threat to freedom, he believed, was power itself. He noted that, "having banished from our land that religious intolerance under which mankind so long bled and suffered, we have yet gained little if we countenance a political intolerance as despotic, as wicked, and capable of as bitter and bloody persecutions." Though he strongly believed that the majority will should prevail, "that will, to be rightful, must be reasonable," and it would not be reasonable to deny that the minority had equal rights, "to violate which would be oppression."

The fact is, the Republic was not even yet a democracy. The rights of man were limited in many ways throughout the states—for example, with land, property, and taxpaying requirements for voting. In Maryland and the Carolinas, a voter had to possess 50 acres of land; in South Carolina he also had to believe in God and divine punishment. Massachusetts voters had to own property. New Jersey during the early years had allowed the franchise to "all inhabitants of the state" so long as they were over 21 and owned £50—and that included women, aliens and Negroes. But in 1807 the state constitution was altered and those three groups were disenfranchised. Nor did the right to vote necessarily include the right to govern. No atheists, Jews or Roman Catholics could hold office in New Hampshire, New Jersey, Connecticut or Vermont. A member of the South Carolina legislature had to own 500 acres of land and 10 Negroes.

Nevertheless, the leaven of the Revolution was working, if slowly. During the 10 years prior to 1799, South Carolina had opened its polls to Roman Catholics for the first time, while New Hampshire had given suffrage to all males over 21. Democracy was gradually spreading through the land.

REBELLION against tyranny in colonial Virginia had been Jefferson's school of statecraft, the happy informality of his frontier boyhood his school of democracy. At William and Mary College he had learned from books, but he still believed that only farmers, men with their roots deep in the soil, could be relied on to express "proper American sentiments." His father had been such a man of the soil, a giant of Welsh yeoman stock; his mother had been a great lady of the Tidewater aristocracy. This dual heritage was to be reflected in Jefferson's own dualism all his life long.

Much has been made of Jefferson's differences with certain of his great contemporaries. What is more interesting, if less colorful, is how closely the Founding Fathers agreed on the fundamentals of the revolutionary movement in America. Thus neither Jefferson nor Adams had blind faith in human nature. However, Jefferson was convinced that democracy was less corruptible than a centralized oligarchy because with all citizens participating power could be distributed more widely. "If once the people become inattentive to the public affairs," he wrote to a friend, "you and I and Congress and Assemblies, Judges and Governors, shall all become wolves. It seems to be the law of our general nature, in spite of individual exceptions."

Jefferson agreed with Adams in his observation that men's honesty did not increase with their riches. And like Adams, who in the New England town meetings had observed the self-appointed elite taking charge decade after decade, Jefferson had an abiding fear of a ruthless and powerful minority's ability to dominate a helpless and uninstructed majority. For this he had a solution: "The most effectual means of preventing the perversion of power into tyranny are to illuminate, as far as possible, the minds of the people." Out of this philosophical conclusion arose Jefferson's plan for the government to sift out and educate "the best geniuses" of the population regardless of class, through the university level, if need be. The purpose of higher education, he believed, should be to train for leadership. If there was to be an elite, let it be an intellectual elite. Even Hamilton was not more concerned with the development of a ruling class than Jefferson; they differed only on just how and what kind of elite was to be found.

IT was Hamilton who, allowing for his personal prejudices, penned the most illuminating description of Jefferson's mode of operation committed to paper in his time: "I admit that his politics are tinctured with fanaticism; that he is too much in earnest in his democracy; . . . that he is crafty . . . not scrupulous about the means of success, nor very mindful of truth. . . . But it is not true, as it is alleged, that he is an enemy to the power of the Executive. . . . He is as likely as any man I know to temporize." And Hamilton was right; there was no new revolution in 1801, when Jefferson's party assumed power.

Jefferson, it has been said, had a double-track intellect through which two lines of thought could run on parallel lines. Never was he troubled with the need for consistency that besets small minds. "Nothing, then," he wrote two years before his death, "is unchangeable but the inherent and unalienable rights of man." To reach his ultimate goals, Jefferson was prepared to subordinate all else—and as Hamilton had foreseen, he did not hesitate to violate his own avowed principles.

He was a believer in states' rights and strict construction of the Constitution—but he was also perfectly well aware that a nation endures, not because of its written Constitution alone, but because the ideas behind it remain meaningful to the people. He was for an agrarian society because his observations had convinced him that farmers made better citizens than those "panders of vice," the city workers—yet he came to realize that "We must now place the manufacturer by the side of the agriculturist," and he strove to adapt his democratic program to the reality. He was condemned for lack of courage. Yet as President he had the courage to sacrifice his great popularity in a drive for peace, even at the price of a trade embargo.

He was one of the most complex human beings who ever trod the planet. The jarring inconsistencies remain: the intellectual with the rugged, workman's body; the gadgeteer and the Renaissance man; the politician who knew how to use Federalist techniques for Republican goals; the idealist who talked emancipation but freed only five of his slaves, three of them allegedly children

A picture from a 19th Century magazine shows New Jersey women voting in the early days of the Republic. The state took away the feminine ballot after an election scandal in 1806 in which, it was said, every woman seemed to vote just as often as she could change her dress, while some men put on skirts to vote a second time.

of his wife's Negro half-sister; the political dogmatist who was open-minded on all other matters; the skeptic who questioned God and denied that Christianity was part of the common law, yet based the rights of man on a tenuous theory of natural rights.

It is easy to see how he became all things to all men, how his means have been confused with his ends, how parts of his thinking—his states' rights doctrines, for instance—have been misappropriated for goals very different from his, how in the great conflict of 1861 his name was called upon not only by slaveholding agrarians and states' righters, but also by Lincoln Republicans who looked to the Declaration and the Ordinance of 1787. He has been invoked by William Jennings Bryan and by Henry George, by Woodrow Wilson and the New Freedom, by Franklin D. Roosevelt and the New Deal, by Jeffersonian Democrats and staunch Republicans, by Communists and by members of the American Liberty League.

Jeffersonian democracy—at least in its culmination under Andrew Jackson —was no unmixed blessing. Jefferson left not so much a program as a faith or an ideology and a realization that government could be either a threat or a refuge. He had no clear-cut plan for setting up a Federal Republic. His views, carried to their logical conclusions, would lead to what has been called the "Jeffersonian Puzzle," in which the South would invoke states' rights to the injury of democracy, and the North would counter by invoking democracy to the detriment of states' rights.

The fact is that although Jefferson's philosophical goals never changed, his methods of achieving them did; he could always adjust to what had to be done. In Europe in 1787, confronted by a law forbidding anyone to take fine Lombard seed rice out of Italy, he invoked the principle that a man's own country comes first, stuffed his pockets and got the rice out under cover of diplomatic immunity (the grain later prospered in South Carolina).

Elbridge Gerry's term as governor of Massachusetts gave rise to a new political word that endures today. When the state was redistricted in 1812 so as to insure election of Republicans, an artist for the Boston "Weekly Messenger" added fangs, wings and claws to one odd-shaped district, creating the "Gerrymander" (above). The cartoon helped to defeat Republican Gerry.

JEFFERSON'S very ability to adjust proved his salvation as President. Had he retired to Monticello at the end of his first four years of office, during which most of the legislation he supported was inexpensive and widely beneficial, history might well have recorded that there was never a more popular or successful Executive. He reduced the armed forces, slashed the diplomatic corps, balanced the budget and cut one million dollars from the public debt (while spending $15 million for Louisiana). Toward the end of his first term, Jefferson happily announced that it could be "the pleasure and pride of an American to ask what farmer, what mechanic, what labourer, ever sees a tax-gatherer of the United States."

His invaluable aide in the field of economics was the Swiss-born Albert Gallatin, who successively served Jefferson and Madison as a distinguished Secretary of the Treasury from 1801 to 1814. Gallatin thought his role was not "to act the part of a mere financier, to become a contriver of taxes, a dealer of loans . . . fattening contractors, pursers and agents," but rather to act as a financial statesman, spending money only as specifically appropriated, taxing as lightly as possible, and using surpluses both to reduce the federal debt and for long-range public improvements. Few public servants have ever accomplished so much so smoothly and so well.

Gallatin was not the only outstanding figure enlisted by Jefferson. As Secretary of State he selected his fellow Virginian, James Madison. The "Father of the Constitution" was a quiet, mild-eyed little man who wore "a queue no bigger than a pipestem" and who had an unexpected gift of laughter. For eight years he would serve as Jefferson's right arm and heir apparent, and the President would eventually pick him as a successor.

Inevitably, the holder of this post would incur criticism. Jefferson's cousin, Congressman John Randolph of Roanoke, sneered of Madison: "We ask for energy, and we are told of his moderation; we ask for talent, and the reply is his unassuming merit; we ask what were his services in the cause of Public Liberty, and we are directed to the pages of the *Federalist.*" Actually, as Randolph was well aware, Madison's services in the cause of liberty were many, and his co-authorship of the *Federalist* was not the least of them. No man was his peer in knowledge of constitutional history, and none worked harder for his country or with less thought of personal gain. In naming him as Secretary of State, Jefferson knew exactly what he was about.

UNLIKE some of his successors, Jefferson took scrupulous care with all his appointments. He would not employ his heroic old friend George Rogers Clark, who had, unfortunately, taken to alcohol. Nor would he get rid of the perpetually troublesome Randolph by shipping him off (as he was urged) to England. When Robert Livingston, the minister to France, became deaf, Jefferson politely recalled him. He rescued the unstable and eccentric Thomas Paine from squalor and disgrace in France and brought him home— the Revolutionary philosopher was facing possible imprisonment because he had dared call Jefferson's inaugural address superior to the words of Bonaparte. But Jefferson was well aware of the contrasts between Paine and his work, of both the baseness and nobleness in him. Although he enjoyed Paine's company and entertained him at the White House, he would not appoint to public office a man who rarely washed.

Albert Gallatin, Jefferson's Secretary of the Treasury, was a Swiss aristocrat who emigrated at 19 to America, where he got his start selling tea. Federalists chided him (in the cartoon above he says "Stop de Wheels of Government!") for his financial parsimony and foreign accent. But he outlasted many a critic, living on to a ripe old age (below), "bald, courteous, toothless."

The Republicans made gains in the off-year elections of 1802 and 1803, and it was clear that thousands of fair-minded Federalists were coming over to Jefferson's side. Jefferson peacefully went on being himself. Informality was the keynote of the Administration. The President startled Washingtonians by taking a young nephew shopping to get him ready for school. When he abolished the weekly levees at the White House, some malcontents decided to come anyway. Jefferson arrived home from a horseback ride to find the house full and marched in, booted, spurred, splashed with mud and smiling, as if it were just a happy coincidence to find so many friends there. Everybody laughed and that was the end of the levees.

He would not accept any gifts. He would not permit presidential birthday balls—or even allow the date to become known when well-wishers desired to celebrate it. He was tired of crowds and socializing; the presidency had already become a strain, even in those simpler times and even for as vigorous a man as he. He had had books sent from Monticello, but it was hard to find time to read them. One visitor who stayed two weeks reported that the dining room table was "chockfull" of congressmen, diplomats and officials every single night. Jefferson's wine bill alone for a single year of his Administration was $2,800, a vast sum for those days.

Yet Jefferson thrived during his first term in the presidential office and the country thrived with him. In the presidential election of 1804, the Republicans carried every state but Connecticut and Delaware, and Jefferson scored an electoral triumph of 162 to 14 over the Federalist candidate, Charles Cotesworth Pinckney. Never again were the Federalists to come even close to carrying the country as a whole.

Yet the old saying that he whom the gods would destroy they first make mad is applicable to some degree even to the moderate and well-balanced Jefferson. He did not become mad, of course, but even he could not resist the taste of power. He resented and distrusted the Federalist-controlled judiciary. There was a danger—as he later put it—that they would prove the "sappers and miners" of the nation; they were "irresponsible" and contained "the germ of dissolution of our federal government." He decided to declare war on the judiciary and thus "to sink Federalism into an abyss from which there shall be no resurrection for it."

To be sure, his predecessor John Adams had supplied much fuel for Jefferson's fire. The Judiciary Act of January 1801 had assured comfortable lifetime offices for a number of federal judges—and Adams had spent the last hours of his term filling these posts with the so-called "midnight judges," an act that enraged Jefferson. Despite all the checks and balances in the Constitution, the new President had good reason to fear what such a judiciary might do to cripple his program.

Once in office, Jefferson tried to block off some of these appointments by simply instructing Secretary of State Madison not to issue the necessary documents. Aggrieved, the Federalists tried for a test case. One appointee, William Marbury, sued for a Supreme Court writ compelling Madison to give him his commission. In the resulting case of *Marbury vs. Madison*, finally decided in 1803, Jefferson won—or did he? For Marbury had cited the Congressional Judiciary Act of 1789 as his grounds for seeking the writ; this part of the act Chief Justice Marshall, himself a recent Adams appointee, declared to have been unconstitutional all along—and the Constitution, he said, is a "paramount law," to be interpreted by the courts alone. For the first time, the Supreme Court voided a law of Congress. The court therefore asserted its authority to strike down the act of a coordinate body, the Congress, if it

THE AMERICAN NAVY
ON THE BARBARY COAST

America waged two naval wars against the Barbary pirates of Morocco, Algiers, Tunis and Tripoli. During 1801 to 1805, three commodores—Preble, Barron and Rodgers—blockaded Tripoli. This, with a land attack from Alexandria against Derna (arrow at right) led by American consular agent William Eaton, won a truce. But it was broken after the fleet withdrew. Ten years later Stephen Decatur returned with nine ships to defeat the Algerian flagship "Mashuda" on June 17, 1815. On June 30 he negotiated a treaty. This time the fleet stayed on to keep the peace.

deemed such an act illegal. This decision was a landmark in American judicial history. But in the process of making his ruling, Marshall went behind the requirements of the case at hand to deliver a stinging rebuke to Madison for not giving Marbury his commission. "Is it to be contended," the Chief Justice asked tartly, "that the heads of departments are not amenable to the laws of their country!"

Angered by this judicial slap, Jefferson renewed his attack on the courts. He now turned his attention to Judge John Pickering of New Hampshire; at the President's urging the Republican-controlled House impeached Pickering on the charge of "high crimes and misdemeanors." Now Pickering was undoubtedly guilty of being drunk, profane and probably insane. He certainly was unsuited for the bench. It would have been possible to pass a law dealing swiftly and humanely with such cases of incompetence (such legislation had actually existed, but had earlier been repealed by the Republicans because it was part of the contested "midnight judges" law). But to impeach and try the hapless jurist was a petty act. The judge was too poor to come to Washington for trial, and the House refused depositions of his insanity, so the impeachment ground on. The country read the details, fascinated; it was obvious that the President and the judiciary were truly at war. In March 1804, the Senate ousted Pickering by a strict party vote, but several Republican senators were so unhappy at this obvious misuse of the impeachment procedure that they declined to vote at all.

POLITICALLY speaking, Jefferson made a still greater mistake in going after his next victim within the federal judiciary, Associate Justice Samuel Chase of the Supreme Court. Like Pickering, Chase was loud-mouthed, abusive and sometimes profane. Unlike Pickering, he was entirely in his right mind, and happened also to have been a signer of the Declaration of Independence. The charge against him was injudicious conduct on the bench and holding opinions "hurtful to the welfare of the country," or, to be more literal, hurtful to the Republican party.

Chase's handling of the sedition trials of the Adams Administration had unquestionably been high-handed and arbitrary—and most of the defendants had, of course, been Republican. Chase, a gargantuan bull of a man, had roared out his private opinions in scandalous fashion from the bench itself. His private opinions were violently antidemocratic. Universal suffrage he said was only "mobocracy," and the doctrine of equal rights for all men had brought "mischief upon us."

The angry Jefferson wrote Congressman Nicholson of Maryland proposing impeachment. Chase was to be tried for having abused his official capacity to a point where he was dangerous to the liberties of the people. Vice President Burr, now under a cloud and in the closing days of his term, presided over the trial in February 1805, showing a serpentine grace and a dignity that won applause from even his detractors.

The question at issue in Chase's trial—as in Pickering's earlier—was whether the judge's actions met the Constitutional definition of "high crimes and misdemeanors" necessary to oust him from the bench. Although 25 of the 34 men in the Senate were Republicans, and there was no doubt how Jefferson wanted them to vote, it was clear that proof of "high crimes and misdemeanors" could not be established. Justice Chase was acquitted in a historic

Stephen Decatur, prone on the deck, is saved from death by a heroic seaman while waging war against the Barbary pirates. Just as a scimitar was about to descend on the 25-year-old captain's head, the seaman jumped into its path. Miraculously, both men survived. In this battle Decatur led 10 sailors aboard a Tripolitan gunboat in a raid to avenge his brother's death.

61

vote; in all likelihood a verdict of guilty would have encouraged the Administration to aim next for bigger game—probably Chief Justice John Marshall himself. As it was, an uneasy feeling was beginning to arise in the nation that perhaps the judiciary should not be torn hither and yon at the behest of the Executive. The Federalists might even be right in contending that moves of this kind were a threat to the independence of the entire judicial branch of the government.

After the ignominious collapse of the case against Justice Chase—and even Jefferson admitted that the trial had been a "farce"—the President abandoned impeachment as a political weapon and made no further effort to harass the Federalist judges.

Talleyrand, Napoleon's agent in the sale of Louisiana, has been called "a nobleman gone astray." An excommuncated bishop and corrupt public official, he was also an ardent spokesman for peace and constitutionalism. In the midst of the French Revolution he prudently fled to America, where he traveled for 30 unhappy months. President Washington refused to receive him.

FOREIGN affairs were a major concern in both of Jefferson's presidential terms. But in this respect he was less successful as President than he had been as Secretary of State under Washington. During the world power struggle that accompanied Europe's Napoleonic Wars a stripling nation like the United States could only lead from weakness, and Jefferson's primary concern was to keep America from being engulfed. This could be done only if the United States stayed neutral, out of the fighting. And keeping the nation neutral was no easy task.

French, British and Spanish ships, along with assorted pirates, were preying on American commerce; cargoes were seized, vessels sunk, crews set adrift in open boats. American seamen were being seized from American vessels by British captains right in sight of American lighthouses. American diplomats were insulted, ships searched and coastal ports blockaded. Foreign troops were gathering along American frontiers; the Empire of Spain seemed to loom alarmingly close from its Gulf Coast possessions of Louisiana and Florida. This whole border area was a wild land of riffraff, fugitives from justice, runaway slaves, half-breeds and marauding Indians, whose forays over into Georgia made life hideous. Shortly after Jefferson became President, France took over Louisiana, but Spain still held East Florida (which had much the area of the present state) and West Florida (part of present-day Alabama and Mississippi). America tried to buy Florida, but Spain would not sell.

More successful was Jefferson's war against the Barbary pirates. For years, the North African Moslem States of Morocco, Algiers, Tunis and Tripoli, the so-called Barbary States, had been making a comfortable living seizing the crews of "heathen" ships entering the Mediterranean, clamping them into irons and holding them for ransom. In 1784 Jefferson had suggested that war was the only solution. "We ought to begin a naval power," he wrote to James Monroe, "if we mean to carry on our own commerce. Can we begin it on a more honorable occasion, or with a weaker foe?" In 1785 the exasperated Jefferson, negotiating with the pirates as an American commissioner in Paris, had complained that his mind was "absolutely suspended between indignation and impotence." Sometime afterward he had secured the release of a certain number of the prisoners by paying $30,000. By 1794, rates had been officially set: $4,000 for each cabin passenger, $1,400 for each cabin boy. Sunday after Sunday, the sad roll of names was read out in the churches of Salem, Newburyport and Boston, listing more men in irons. Congress would pay $200 each for their redemption, but the rest of the money had to be raised privately, and sometimes the process took years.

Jefferson determined to stop the indecent and undignified practice of ransoming Americans from pirates. In 1801 he sent warships to the Mediterranean. After four years of fighting, highlighted by the exploits of the younger Stephen Decatur, the Americans were able to sign a satisfactory treaty with Tripoli and to reduce considerably their payments to the other Barbary states. But owing to delays caused by the War of 1812, a final settlement was not reached until 1816.

Meanwhile the warring European powers came even closer to wrecking the commerce of the United States. This, of course, was not their avowed objective. Great Britain was fighting for her own survival and to prevent the permanent conquest of Europe by France. In this situation it was virtually impossible for the United States to maintain neutrality. Each side was trying to starve the other out; in the process both were strangling American shipping. The British, who held command of the seas, would not permit any American or neutral vessel to trade with continental Europe unless it stopped first in England—while Napoleon, in his turn, was prepared to seize any vessel that did stop there.

The United States was saved from open involvement in the war at this stage chiefly by its overpowering reluctance to ally itself with either side. Nevertheless there was a harsh and continuous trade war between both combatants and the United States, and about 1,500 United States ships were seized by the belligerents from 1803 to 1812. Even so, America prospered in trade until Jefferson got Congress to pass the Embargo Act in December 1807. In putting forward the embargo Jefferson's thought was that, since the warring states showed no respect for American shipping, all American vessels should be barred from foreign ports, and all foreign trade, going and coming, should be virtually outlawed. The Americans could trade with no one but themselves.

THE embargo hurt the United States far more than it hurt Britain or France. American exports dropped from $108 million in 1807 to $22 million in 1808. Warehouses were crammed with unsold goods, harbors filled up with idle ships, unemployment was rife, while merchants, manufacturers and farmers alike suffered heavy financial loss.

The law was enforced with a ruthlessness that Jefferson would have condemned had the Federalists been guilty of it. Congress passed an enforcement act under which the Federalists claimed Jefferson exercised just the sort of arbitrary power and infringement on individual liberties for which he himself had denounced George III years before. Not without some reason, he was accused of ruining the country, even though that was the last thing he had ever intended.

Not since the Alien and Sedition days had any measure been so hated. The first anniversary of the embargo's enactment, December 22, 1808, was observed everywhere as "Embargo Day." In the harbor at Beverly, Massachusetts, flags drooped to half-mast; in Boston the boats were shrouded in mourning. Petitions of protest flowed into Washington. Jefferson had split the nation and driven the Northeast close to secession. After 14 months of privation, popular pressure forced an abandonment of the embargo policy. On March 1, 1809, only three days before the end of his second term and his retirement from public life, Jefferson signed a law repealing the act.

"The Death of the Embargo"— sometimes called the "terrapin policy" by those who felt that it forced the U.S. to draw into a shell—depicts President Madison as a last victim of the hated act, being felled by the dead terrapin's snap. This wishful Federalist sketch, by a well-known portrait painter of the time, John Wesley Jarvis, appeared in the "New-York Evening Post."

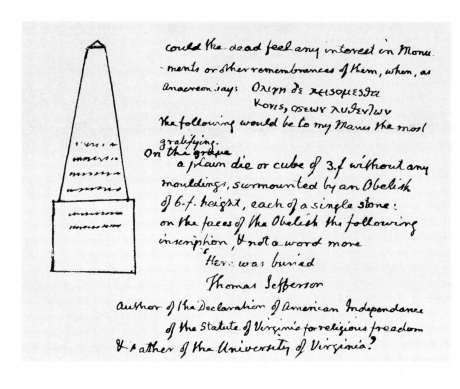

could the dead feel any interest in Monuments or other remembrances of them, when, as
Anacreon says: Ολιγη δε κεισομεθα
Κονις, οσεων λυθεντων
the following would be to my Manes the most
gratifying.
On the grave
a plain die or cube of 3.f without any
mouldings, surmounted by an Obelisk
of 6.f. height, each of a single stone:
on the faces of the Obelisk the following
inscription, & not a word more.
Here was buried
Thomas Jefferson
Author of the Declaration of American Independance
of the Statute of Virginia for religious freedom
& Father of the University of Virginia.

JEFFERSON THE PLANNER (*above*, in his first known portrait at age 33) is reflected in his original designs —for Monticello (*right*, with the building itself visible in the distance through the window) and for his gravestone (*left*), which he ordered erected after his death at his favorite place in the world, Monticello.

Monticello: a founder's memorial

THOMAS JEFFERSON was a many-sided man who spent almost a lifetime creating a house in his own image. He called it Monticello, and it was more than just a gracious home. Rather it was an extension of a single astonishing human being, displaying its creator not only as a statesman and politician, but also as architect, farmer, anthropologist, tinkerer, philosopher, art lover, inventor, musician.

Jefferson's interest in Monticello began in his boyhood when it was merely his "little mountain" (in Italian, *monticello*)—a hilltop 800 feet high in the midst of 2,750 acres owned by his father near Charlottesville, Virginia. Even as he played he dreamed of someday building a house on the summit. The property came into his possession on his 21st birthday, and work was begun only three years later, in 1767, the year he began to practice law.

Not only was Monticello built according to Jefferson's own plan (*opposite*), but it was constructed with wood sawed from his trees, bricks molded from his earth, stones dug from his mountain and even nails made on the spot. Jefferson moved into Monticello around 1772, and it was his home for the next 54 years. But the house was never really finished. For Jefferson, there was always something to add or change or improve. The most extensive of these remodeling jobs took almost a dozen years to complete. Consequently, as the decades passed, Monticello took on a uniquely personal flavor. The hand of Jefferson is visible everywhere, not excepting his own gravestone (*above*). However, to the three accomplishments he wished to have inscribed as a final memorial, he might fittingly have added a fourth: "Creator of Monticello."

Beauty achieved
by an exercise
in artful restraint

When he designed Monticello, Jefferson characteristically broke with tradition. Most plantations of his day consisted of a manor house surrounded by outbuildings—servants' quarters, workrooms, storehouses. Jefferson considered such a clutter unsightly and he artfully hid the outbuildings at Monticello by tucking them into the hillside on a level below the main plateau. Furthermore, hillside passageways interconnected all of them, including the main house, the law office *(left background)* later used by his son-in-law and the "Honeymoon Cottage" *(below main house)*, where Jefferson and his bride lived while Monticello was being constructed. Thus the view at right is all the more remarkable for what it does not show.

JEFFERSON PLOW, which he designed, bites into the red soil of the Piedmont area he loved. The plow was easier to handle and turned a deeper furrow than other models.

Tasteful testimony
to a wide-ranging intellect

WHILE the exterior of Monticello is stately and impressive, the interior is where the spirit of Jefferson really comes alive. Its strongly individualistic mood may be due in part to the fact that Jefferson was a widower during most of the years Monticello was his home—and thus had a free hand to do with it whatever he wished. He turned his entrance hall *(below)* into a personal museum, with elk and moose antlers brought

back by Meriwether Lewis and William Clark from their expedition to the West, the fossilized bones of a mammoth (on the marble-topped table), and a clock over the door that registered both indoors and out. The clock's cannon-ball weights, visible in the corner, marked the day of the week as they descended. And although Monticello may have lacked the wifely influence, these pictures testify that it did not lack for beauty.

THE PARLOR, with its 18-foot ceiling, exhibits a distinctly French influence *(right)*. It was used primarily for entertaining visitors. The parquet floor is thought to be the first of its kind in this country. It cost $200, which Jefferson considered very extravagant.

THE ENTRANCE HALL, Jefferson's own museum *(left)*, displays objects of natural history, plus busts of Voltaire, Jefferson himself and his old adversary Alexander Hamilton. The sculpture at the right is a copy of a Vatican statue, *Sleeping Ariadne*.

THE MUSIC CORNER of the parlor reflects one of Jefferson's greatest interests. His wife Martha played the piano and he the violin. Jefferson complained that music in the United States of his day was "in a state of deplorable barbarism."

69

A place for work and slumber

Jefferson's sleeping quarters were as much a place for scholarship as for slumber, in keeping with the reported boast of his old age that the sun had not caught him in bed in 50 years. The bed is in an alcove which opens on two sides for equal access to his study (above), or the bedroom beyond. Jefferson's day

began soon after dawn, when he sat down to answer correspondence in the candleholding swivel chair he is believed to have invented. It faces another Jefferson design—his revolving table, which allowed quick access to a variety of papers. Jefferson was busy here until breakfast, then later returned to work until about 1 o'clock. He referred to his voluminous correspondence as a "persecution of letters." One year he replied to 1,267, "many of them requiring answers of elaborate research." In this bed Jefferson died on July 4, 1826, a few hours before the death of John Adams, whose bust is in the background.

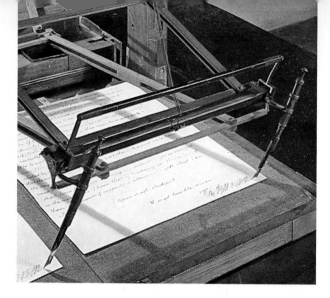

THE STYLUS of the polygraph above makes duplicates as the writer pens the original. Jefferson called it the era's "finest invention" and he contributed ideas to its design.

THE STAIRCASES at Monticello are only about half the ordinary size and there are only two in the entire house. Both are in inconspicuous—and inconvenient—locations.

THE SPECTACLES which Jefferson used cast their shadow across a diagram on tree-moving in a French book on agriculture. Gardening was one of Jefferson's chief delights.

Afternoon sunlight floods the dining table, set with 10 places. Dinner began before 4 p.m., for Jefferson liked to eat while it was still light.

The mind and courage to be different

THE incomparable flavor of Monticello is mainly a reflection of Jefferson's highly practical intellect—but a few sheer idiosyncrasies are also in evidence. Unlike most Southern mansions, Monticello has no grand stairways. Jefferson felt that all stairs were a waste of space, and made his so narrow that two people could not pass and women with hoop skirts complained. He also had an aversion to the interruption of good conversation, so he installed hidden dumb-waiters in his dining room so refreshments could be brought from the cellar without the intrusion of servants. However, these are not mere crotchets but evidence of a strong-minded originality which was always quick to try something unorthodox or new, such as the passageways connecting his hidden outbuildings, and the polygraph with which he signed letters. Jefferson both satisfied and stimulated his powerful curiosity by avid reading. In 1814 he sold more than 9,000 books to the Library of Congress but he still owned thousands when he died.

THE SUBWAY shown here leads from Monticello's basement to the servants' quarters. There are two of these passageways, one on each side of the house, located beneath long terraces.

A heritage preserved

Monticello, with its famous dome and west entrance, reflects the warm glow of the Virginia twilight. The finished design was a far remove from the dwelling Jefferson originally planned *(page 65)*. In 1789, after five years as the American minister to France and extensive study of European architecture, Jefferson

returned with plans to remodel Monticello. He virtually doubled the size of the house and added the dome, patterned after the Roman Temple of Vesta. The parlor is behind the portico. The wing to the right contains his bedroom, with the library to the rear. The dining room and tea room are to the left. Both wings open onto terraces. Jefferson's favorite was the northern one *(right)*, and he loved to sit there after dinner with his guests. One member of his family observed: "Here, perhaps, has been assembled more love of liberty, virtue, wisdom and learning than on any other private spot in America."

4. REACHING
TO THE WEST

WEST is the widest-stretching word in the American language. From the days when the first Yankees peered beyond the Berkshires and the first Southerners peered beyond the Blue Ridge, Americans have looked to the West, to the horizon beyond the mountains, to the unmarked line where earth and sky become one. For generations, the West was an outlet for the landless, a challenge to the pioneer, and a route of escape from the law, from taxes, from failure, from intolerance, from the old limitations and boundary lines.

In 1790 there were some 4,300 white people settled north of the Ohio River and east of the Mississippi; by 1800 there were 45,000 in Ohio alone. Hardship, coarse food and rough clothes reduced life for everyone—the idler and the worker, the judge and the lawbreaker—to a common denominator. The roads were blazed trails. Cash hardly existed; payment was made in hemp, hides, pork or ginned cotton. In 1800 a man advertised in the Tennessee *Gazette* that he would buy all manner of products, including cotton, sell them where he could and bring back cash: the middleman had arrived.

While carpenters in the long-settled coastal regions were carefully framing Federal-style houses, in western "raisings" whole communities turned out and entire cabins were erected, roofed, their log walls chinked and their rough chimneys coated with mud in a few hours. The floors were rough planks; often there was no window, or at most one covered with greased paper instead of glass. In the East men wore knee breeches and silver buckles; in the West they

A PLANNER OF EMPIRE, James Madison, the future President, is depicted here as Jefferson's Secretary of State—a role in which he helped add a vast domain to his country.

wore deerskin pants and homespun shirts. Back East was the world of the theater, the concert, the assembly dance and steepled churches; the West had gamblers, fights that featured eye gouging, and occasional religious services conducted by occasional circuit-riding preachers.

The people who settled Ohio, Illinois, Indiana, Wisconsin and Michigan— the old Northwest Territory—were mostly respectable citizens, many of them veterans of the Revolution using their war bounties for land claims. But few were well off, even fewer educated. Some were criminals, potential and actual. That this chaotic mass of people should shape states equal to the first 13 seemed unthinkable to some citizens of the old states. It was said that they had no political principles, and no ties to the East but debts.

The ways and means for new states to enter the Union had been worked out by that most westward-looking of American statesmen, Thomas Jefferson. Under a plan of his adopted in 1784, the Western regions would be governed as territories until their populations grew large enough for them to apply for statehood. The Northwest Ordinance of 1787 set the number of states that could be carved out of the Northwest Territory at no more than five and no less than three. It also spelled out an interim system of territorial government. Finally, the Harrison Land Act of 1800 provided procedures by which individual settlers could get title to their Western landholdings.

These were farseeing measures, and under them the West prospered. But there were still problems. Not the least was the fact that the region's chief waterway was effectively controlled by a foreign power. The Louisiana Territory, which stretched north up the Mississippi and west through a vast uncharted area, had been first French, then Spanish. Early in Jefferson's first Administration the Spaniards closed the port of New Orleans to American traffic, bringing great hardship to Western settlers—to whom, as Secretary of State Madison put it, the Mississippi "is the Hudson, the Delaware, the Potomac and all the navigable rivers of the Atlantic states formed into one stream." In 1800, the Spaniards secretly ceded the region to Napoleon. Reports of this soon reached the President. Despite his sentimental attachment to the French, Jefferson felt that any strong nation which held the mouth of the Mississippi was a threat to the United States. In 1803 the President sent James Monroe to France with an offer to buy New Orleans, and if possible West Florida, for two million dollars. Monroe failed to get West Florida, but he presented the President with New Orleans, the entire Louisiana Territory —and a bill for $15 million. "A truly noble acquisition," exulted Madison.

Robert Livingston, who helped negotiate the Louisiana Purchase, cut a tall figure in New York as well as in national affairs. As the Chancellor, or Chief Justice, of New York he administered Washington's first oath of office. He later backed Robert Fulton in the building of his famous steamboat, the "Clermont," named after Livingston's New York estate.

THE Louisiana Purchase confronted Jefferson with a dilemma. The Constitution said nothing about the acquisition of foreign territories—and as a strict constructionist Jefferson had long held that the Constitution must be rigidly observed. But a capable Executive must know when to put aside principles for the sake of country. Louisiana was necessary to the United States, not only politically but also militarily and strategically in a world racked by Napoleon's wars. Offered an empire that would double America's size, Jefferson let his common sense triumph over his constitutional scruples. He approved the purchase in what was probably the greatest single act of his presidency.

At first he proposed to legalize matters by a constitutional amendment. But his friends, fearful of a party fight and concerned lest Napoleon change his mind if there were any delay, urged him not to press for this. So Jefferson lamely proceeded to justify the purchase under the Constitution's treaty-making and war powers clauses—a loose-constructionist tactic that would have enraged the Republicans had the Federalists used it. As it was, Jefferson's use of Federalist means to promote Republican ends angered the Federalists—particularly those of the Northeast. If Louisiana were to be carved into new states, the threat to the Northeastern states was perfectly clear. They might become a helpless minority in the Union, outvoted and subjugated by Western sugar planters and fur trappers. It was said that the South had wrought this act to extend its own influence in the Union. Furious, certain Federalists even proposed that the Northeastern states prepare for secession.

Now that he had Louisiana, a host of questions pecked at Jefferson's restless brain. He had no information about the vast territory except fantastic tales of trappers. He wanted factual answers. He knew that in 1792 the Boston skipper Robert Gray had sailed his ship up the Columbia River and seen the edge of the Oregon country. Now Jefferson wanted this region explored overland. And Congress, by voting money to extend American trading posts with the Indians up the Missouri River, gave him the opportunity.

He would send a corps of exploration to the new Northwest, headed by his secretary, Meriwether Lewis. Then 29, Lewis had first seriously thought of exploring the Far West when he was 18. As his associate, Lewis chose a man born to distinguish himself: red-headed William Clark, younger brother of George Rogers Clark, a hero of the Revolution. They were completely unalike, Lewis and Clark, though they had shared some military experiences on the frontier. Lewis was shy and awkward and had a frightening moodiness; a shadow hung over him. A seeker of the wilderness, rather than native to it like Clark, he found his innermost needs satisfied by the challenge of nature. Clark, outgoing, forthright, practical, was a wilderness craftsman and a born leader who understood both the woods and men. It was essential that these two get along. They did. In all the vicissitudes they shared, they differed only on the palatability of dog meat and the necessity for salt.

Jefferson drew up their instructions: to find the source of the Missouri, to cross the mountain barriers, to reach the Pacific. Waterfalls, rapids and islands were to be located; weather, animal life, minerals were to be noted, as well as the kinds of furs. The President wanted to know about Indians and their customs, and he wanted specimens: the hides of strange creatures, perhaps some mammoth bones. These were the specifics. The grand design was even more sweeping: to discover the overland water route to the Pacific, to challenge the British fur trade, to fill in every possible blank place on the map.

The expedition got under way on May 14, 1804. It took off from St. Louis, then a frontier settlement and the center of a fur trade that encompassed a great network of posts running west along the Arkansas and north into upper Michigan. Since only traders would be understood or expected by the Indians, the explorers loaded their boats with such bartering necessities as mirrors, curtain rings and knives. They also took a fiddle (which some of the Indians they later met politely said they enjoyed).

The 23 men of the expedition were young, timber-tough frontiersmen. Lewis' dog Scannon went along, as did Clark's slave York, a black giant of a man whose unusual color the Indians vainly tried to rub off. The first test for the explorers was the Missouri, which—as one chronicler of the Lewis and

This "Portrait of a distinguished Mississippian" in an Eastern magazine pokes fun at frontiersmen's boastful description of themselves as "half-horse, half-alligator." The backwoods braggarts often added other ingredients: "a little of the steamboat," "a small sprinkling of earthquake," "a cross of the wild-cat," or, Davy Crockett's specialty, "a touch of snapping turtle."

Clark expedition put it—was not so much a river as a calamity. The channel currents could spring like unbroken colts, and as the men poled their way up they saw huge torn limbs of trees thrashing about in the river as if alive. Slowly the expedition struggled its way up through the center of the continent, past islands fringed with feathery forests and river bluffs resembling old forts.

It took the men five months to travel the 1,000 miles from St. Louis to their winter camp, near what is now the city of Bismarck, North Dakota. It was there, in the Mandan Indian country, that they made two important additions to the expedition's roster: a middle-aged French-Canadian guide named Charbonneau, who knew the language of certain river Indians, and his wife, a 17-year-old Indian girl named Sacagawea, who spoke the language of some of the mountain tribes. More to the point, Sacagawea knew something of the country into which the travelers were heading. We have Clark's testimony that "Janey," as he called Sacagawea, was "of great service . . . as a pilot through this country." For the Indian girl was a Shoshoni from the mountain regions. She had been kidnaped four years before by the Hidatsa, but could still remember some of the old landmarks, the river, the plains and "the pass through the mountains." Before the expedition left its winter camp the Indian girl gave birth to a boy, Pomp, who became the pet of the corps. In the spring, boxes were sent back to Jefferson laden with the scientific spoils of the first 11 months—the bones, skins and horns of strange animals, Indian clothing, live prairie dogs, a prairie hen and some magpies.

O N April 7, 1805, the expedition moved west, across the great flat country that unrolled, maplike, toward the horizon. Here the pleasant days faded off into cool nights, with the moon like a shining powder horn. Now the travelers knew how the birds must feel—from the top of a hill it was as if they could see forever, the sky above and the earth below, with the antelopes moving across the plains, light as blown dandelion dust. There was still snow in the mountains, and sometimes the wind came keening off the fields, driving at the men so they could hardly breathe. All the more joy did they take in a comfortable, dry night on beds of willow boughs, after a good supper of "broiled buffaloe well seasoned with pepper and salt and rich soope of the same meat."

The men hoped to find and make friends of the Shoshoni, for they knew the pass through the mountains. But finding the Shoshoni was no easy task; they hid from strangers. Finally, the day came when Sacagawea recognized a hill that looked like a beaver's head. This was Shoshoni country, then—and soon the travelers met the Indians themselves. Sacagawea provided the necessary introductions, and the Shoshoni agreed to make available the horses and guides the white men needed.

Now, crossing the backbone of the continent, for the first time they saw waters flowing west to the Pacific. They pushed on, through range after range, through the immense unspoiled forests. They drank from the Salmon, from the Snake and the Columbia Rivers, and built canoes that carried them down to the Columbia's mouth. On November 15, they saw the shine of the Pacific and the waves rolling in all the way from the China Sea.

The mountain country was obviously rich in beaver and otter, and Lewis and Clark saw that furs could be taken down the Columbia for the China trade far more quickly than they could by the route the British were using, through Montreal in eastern Canada. But if the British or any other power

Meriwether Lewis, co-leader of the great Western expedition, learned folk medicine from his mother, a famous Virginia "yarb [herb] doctor." Whenever illness struck the expedition he was ready with a remedy—such as a steaming brew of chokecherry twigs. Few of the men escaped his herb soups and bitter broths—and in 28 rugged months only one of the men died.

were to settle along the Columbia the whole area might well be lost to the United States. So a tall pine was carved to bolster the American claims: "William Clark December 3rd 1805 By Land from the U. States."

They spent a hard winter on the coast. Food was scarce, and Sacagawea gave Clark some bread she had intended for her child. Next spring the expedition started back across the Rockies, then dividing up so as to explore Montana. They reunited near the mouth of the Yellowstone, then moved on across the high plains. They lost their blankets when a raft overturned. One man had a hand-to-hand encounter with a grizzly. Little Pomp almost died. But finally they saw the Stars and Stripes floating over the village of La Charrette on the Missouri. They shouted when they saw some cows. On September 23, 1806, the explorers reached St. Louis.

Soon Thomas Jefferson read these words from Lewis: "In obedience to your orders we have penitrated the Continent of North America to the Pacific Ocean." The President was deeply moved. They had been gone 28 months and many had given them up for dead. But they had done it; they had filled in the empty spaces and charted the unknown. They came home without a man killed, although Lewis had been shot in the rear of his leather breeches by one of the group who had mistaken the two-legged animal for a four-legged one. One man, Sergeant Charles Floyd, had died, apparently of appendicitis. Sacagawea had twice almost died, once in childbirth and once from overeating. Congress voted a due reward, 1,600 acres each to Lewis and Clark, with double pay and 320 acres to every man who had accompanied them.

In the years afterward, Clark married and settled down happily. Lewis became governor of the Louisiana Territory. Most of the others dropped out of sight—but not all. One of the corps was later arrested for murder but was acquitted by a court in St. Louis. One became a judge. Another fought in the Black Hawk War. One, Paddy Gass, lost an eye at Lundy's Lane in the War of 1812, drank up his pension, married at 60 and had seven children, was baptized when 86 and was on hand during the Civil War to harangue the troops going off to fight. He was then 90.

And Sacagawea? When over 80, she seems to have persuaded the Shoshoni to move from the South Pass to the valley of the Wind River, to keep peace with the white men. There she lived, keeping some papers she had received from some "great white chiefs." In 1884 she died on the Wind River Reservation in Wyoming and her precious papers were buried with her. Her journey had ended; it had been nearly 80 years since a girl with swinging braids and a baby on her back had gone on an expedition that opened a continent to the sea.

THE explorers had returned home to shocking news. On the morning of July 11, 1804, Vice President Aaron Burr had mortally wounded former Secretary of the Treasury Alexander Hamilton in a duel at Weehawken, New Jersey, across the Hudson from Manhattan. Though Burr had been the more popular of the two, he was suddenly viewed with abhorrence. "No one wished to get rid of Hamilton in that way," old John Adams is said to have exclaimed.

Since his clashes with Adams, Hamilton had been living in semiretirement, practicing law in New York. Those years had not been good to him. Although he had a profitable practice, by 1804 he was deeply in debt. The chief reason was a series of unfortunate investments in land. Another was the house he had built on Washington Heights in northern Manhattan. He called it The

Sacagawea points out a route to Lewis and Clark. Lewis wrote of her: "If she has enough to eat and a few trinkets to wear I believe she would be perfectly content anywhere." Once, when the expedition's boat almost capsized in a gale on the Missouri, she sat calmly in the stern and rescued every possible piece of equipment as it floated past on the foaming water.

William Clark, who shared command of the journey west, kept up a family tradition that all carrot-topped Clarks would be renowned. The Indians called him "Red Head Chief." Clark named the Judith River in Montana after his sweetheart Judy Hancock, and married her upon his return to the East.

Grange, and even in a state of decay a century and a half later it retained a ghostly beauty. In an era of sumptuous Federal mansions, the greatest Federalist living had built a small, graceful house. With exquisite taste, he had scaled the dwelling to himself and his tiny, pretty and piquant Betsy.

Although Hamilton was no longer active in government, he had kept up his interest in politics—and in the process had run afoul of Burr. In 1802, Jefferson and Hamilton, in a rare moment of complete agreement, had worked separately to halt Burr's drive to become governor of New York. Hamilton had at least indirectly taunted Burr into action, describing him as "a dangerous man and one who ought not to be trusted with the reins of government." Burr, he implied, would stop at nothing in his drive for power. And so there came the tragic collision of two lives that had been strangely intertwined, of two men who were strangely and ironically alike.

They were both slight and handsome, although Burr was dark and Hamilton fair. Both were separated from their parents early in life—Burr orphaned when he was only two, Hamilton left on his own by his mother's death when he was 11. Both were prodigies, gifted writers, heroic soldiers. Burr was a youthful senator from New York when Hamilton was Secretary of the Treasury; from there on the differences grew. Burr had talent, real talent in his concept of politics as the art of the practical, but Hamilton had genius of a very rare kind: he possessed to an overwhelming degree the ability to get things done. Both were overambitious, but again there was a significant difference: Hamilton basically equated his ambition with the greatness of a great and growing nation; Burr basically used his country to further his own glory. Their lives ran on almost parallel tracks; then the tracks crossed and there was not room enough for both Alexander Hamilton and Aaron Burr.

The fateful "meeting" was held on a grassy ledge above the Hudson. Ten paces were measured; the cry rang out; Burr fired. Hamilton rose a little, spun on his toes, then reeled forward as his pistol went off, the ball clipping a limb seven feet above Burr's head.

The duel and its tragic outcome created a sensation, especially in the Federalist North. Both New Jersey and New York wanted to try Burr, New Jersey on a charge of murder. The Vice President was forced to flee, finally taking refuge in Spanish Florida. At last the furor died down and he boldly returned to Washington to resume his place as presiding officer of the Senate.

Burr knew now that he could never become President. In the last few

These four fanciful etchings decorate Patrick Gass's "Voyages and Travels of a Corps of Discovery." This first account of the Lewis and Clark expedition, printed in 1807, sold widely and included British and French editions. Lewis and Clark's own writings did not appear until 1814—after Lewis' death.

Captain Lewis & Clark holding a Council with the Indians

A Canoe striking on a Tree

months before his term as Vice President ran out in March 1805, he approached the British minister in Washington, seeking funds for mysterious purposes in the West. The envoy gave him no money, but apparently the Spanish minister later did give him some. Burr's purpose is unclear, but it seems that his plan involved an old friend, Major General James Wilkinson. Wilkinson, who had a sizable slice of the army at his disposal as commander of the American troops in the Mississippi Valley, was a scheming, red-faced, high-living man, secretly a paid agent in the employ of Spain. In the 1780s, before the Constitution was ratified, he had been planning to start an independent nation in the West. In 1796 he had dreamed of forming a Western Republic in the Mississippi Valley, with himself as "the Washington of the West."

Such notions fascinated many Americans, by no means all of them rascals; there was a real fear that the West might be taken over by Spain unless the United States moved first, or a rival power were formed. Even Jefferson, before the purchase of Louisiana changed his views, had seriously considered the possibility of two separate Atlantic and Mississippi Confederacies, wondering if the continent were too big to be ruled by a single power. In 1798 Hamilton had thought that a United States conquest of Louisiana and the Floridas might be the solution to the Spanish threat. The details of Hamilton's plan had been worked out with Wilkinson: the rendezvous at Cincinnati, the flatboats to go down-river to New Orleans and later a bold strike through the Caribbean. This plan failed for lack of support from President Adams. But there were many other plans and almost all had one element in common. The figure of General Wilkinson was always in the picture, sometimes as the Man on Horseback, sometimes as second-in-command to a more compelling leader.

From May to September in 1805, this leader was Aaron Burr. He moved about the Mississippi Valley, meeting with Wilkinson and others, gliding from settlement to settlement, leaving a trail of rumor. Everywhere, the former Vice President was toasted and received as a hero; the West had no love for Alexander Hamilton. Burr was as captivating as ever, and full of promises. He hinted of an empire to be set up in the West, and of fortunes for all who would follow him. He gave the impression that the government in Washington at least secretly approved his plans, which seemed to be based on war with Spain.

A newspaper hint that Burr would soon be enticing young men to follow him as "the head of a revolutionary party" was ignored in official Washington. But that winter Burr began openly seeking out money and recruits right in

Zebulon Pike never got closer to Pikes Peak than the summit of Cheyenne Mountain, 16 miles distant. From there, he said, "The unbounded prairie was overhung with clouds . . . like the ocean in a storm. . . ." Later the Colorado peak was named after him by another pathfinder, John C. Frémont.

Captain Clark & his men building a line of Huts

Captain Lewis shooting an Indian

the national capital. His blandishments even enticed a wealthy eccentric named Harman Blennerhassett into laying his fortune at the feet of Burr to build his empire. Blennerhassett's private island on the Ohio River—near what is now Parkersburg, West Virginia—was to serve as the port of embarkation. Flatboats were a-building at Marietta, Ohio, and at Beaver, Pennsylvania. More money was coming in; the one sure thing Burr seems to have done was to have enticed a great deal of money out of a great many people.

Now and then madness crackled across the scheme. One moment Burr talked of empire, then of real estate developments. Once, it is said, he burst out that, given 200 men, he could drive Congress and the President into the Potomac. With his new friends, as with his old, his stability was questioned. Perhaps this was what frightened Wilkinson, who wanted a winner, not a dreamer. Determined to save his own skin, he suddenly betrayed Burr to Thomas Jefferson—convinced, he said, that Burr's aim was treasonable. Whether it was or not, the opportunity had at last arisen to get Burr out of the way.

At this point Jefferson's tolerance for "Western Confederacies" evaporated. With Napoleon loose in Europe, it would be folly to let a would-be Napoleon loose in America. Then the inanity of the scheme began to unfold itself—"the most extraordinary," Jefferson thought, "since the days of Don Quixote." The President believed that Burr wanted to put himself on the throne of the Montezumas in Mexico, while extending his empire to the Alleghenies. In November 1806, Jefferson issued a proclamation warning all Americans not to take part in any such illegal expedition. Orders went out to arrest every man who looked suspicious. Burr's little group, in several flatboats, had almost reached Natchez before Burr learned of Wilkinson's accusations. In February 1807, the former Vice President, disguised as a Mississippi boatman, was arrested in Alabama while fleeing toward Spanish Florida. First he was charged with a misdemeanor, then with treason—specifically with levying war against the United States and with launching an expedition against New Orleans.

In August, Burr went on trial at the United States Circuit Court in Richmond. The presiding judge was Jefferson's old antagonist, Chief Justice John Marshall. Everybody who was anybody flocked to attend. Many of Burr's former friends had been called to testify for the prosecution. Others came uninvited. One day (an eyewitness later related) there sounded "a great noise of haranguing" outside a store not far from the courtroom. It turned out to be "a great blackguard from Tennessee, making a speech for Burr and damning Jefferson as a persecutor." The blackguard's name was Andrew Jackson.

Sequoyah, the son of a Cherokee woman and an itinerant white trader, was struck by the written language that settlers brought with them through the primitive wilderness. Though at first suspected of witchcraft by the Cherokee, he copied the white man's use of symbols for spoken language and made it possible for his tribesmen to read and write their own tongue.

WHETHER such street-corner testimony helped Burr is questionable. In any case, he did not need much help. The prosecution compared Burr with "the serpent in the garden"—the garden being Blennerhassett's Island. But this was hardly evidence, and as the trial progressed it became apparent that little real evidence existed. It was claimed that Burr had started an expedition from the island, but it was shown that he had not even been there when the "expedition" set out. Wilkinson's uneasiness as he testified against his former friend added no strength to the state's cause. Blennerhassett's papers seemed to show that Burr's "ultimate object was the throne of Mexico," but again, there was no proof that he meant to draw off the Western states.

Once again, John Marshall turned a case against Thomas Jefferson, and once again his was a precedent-making ruling. In his charge to the jury Marshall cited the Constitution's provision that "No person shall be convicted of treason unless on the testimony of two witnesses to the same overt act, or on confession in open court." There had been no overt act witnessed by two persons, said Marshall, and in this respect he proved himself as strict a constructionist as Jefferson had ever been. Burr was acquitted.

Nevertheless the former Vice President was ruined. Never again would he be a threat to Thomas Jefferson. He exiled himself to Europe to avoid being prosecuted by any of the several states eager to challenge his actions within their borders. He was virtually a man without a country, and had to pawn his belongings to live. Years later, when the news came that Texas had freed itself from Mexico, the aged Burr shouted: "I lived before my time!"

T HERE were other postscripts to the story of the opening of the West under President Jefferson. In 1805 Wilkinson had sent out his own corps of exploration, headed by Zebulon Pike, to search for the source of the Mississippi. The expedition failed when Pike mistook his rivers. The next year Wilkinson sent Pike out again on a more mysterious errand. Whatever Pike's purpose, his route took him up the Arkansas River into Colorado. There he saw—but did not climb—the great peak that now bears his name, then moved west and south. Winter closed down with hideous fury; Pike and his men sometimes went without food for days at a time. Nine men's feet froze. Yet they endured. In January 1807, Pike saw the Rio Grande, in Mexican territory, and once again got his rivers confused. Thinking it was the Red River, he put up a fort on one of its tributaries that he said was on American soil. That was what he said. But men would argue later that Zebulon Pike knew exactly what he was doing—which was gathering information inside Mexico for James Wilkinson. The Spaniards captured him and took him to Santa Fe, but they finally let him return. Pike had acquired much valuable information for Wilkinson's purposes, but Wilkinson's dream of empire had by then collapsed.

These pistols, owned by Alexander Hamilton's brother-in-law, Colonel John B. Church, were probably used by Hamilton in his duel with Burr at Weehawken (below). They may also have been used in two other duels involving the same families—a political row in which Hamilton's son Philip died, and a bloodless affair of honor involving Colonel Church—and Burr.

Meanwhile, less ambitious and less calculating Americans were pouring westward simply to settle the land. Great stretches that had been Indian hunting grounds were beginning to fill with cabins. But the West still was not without its mysteries. On the night of October 10, 1809, to a wretched tavern on the Natchez Trace, there came riding a man who had known fame, but for whom life in recent months had become almost more than he could bear. Meriwether Lewis had succeeded James Wilkinson as governor of the Louisiana Territory, armed with orders from Jefferson to get rid of Burrists. This he had done, with wholesale removals. Naturally, he had made enemies. He still suffered from terrible black moods. He feared that his health was failing. He was in financial difficulty. He had recently been unjustly reprimanded by Washington bureaucrats regarding some minor matter. At suppertime in the dirty tavern he ate only a few mouthfuls of food. When he went to his room he found that his wallet, his papers and his watch were missing. He went out, and men heard him muttering in the darkness: "They want to ruin me."

That night, distrusting the linen, Lewis bedded down on the floor, in bearskin and buffalo robes. Suddenly shots were heard. But for some reason, never adequately explained, no one investigated. The next morning the body of Meriwether Lewis was found lying 150 yards from the inn; apparently he had dragged himself there while mortally injured. Suicide or murder? His death was one of the great unsolved mysteries of the new and violent West.

Emigrant wagons rattle through Independence, Missouri, a starting point for the West, in 1853.

A vast, beckoning wilderness

THE typical American of the early 1800s lived in a strange land. The nation he knew was mainly a slender fringe of civilization along the East Coast; everything else was a mystery. He had heard of Jefferson's Louisiana Purchase, and some people said the country now extended all the way to the Pacific. But such vastness was inconceivable. West of the Mississippi lay an enormous void, a misty land of legends filtering back from frontiersmen like the trapper opposite. Americans heard all sorts of rumors about this wilderness. There was a story that it contained a lost tribe of Israel and possibly another lost tribe as well—of Welshmen. Thomas Jefferson asked one early traveler to the western regions to check a report that "The Lama or Paca of Peru, is found in those parts of this continent. . . ." Even when rumors were based on fact they seemed scarcely more credible—like the stories of prairies that stretched beyond a hundred horizons and of buffalo in such immense herds that they made a veritable sea of cattle.

But when Lewis and Clark returned from their westward journey just three years after the Louisiana Purchase, they stripped much of the mystery from the wilderness. They had blazed the trail to Oregon, and soon little Independence, Missouri *(above)*, would become the gateway through which thousands of Americans would venture, to see and settle the great West for themselves.

A TYPICAL TRAPPER sits astride his restless horse, carrying a muzzle-loading rifle and wearing buckskin trousers. The leather of the fringe could also be used for thongs.

A FRIENDLY MEETING with Flathead Indians interrupts the expedition of Lewis and Clark, shown at right with the Indian girl Sacagawea. The Flatheads were named by tribes who deformed their own heads into points and found normal skulls peculiar.

A HOSTILE MEETING with the Gros Ventre Indians ends happily for an 1833 expedition of the touring German Prince Maximilian. The Indians swarmed aboard, stole everything within reach but hurt no one. Lewis and Clark traveled in a similar vessel.

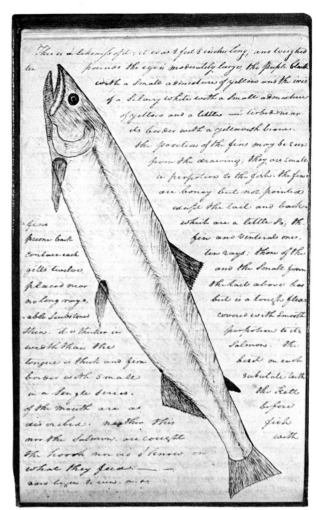

CLARK'S DRAWING of a salmon decorates his journal. In the same way that birds showed Columbus land was near, salmon convinced Clark the expedition was approaching the Pacific.

The ageless secrets of a continent unlocked

WHEN Lewis and Clark set off on the first major American exploration of the Far West they were hampered by nearly three centuries of misconceptions. Their main purpose was to find the fabled Northwest Passage—the transcontinental water route that men had long dreamed of. The dream had persisted so long that much of it had been accepted as reality. There was, many thought, an undiscovered "River of the West" which led to the Pacific; this notion had taken on such substance that the river even had a name, the Oregon.

However, the cruelest misconception concerned the immensity of the Rocky Mountains. It was said that a man could get over them with a portage of "about 20 miles." Lewis and Clark might have had even more

trouble getting through than they did had it not been for an improbable coincidence. One day in western Montana, Sacagawea, 17-year-old wife of the expedition's interpreter, saw some Indians and "began to dance and show every mark of the most extravagant joy. . . ." They were friendly Shoshoni—her own people, from whom she had been captured years before. Not only that, but their chief turned out to be her brother. The Shoshoni provided the party with horses and guides through the mountains. Three months later Clark jotted a historic line in his notebook, *"Ocian in view! O! the joy."* Returning eastward Lewis and Clark encountered a team of trappers already making use of the route they had blazed—the first of thousands who were to follow.

AN INDIAN PRISONER, Black Hawk *(right)* reflects un-dimmed pride, although he and his son are seen here in defeat. Caught in the Black Hawk War, they were displayed throughout the U.S.

Bold, flamboyant savages of the Western plains

WITH the great westward expansion of the early 19th Century, Americans met a new red man, the Plains Indian. He was a tall, independent, wild-riding figure *(right)*, to whom, generally, war was a sacred ritual, an exciting sport and a glorious way to die. His belligerence usually involved ancient feuds with other tribes and at the start he had no dispute with the white man. In nearly two and a half years, Lewis and Clark's little band met thousands of Indians of many nations, and were involved in only one hostile incident—at the hands of the notoriously bad-natured Blackfoot tribe.

The peace lasted while the white man remained just a visitor. But before long the wagon trains were rolling, and the Indian saw his land being appropriated in fulfillment of the white man's ambitions. The Sauk and Fox tribes of what is now the Middle West were among those who struck back. Their great leader Black Hawk *(above)* was defeated, but peace was ended—and in the Western Indian the white man had found a potent foe.

AN INDIAN RAID erupts outside Fort McKenzie as Assiniboin attack the Blackfoot. Painter Karl Bodmer, traveling with German Prince Maximilian, was an eyewitness as 40 Blackfoot were killed.

A Sioux rider, attacked by Snake

enemies, takes refuge behind his horse—secure in the knowledge that his foes would much rather capture his valuable mount than injure it.

TRAPPING BEAVER, mountain men invade an icy creek in the Rockies. One is preparing the pole to which the trap was fastened. The other baits a second trap. Of all the trapper's risks, perhaps the greatest of all was the Blackfoot Indians, who killed on sight, apparently urged on by the Canadian traders who employed them and who wanted to stifle competition.

TRADING THEIR FURS, Sioux Indians set up their tepees outside Fort Laramie. The Indians exchanged beaver pelts for dry goods, tobacco and watered alcohol. As a safety measure, the Indians were rarely allowed inside the fort. It was built in 1834 on an expanse of flat land with little growth that might hide an enemy, and a cannon was mounted in the gate blockhouse.

HUNTING GRIZZLY, members of the Maximilian expedition warily approach a snarling beast. Trappers, carrying only single-shot rifles, dreaded these hard-to-kill predators.

A fad of fashion that helped populate the Wild West

THE exploration and later settlement of the American Far West owed much to the seemingly insignificant fact that the fur of the beaver is uniquely barbed. As a result, beaver fur can be worked into a particularly luxuriant kind of felt. And because of the popularity of the high-crowned fur hat—which had been a European status symbol for generations—there was an enormous demand for beaver pelts. The high price paid for beaver sent a special breed of men westward into the American wilderness to search out every valley and swale where the rodent might build his dam.

These were the "mountain men" who roamed the Rockies. Usually they went singly, though sometimes in pairs. It was an incredibly hard life, lonely and perilous, and it demanded a degree of self-reliance rarely found even among Indians. Its appeal was its independence. Some mountain men grew to enjoy their solitary existence so much they disliked even visiting frontier settlements to obtain supplies.

But in the 1840s the vogue changed. Top hats were now made of silk rather than felt, and the fur trade declined. Yet there was still a need for the mountain men. The emigrant trains had begun to roll, and the trappers, because of their intimate knowledge of the Far West, were needed as guides. So, by a twist of fate, they wound up helping to bring an end to the solitude they loved.

93

The last great rendezvous

A caravan of trappers' supplies creaks across the plains on its way to the rendezvous at Green River in the mountains of west-central Wyoming. The rendezvous was a get-together that was sponsored every July by a fur-trading company. Trappers gathered at this meeting to exchange their year's catch of pelts for

the supplies they would need for another season in the mountains and to await the coming of their mail and newspapers. It also afforded the lonely trappers a rare opportunity for socializing, and the amount of whiskey consumed during the several days of the rendezvous was legendary. With the fur trade declining, this 1837 caravan, sponsored by the American Fur Company and made up of about 150 men and 20 wagons, marked the last of the large-scale rendezvous. But the route of most caravans was the Oregon Trail, which in a few years would feel the first wagon wheels of the coming flood of permanent settlers.

5. A SECOND STRUGGLE FOR INDEPENDENCE

WHEN Congress met in Washington late in 1811, the shadow of the Napoleonic Wars stretched darkly across the Atlantic. England needed seamen and was seizing them—"impressing" them—from American vessels. France needed ships and was commandeering numbers of American merchantmen. Both sides in the international conflict were demanding that America stop trading with the other. Both ignored the American slogan of "Free Trade and Sailors' Rights." "The Devil himself," wrote one congressman, "could not tell which government, England or France, is the most wicked." Madison's presidential message to Congress attacked them both.

The Embargo Act devised by Jefferson to cope with the situation had been repealed just before he left office, but the Republicans had not given up the idea that economic pressure might solve the American dilemma. In 1809 and 1810 Congress passed laws stating that if either France or Britain would agree to end its interference with American shipping, then the United States would immediately stop trading with the other. Napoleon quickly announced his compliance—but although the United States took him at his word, his navy continued to seize American ships. For 19 months Britain held out. At last, driven to the wall by crop failures, closing factories, unemployment and great backlogs of unsold goods, the British agreed to leave American ships alone. But it was too late. War with America was upon them.

Since June 22, 1807, when the British man-of-war *Leopard* had attacked the

A WESTERN WARRIOR, General William Henry Harrison is resplendent in military attire. Harrison built a political career on a handful of victories in the War of 1812.

97

John C. Calhoun was a moderate man who drank little and did not smoke or play cards. But he held strong views, and after a hot debate in 1813 Representative Thomas P. Grosvenor challenged him to a duel. A settlement was negotiated by a lawyer whose fame was yet to come—Francis Scott Key.

Brilliant but eccentric, John Randolph strutted about the House of Representatives with a whip in his hand. He was a vitriolic man who scandalized an era by referring to the marriage of the President and Dolley Madison, for no apparent reason, as being "an unfortunate matrimonial connection."

United States frigate *Chesapeake*, killing or wounding 21 men and impressing four, war fever had been mounting steadily in the United States. The impetus came not from the shipowners and seamen of New England, who knew they would suffer even more from open hostilities, but from Western frontiersmen who mistrusted Britain and hoped that war would bring the St. Lawrence and the Mississippi, Canada and the Floridas under the same flag. Frontier hatred of England was powerfully strengthened in November 1811, when troops under General William Henry Harrison, governor of the Indiana Territory, encountered hostile tribesmen at Tippecanoe, 50 miles from Fort Wayne *(see pages 110-111)*. After forcing these followers of the bold, eloquent and energetic Indian chief Tecumseh to retreat, Harrison's men captured British-made guns complete with ample supplies of excellent British powder. Harrison and many other Americans were convinced that England was plotting with the Indians to reconquer the United States.

THE Louisiana Purchase of 1803 had not only doubled the young republic's size, but had impressed the nation with a sense of its own importance. In this period of developing nationalism it was appropriate that the leader of the House of Representatives was Henry Clay of the frontier state of Kentucky.

Twenty years before, Clay had been a lanky, rawboned boy in southern Virginia. When his family sold the farm, he had turned to selling imported corsets and brandies in a Richmond store. He had migrated to Kentucky and had served as speaker of its legislature. Elected to the House in 1811, this buoyant, breezy young man with the light hair and impudently curling mouth had stepped almost straight from the door of the chamber to the Speaker's chair. Clay was the spokesman for the "War Hawks," a group of congressmen who were convinced of the necessity and inevitability of conflict, both for expanding young America and for national pride.

As his second-in-command in the looming debate over war, Clay chose young John Calhoun of South Carolina, a man completely unlike himself. It was part of the genius of Henry Clay, soon to be recognized as the most talented politician of his time, that he was able to utilize so well the very different talents of Calhoun: where Calhoun's great intellect could see exactly what *had* to be done, Clay could see, as if by instinct, what *could* be done —how far the people would be willing to go.

A driving seriousness of purpose animated Clay's group of young congressmen. In the muddy streets and half-finished buildings of Washington, "falling rapidly to decay," as one visitor wrote, they sensed a matching decay of the national spirit. They had no patience with Madison's long, careful diplomacy with the warring European nations. They were weary of his sending envoy after envoy to negotiate in the face of constant insults and injuries. In November 1811, the same month as Tippecanoe, the House Foreign Affairs Committee issued a report demanding that an army of 50,000 volunteers be raised and that United States merchant ships be armed. Calhoun took the floor to support the plan. He lacked Clay's easy charm and musical voice, but he spoke with a fierce intensity. The cost of war might be great, he said, but who would count in mere money "the slavery of our impressed seamen"? If the country was unprepared, it should be made to prepare. If it was not united, the common danger would unite all.

Calhoun was also mindful, as always, of the interests of his Southern planting constituency. British trade restrictions and embargoes had injured the South even more than New England. New England could cut back its trading and manufacturing, but Southerners could not cut down their slaves, nor reduce their expenses. Andrew Jackson of Tennessee asked, "Shall we, who have clamored for war, now skulk into a corner?"

This second generation of American statesmen coming to the fore in 1811 had all been marked to a greater or lesser degree by childhoods spent in the shadow of the Revolution. They had talents which set them above even many of the Presidents under whom they would serve. Yet they lacked the culture and the sense of a world beyond American continental frontiers which characterized the group to whom they already referred in reverence as "the Fathers," and whose work they felt dedicated to carrying on. No longer Englishmen, they were cut off from the cultural heritage of England. The frontier was of more concern to them than France, the Indians a greater threat than Napoleon. Clay had seen his father's grave violated by British dragoons. Congressman Felix Grundy of Tennessee had watched Indians scalping and murdering his relatives. Jackson bore the saber scars he had incurred as a boy when he defied a British officer. Calhoun grew up in the South Carolina hill country that was peopled with the ghosts of those who had died in the Revolution, in Indian raids, in Tory skirmishes. Consumed by hatred of the British, the War Hawks of 1812 understood almost nothing of the international implications of the war into which they were plunging their country. They understood only that this was to be a second war for independence.

They did not see, as others did, that neutrality had brought the United States prosperity. They saw only the humiliations suffered by their country. They were deaf to John Randolph's plea not to let the "last republic of the earth" become "enlisted under the banners of the tyrant"—to join against Britain with the dictator Napoleon, whose armies had overrun the once-free nations of continental Europe. The war Napoleon was waging was no ordinary war, Randolph insisted; it was against the liberties of all humankind.

Randolph's argument made no sense to the War Hawks. To them the French danger was imaginary, the British threat very real. "We are invited, conjured, to drink the potion of British poison, actually presented to our lips," said Henry Clay, "that we may avoid the imperial dose prepared by perturbed imaginations." Madison, who had no love for Napoleon but who accepted the inevitability of conflict with Britain, attacked Randolph angrily. "The damned rascal!" he snapped. "I wonder how he would conduct the government. It is easy . . . to make speeches." There was widespread public reaction against Randolph. The town of Randolph, Georgia, changed its name to Jasper.

On June 17, 1812, the British minister called on the President. He found him pale, with Clay and Calhoun flushed and excited beside him. They knew what the minister did not: a declaration of hostilities had passed the Senate. The next day the House approved. Britain and the United States were at war.

A patriotic kerchief commemorates America's second naval victory of 1812. In this encounter the frigate "United States" fired so fast that her shots appeared as "sheets of liquid fire," fooling British sailors aboard the "Macedonian" into thinking they had won. Instead their ship became a victory trophy.

T HE war vote in Congress was one-sided. Until the showdown, even the New England newspapers had been agitating for conflict—and then belatedly had come the realization that of all sections of the country, New England would be hurt the most by the war. Therefore the vote of the maritime states was divided, and influential New Englanders never gave real support to the war. The representatives of the interior could afford to vote for war:

they had no ships to be sunk, they could not be invaded or bombarded. The evidence is clear that almost all Congress members, regardless of individual votes, believed the grounds for war just.

It is plain too that despite the dreams of land-hungry young imperialists for "the whole of Canada," the real reason for the invasion the United States immediately planned was that Canada was the one place where the British were vulnerable. Britain would attack by sea; the United States would attack by land. The American decision to risk everything on a land war was an ironic one, for the young republic went to war in financial chaos, with an ill-prepared army of fewer than 10,000 men. On the other hand the American navy, though small, was, ship for ship, as good as any in the world—a fact the Americans themselves were the last to realize.

So the strategy was drawn. The Americans planned to invade Canada along the line of the Great Lakes. Major General Henry Dearborn with 6,000 men at Lake Champlain was to join General William Hull at Detroit and Major General Stephen van Rensselaer at Niagara in a pincers movement aimed at knocking Canada out of the war. For their part, the British mapped defensive action to beat back any threat to Canada, to blockade America's coast, crush its navy and finally invade the country.

The fledgling American navy struck some of the first and best blows of the war, notably through the exploits of the 44-gun frigate *Constitution*. Launched in 1797 and copper-sheathed in 1803 by Paul Revere, she was a beautiful sight: boldly painted in black and white, brave with gilt trim, and with towering masts that could carry almost an acre of white canvas. The *Constitution* got off to a lively start that summer of 1812, dodging a whole British squadron off New England in a wild chase from July 18 to July 20, then a month later sinking the frigate *Guerrière* as the British shot thudded off her planks, and finally slipping back to Boston with a load of 250 prisoners. Thus the legend of "Old Ironsides" was born. A succession of American naval victories followed. The *Essex* cap-

THE WAR IN THE NORTH:
VICTORY ON THE LAKES

The combatants of 1812 shared a common border—the U.S.-Canada boundary—and they waged war on both sides of it. The Americans launched a three-pronged invasion from Detroit, Niagara and Plattsburg, but inept leaders and green troops caused it to fail. Indecisive fighting continued all the way from Frenchtown in the west to La Colle Mill in the east. The U.S. finally gained control of the Great Lakes through Perry's victory at Put-in Bay. In the climactic battle the British, invading by the historic Lake Champlain route, were badly beaten at Plattsburg.

100

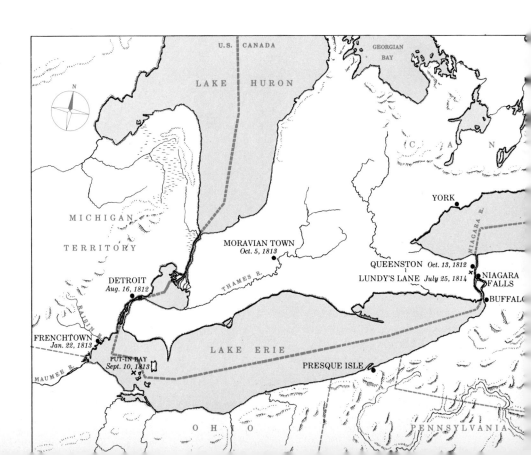

tured the *Alert*. Captain Stephen Decatur on the *United States* took the frigate *Macedonian* after a bloody battle. In October 1812 the *Constitution* sank the *Java*. In February the *Hornet* took the *Peacock*. British courage and experience, it seemed, counted for little against new ships and superior seamanship.

The two navies also clashed on the Great Lakes. Captain Oliver Hazard Perry, son of a privateersman of the Revolution and himself a veteran of the war with Tripoli, became a kind of young Nelson, eager only to be where the fighting was. At Presque Isle on Lake Erie, where he was ordered to support the Canadian campaign, he had found total unpreparedness: few boats, no guns, not a yard of canvas. He set to work. A white oak that was standing in the morning was part of a boat frame by afternoon. Iron hinges were ripped from the doors of barns. In all he built five new vessels. Five more were dragged by oxen up the Niagara River rapids outside Buffalo, where they had been hemmed in by the British, and were sailed over the great inland sea to Presque Isle. With his fleet assembled, Perry anchored at Put-in Bay at the western end of the lake. At sunrise on the morning of September 10, 1813, he saw the sails of the British ships loom over the horizon.

The British squadron was smaller and its men, cut off from the bulk of their supplies for about a month by the American fleet, were weak from hunger. And though the British had more guns, the American cannon were heavier. Perry bore down before a light breeze. As the ships came into range fierce firing broke out. The larger vessels in each fleet literally ripped each other apart. Perry's own flagship, the *Lawrence*, was sunk, and he had himself rowed over to the *Niagara* where he raised his flag. The *Niagara* broke the enemy line and was able to rake the British with both port and starboard batteries. With the smoke of battle still hanging heavy about him, Perry sat down and wrote his famous report: "We have met the enemy," he said, "and they are ours." Ship for ship, man for man, gun for gun, the Americans had outmatched the representatives of the proudest navy in the world. Now the bells could ring and the

War Hawk Henry Clay, known to history as one of Kentucky's most famous sons, was actually born in Virginia. He moved to Kentucky at 20, and before going into politics was the state's leading criminal lawyer. He had an enviable record in capital cases: it was said that no client of his was ever hanged.

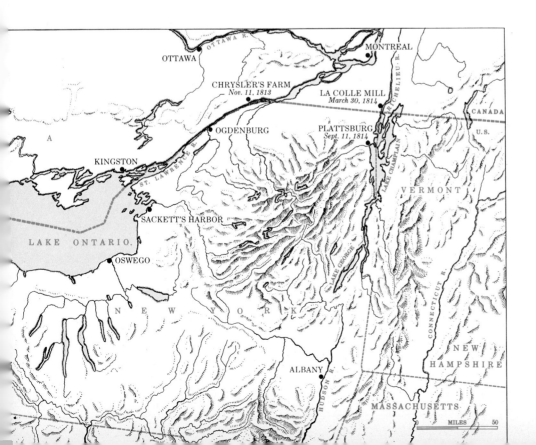

101

cannon boom in triumph. In the House of Representatives, John Calhoun exulted: "The charm of British naval invincibility is broken."

But the British were still powerful, and they found the course of the naval war intolerable. When the *Java* was destroyed, the *Naval Chronicle* in London merely said: "The subject is too painful for us to dwell on." No upstart power could defy the entrenched majesty of England; America must be swept from the seas. Grimly the British struck back. They ranged up and down the American coast, and succeeded finally in bottling up the ports and the fighting ships. American privateers, which had been active from the start, managed to evade the blockade, capturing cargoes, dogging and teasing the British fleet. But most of the Yankee warships were effectually sealed in their own harbors, and England was again mistress of the seas as Napoleon was master of the continent.

Charming Dolley Madison was one of the earliest, most brilliant Washington hostesses. Washington Irving, who attended one of her parties, found "a crowded collection of great and little men" and "ugly old women." He thought the hostess was "a fine, portly, buxom dame," but of her husband, Irving commented: "Ah, poor Jemmy!—he is but a withered apple-john."

ON land, matters did not come off at all as planned by either side. The hostilities got under way at Detroit in the summer of 1812. There the elderly American General Hull crossed into Canada, issued a ringing appeal for the Canadians to come over and exchange British "Tyranny and Oppression" for the blessings of American liberty, and then hurriedly fell back to the American side on receiving a false report that his troops were outnumbered. Eight days later he surrendered Detroit to a modest enemy force without firing a shot. At Lake Ontario General Van Rensselaer, commanding the second prong of the planned United States invasion, found the spirit of his men so high they could hardly wait to enter Canada. He turned them loose before dawn on October 10, when the first rowboat pushed off from the American side of the Niagara River. At that point it was discovered that an officer had stacked all the oars in that boat, so not another could follow. The American invasion had to be postponed.

Three days later, 325 men crossed over in 13 boats and drove the British back toward Queenston. Four hundred more Americans crossed behind them. Then the British rallied. Van Rensselaer was severely wounded. His men held and might have won—except that the rest of the troops would not cross. They had seen the dead being brought back in the boats. They had heard the screams of the wounded. Ignoring their officers' pleas to act like men, they stood by and watched the British defeat their compatriots across the river.

This pattern was repeated over and over again throughout the land battles of the northern frontier—at Stony Creek, at Beaver Dams, at Chrysler's Farm. There were men enough on the American side, but they would not fight. It was whispered that no volunteer should cross into foreign soil because this automatically made him a regular, liable for five years' military service. Many of the troops obviously had come to see a show, not to fight a war. Quickly it became clear that all hopes for the conquest of Canada were futile.

There were a few bright spots, but even these shone only by contrast to the general picture. On the evening of July 25, 1814, a force of Americans, including a brigade commanded by Winfield Scott, fought the British to exhaustion at Lundy's Lane in Canada, firing at such close range that in the flash of muskets the Americans could see the shining buttons on the red coats. Both sides claimed victory. And at Moravian Town, Ontario, on October 5, 1813, William Henry Harrison routed a mixed force of British and Indians in the Battle of the Thames, and finally ended Tecumseh's dream of a great Indian confederacy. This victory did at least remove the Indian menace in the Northwest.

Small triumphs in the interior were of no help to the besieged coast. The British were tightening their blockade from Maine to the Mississippi. Maine was invaded from Canada. By September 1814, the whole area east of the Penobscot was conquered and annexed. From the sea Admiral Thomas Hardy (to whom the dying Nelson had whispered "Kiss me, Hardy" at Trafalgar) landed at Eastport. Bangor surrendered with all its guns, food and ammunition—and the town even had to finish ships under construction and turn them over to the enemy. Farther south, Cape Cod was plundered and its townspeople made to pay tribute. When Stonington, Connecticut, refused to give in to Hardy it was bombarded half into ruins. At Hampton, Virginia, the British landed, pillaged the lightly defended town, raped a number of women and killed an old man in his bed. Another force of invaders swept in at Havre de Grace, Maryland, and burned two taverns, 13 houses and 10 stables.

Then came a major change in the balance of strength. On April 12, 1814, a defeated Napoleon abdicated as Emperor of France. An uneasy peace settled over Europe, leaving England free to send far greater forces to the New World.

In some places Americans made anxious preparations for the impending attack. The forts and entrenchments around New York City were like those of Revolutionary days, and men were forced to "volunteer" and dig, even to work at night. But elsewhere little was done. On July 4 Maryland called out 3,000 militia. Fewer than 300 showed up.

When a powerful British fleet appeared in Chesapeake Bay, Washington was virtually without defense. Citizens began to pack up and government clerks hid the public papers. Every available man had joined a makeshift force assembled to attempt a stand at Bladensburg, Maryland, but the disorder among them was chaotic. Women and children poured in a steady stream across the bridge to Virginia. Forty miles below the city, the British veterans landed undisturbed and marched on for hours as peacefully as if on their way to a picnic. At Old Fields, Maryland, they encountered a force gathered for battle, but the Americans promptly fled. Again at Bladensburg, a little army of clerks, mechanics and regulars turned and ran.

MADISON had left for Maryland to join the army, and the rout. His wife remained at the White House, to pile a wagon with curtains, silver, books and Cabinet papers. She could hear cannon muttering in the distance. Standing with a spyglass, Dolley Madison watched groups of military wandering about "as if there was a lack of arms or of spirit to fight for their own fireside." At 3 o'clock on that afternoon of August 24, two messengers, gray with dust and weariness, came and urged her to flee. Dolley hesitated. She was remembering a promise she had made to George Washington Parke Custis, Martha Washington's grandson. The Gilbert Stuart portrait of Washington must not be allowed to fall into British hands. Swiftly she gave the order, and the great frame was broken and the valuable canvas removed.

Panic was spreading. When a British squadron came up the Potomac River, the terrorized citizens of Alexandria, Virginia, across from Washington, sought and received terms, and worked for three days to supply the fleet. Not far away, according to one report, Dolley was for a time denied admission to a tavern (she had spent the previous night in a tent). In a woodland nearby, the President, bearing all the odium of defeat, "miserably shattered and wo-begone," seems to have stayed one night in a henhouse.

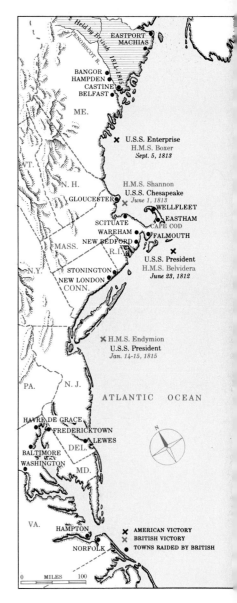

WAR IN THE EAST:

THE BATTLE OF THE COAST

The Atlantic coast of America became one of the most important battlegrounds of 1812. From its ports ventured United States ships to do battle with the British. They won their share of major offshore engagements, but a British blockade extending the length of the coastline virtually put an end to their excursions. In 1814 the British attacked the mainland in force. They invaded and occupied a large part of Maine and raided at will up and down the shore. More than a score of coastal towns were plundered and the capital city, barely a dozen years old, was badly burned.

I Josiah the first do by this my Royal Proclamation announce myself King of New England, Nova Scotia and Passamaquoddy. Grand Master of the noble order of the Two Cod fishes.

Representative Josiah Quincy of Massachusetts had a distaste for democracy. His arrogance inspired cartoonist William Charles to portray Quincy (above) as "Josiah the First, King of New England." When in 1812 war was declared despite his opposition, Quincy quit Congress. He later became president of Harvard and was depicted in more flattering fashion (below).

As the sun dropped lower the British tramped into Washington. Swiftly they began the work of destruction. At the Capitol they burned first the carpets and velvet hangings and the books; then 50 men thrust pikes tipped with fireballs through the windows and set the building ablaze. Next they made for the White House, where they stacked the furniture in the parlor, got a coal from a tavern and touched off another fire. The citizens who remained in the city could see it all like a scene in a play, the columns of flame rising upward, the government buildings "wrapt in one sheet of fire."

Next morning, under a somberly darkening sky, British Admiral Sir George Cockburn, who was riding around Washington on a white horse with a nursing foal, ordered his men to tear down a newspaper office. "Be sure that all the C's are destroyed," he said, "so that the rascals cannot any longer abuse my name." Rain was beginning to fall and high wind to blow. Suddenly an explosion rocked the American capital. A soldier had dropped a torch into a well where barrels of gunpowder had been hidden. A number of men were blown up. Then as a howling storm roared down upon the city, stripping off roofs, clawing up trees and rolling cannon about like logs, someone among the British forces thought he saw a great American army poised for attack on the heights above Washington. There was no army, but the call for retreat sounded. As the invading troops fell back, the Americans returned like ants to a crushed hill. Among them were the President and his wife.

At Baltimore the British encountered much firmer resistance. Their 25-hour naval bombardment of the city was notably unsuccessful. Poet Francis Scott Key, observing that the United States flag still waved defiantly at dawn, was inspired to write the verses that later became the young nation's anthem. Sullenly the British embarked and withdrew to the Caribbean.

IN scorched and blackened Washington came the darkest days of the war. The government needed $50 million if the war was to continue, but the government was bankrupt. Scheme after scheme for a National Bank to help finance the war was considered, reconsidered, rejected and shelved. Few people wanted to lend to a faltering government. As evidence of failing confidence in the currency, every bank from Albany to Savannah had stopped payment in coin. Taxes and prices rose sharply. Other things were going badly as well. The great naval hero Decatur got captured while trying to slip through the British blockade of New York in the frigate *President*. A futile attempt at one more trade embargo against England had failed; lawless smuggling was rampant. As Calhoun conceded, it was a practical impossibility to "say to the most trading and exporting people in the world, 'You shall not trade; you shall not export.'"

As early as 1812, Russia had made an abortive attempt to mediate between England and the United States. Then in the early summer of 1814 a five-man American commission arrived in Ghent, Belgium, to open peace negotiations. The end of summer brought galling news of the British price for peace: the Indian country of the Northwest was to become a neutral buffer state and about a third of America's territory from Maine westward would have to be ceded. The terms could not be taken seriously. Not a man on the commission—which included John Quincy Adams, Henry Clay and former Secretary of the Treasury Albert Gallatin—thought of yielding. They remained in Belgium, rejected the British demands and waited for better war news from home.

At last in October came word that a full-scale British invasion of the United States from Canada had been halted in its tracks near Plattsburg, New York, by a brilliant naval defense of Lake Champlain by 30-year-old Captain Thomas Macdonough. The battle of Lake Champlain was the decisive naval engagement of the war and a stunning blow to the British. In desperation the government offered England's greatest general, the Duke of Wellington, a North American command. Wellington told his government that its recent reverses did not justify the territorial demands it was making on the United States. After that, London was more willing to talk about peace.

Terms were finally signed in Ghent on Christmas Eve, 1814. All prisoners were to be released, all conquered territories returned and the frontier Indians pacified. Nothing was said about "Free Trade and Sailors' Rights" or the other maritime disputes. The British did not even withdraw their "right" of impressment, although by now this had become rather an academic question.

Though this treaty did little more than restore prewar conditions, it contained one important provision regarding disputed boundary lines. These were to be determined later by boards of commissioners. This was done very successfully in 1818, when the United States-Canada boundary was drawn from the Lake of the Woods in Minnesota westward along the line of the 49th parallel to the Rockies. However, the Oregon country, including part of British Columbia, was to be held in joint occupancy by Britain and the United States, thus creating an issue that would arise later to plague both nations.

While peace negotiations were dragging on, General Andrew Jackson was fighting his own kind of war. His immediate enemy was the Creek Indians; his task, to avenge the hideous massacre at Fort Mims, north of Mobile, in the summer of 1813. One thousand Creeks in war paint had stormed the fort's stockade at the very moment the drums were beating for dinner. Fifteen whites hid in the swamp and escaped, but 250 scalps were carried out on poles. The entire Mississippi Territory was in a panic.

Orders went out to quell the Indians. Jackson, a hot-tempered and combative man, was recuperating at the time from a shattered shoulder received in a shooting affray in a Nashville hotel, and somebody said he obviously was not fit to serve. "The devil in hell he is not!" responded Jackson. With his arm strapped to his side, and frontiersmen Davy Crockett and Sam Houston close at hand, he plunged 160 miles into the Alabama wilderness. At Horseshoe Bend, a looping curve of the Tallapoosa River, Jackson bombarded the Indian

"The Star-Spangled Banner" once read "through the dawn's early light" but was changed on the original manuscript (below). It was not designated the national anthem until 1916 and was not confirmed by Congress until 1931. The words were inspired by U.S. valor under British bombardment, but the music, ironically, is from a British song, "To Anacreon in Heaven."

O say can you see ~~through~~ by the dawn's early light
what so proudly we hail'd at the twilight's last gleaming,
to hose bro is stripes & bright stars through the perilous fight
O'er the ramparts we watch'd, were so gallantly streaming?
And the rocket's red glare, the bomb bursting in air,
Gave proof through the night that our flag was still there
O say does that star spangled banner yet wave
O'er the land of the free & the home of the brave?

breastworks, five logs high. Of 900 Indians, 500 were killed. Jackson's men suffered 200 casualties, and Sam Houston was badly wounded. But from that time on the very name of Jackson spread terror in the Creek tribe.

Named a major general to replace Harrison, who had resigned, "Sharp Knife," as the Indians called Jackson, made a harsh, unfair peace with the Creeks. He demanded and won surrender of 23 million acres of land, comprising a fifth of what is now Georgia and three fifths of Alabama. Then Jackson moved on toward the moldering old Spanish town of Pensacola which, he explained to Secretary of War James Monroe, had assumed "the character of British Territory." The nation waited anxiously, for time was running short. A British armada, equipped at a cost of one million pounds, was hovering off Cuba bearing men who had fought with Wellington and Nelson.

Jackson took Pensacola after a brief fight, and on November 11, returned to Mobile, convinced that the British would land there. He was wrong. The British prepared to disembark directly on the Louisiana coast opposite New Orleans. Jackson moved fast. In nine days his men were in the threatened city. Too ill with dysentery to stand, he lay on a sofa at his headquarters, drinking brandy and issuing orders until the city resounded to his vigorous commands. Quickly he transformed New Orleans into an armed camp—although when a Kentucky division arrived, he found to his horror that there were but 700 guns for over 2,000 men. "I don't believe it," he burst out. "I have never seen a Kentuckian without a gun and a pack of cards and a bottle of whiskey in my life."

Jackson ordered his men to set up batteries of naval guns, supporting them on the soggy ground by building wooden platforms on cotton bales that had been sunk deep into the earth. The American commander broadcast an appeal for arms and men, and received an offer of help from a strange quarter. A tall, sun-tanned, Bordeaux-born smuggler and pirate named Jean Lafitte had been lured by the British with the offer of a captain's commission. Instead, he offered himself to Jackson, along with his intricate knowledge of the bays and bayous of the river country and a polyglot mixture of men. Jackson accepted Lafitte—price on his head and all.

JUST after dawn of January 8, 1815, a rocket soared up, signaling the start of the British attack. Behind their frost-covered earthworks, a double row of logs two feet apart and filled in with dirt, lay Jackson's men, peering into the morning mist—pirates, Tennessee backwoodsmen in brown homespun hunting shirts, Kentucky riflemen, a battalion of free Negroes, Creoles in colorful uniforms, Indian fighters, even a few former soldiers of Napoleon, waiting to face the British troops who had beaten their exiled emperor. As the breeze opened ragged patches in the fog, there was revealed an entire field of red tunics, crossbarred in white, a great army bearing knapsacks and scaling ladders, advancing briskly in cheering columns 60 men wide.

Tense but steady, the Americans watched for the British to come into range. Finally the American guns sounded, their flashes lighting the fog into all the colors of a rainbow. "Fire!" came the command again. Rank after rank opened. "Fire!" The solid front was cracking, the men in the red coats falling, one eyewitness reported, like blades of grass beneath a scythe. "Fire!" The British commanding officer, Major General Sir Edward Pakenham, went down. Now the Highlanders moved forward with their swinging kilts, and wider and wider grew the spaces between them. The field, once shining with frost, was now

In an ignominious defeat, General William Hull, with about 2,200 men, gives up Detroit to a smaller force. Hull was an old man whose troops held him in contempt. They were planning to mutiny and go on fighting when he surrendered. Disgraced, Hull spent the rest of his life trying to vindicate himself, and his son and grandson were still trying 37 years after his death.

dirty red. "Fire!" British officers were striking at their halting men with the flats of their swords, but to no avail. They had experienced a disaster.

The British had 2,036 killed and wounded at the Battle of New Orleans. The American casualties were 21. Months later the stench still lingered over the battlefield, with parts of bodies poking up out of thinly dug graves. That bloody morning made Andrew Jackson an authentic American hero.

NEWS traveled slowly, and New Orleans was fought 15 days after the Ghent peace treaty was signed. On December 15, delegates from Massachusetts, Connecticut, Rhode Island, Vermont and New Hampshire, unaware that the final peace terms were being hammered out and that British troops were landing in Louisiana, gathered at the Hartford Convention to vent their spleen against war and the encroaching power of the federal government.

These were angry men. In the 25 years of the republic, New England had had but one President—and he had lasted for only one term. The others were all Virginians and Virginians did not seem to understand New Englanders. Now New England had been invaded and overrun. Northern commerce was being damaged—and that was nothing new; it traced back to Jefferson's 1807 embargo. Echoing the principles of state sovereignty that had been sounded in the Kentucky and Virginia Resolutions of 1798, the Hartford Convention declared: "In cases of deliberate, dangerous and palpable infractions of the Constitution, affecting the sovereignty of a State and liberties of the people; it is not only the right but the duty of such a State to interpose its authority for their protection, in the manner best calculated to secure that end." This threat only echoed the previously expressed sentiments of a New Hampshire congressman, Daniel Webster, who had denounced a proposed conscription act as "a horrible lottery" to "throw the dice for blood." Should such an "unconstitutional" measure pass, he said, it would be the duty of the state governments to resist its execution.

But before any of the states were called upon to perform such a duty, the news of New Orleans spread joyously across the land. Then in early February came the glad word from Ghent. Torchlights flared. Crowds surged shouting through the streets. Bunting rippled across the blockaded ships in the harbors. New England's disaffection was forgotten. Bonfires threw flickering shadows over the burned ruins of Washington. At the Octagon House, the temporary presidential mansion, Dolley Madison queened it once more, her round white shoulders bare and her cheeks bright with rouge.

"A peace! A peace!" was the cry—and the fact that the peace had been signed before New Orleans was fought seemed to matter not at all. From that day to this, the American people have been fully convinced that they defeated the British a second time. As for the British people, they have been barely aware that the War of 1812 ever occurred.

A useless war, many have called it. Perhaps. But to the Americans of the time, fighting this war had been a matter of the young republic's existence, its subsistence, its very being. The United States had to fight, Henry Clay always said, as a proud young man might fight to prevent being bullied. Now that it was all over, the United States could be better friends with Britain than ever before. In any event, Americans emerged from the War of 1812 certain, as they had always suspected, that they were a great nation. And, armed with this happy delusion, they were able to exist most comfortably until they were.

"The last of the great freebooters," handsome Jean Laffite (left), concludes an agreement to support General Jackson at New Orleans. The dashing French-born criminal once had a $500 reward placed on his head by Louisiana's Governor Claiborne. He promptly returned the compliment by posting bills in New Orleans offering $5,000 for the governor. Neither was caught.

The British sack Havre de Grace—one of several atrocities committed by both sides in the War of 1812.

A small war on far-flung fronts

THE War of 1812 was, on the whole, a series of small-scale actions. Rarely were as many as a few thousand men engaged in one place at one time. American casualties in two and a half years were 5,000-odd, fewer than fell in an hour at Gettysburg; and total U.S. war expenditures, including veterans' pensions, came to $127 million, less than the cost of the American Revolution. Yet this small conflict was played out on a world stage. At sea, it produced duels on the China Sea and the Pacific coast of South America, in American harbors and the home waters of Great Britain. On land, it was fought from Spanish Florida north to Maine and west to New Orleans, and along the 1,000-mile border between the United States and Canada.

The sheer distances involved were a constant frustration to both antagonists. Great Britain's high-seas fleet was so huge it could blockade much of the American east coast and easily ignore the loss of an occasional warship (*opposite*), but it was not big enough to safeguard all of England's long supply lines from swift U.S. privateers. Nor could this mighty navy reach inland to secure the Great Lakes from the bold sallies of young American captains. The war's main front, the wild Canadian border country, swallowed up its British garrisons, regulars, militia and Indian allies. But the modest forces the U.S. could send north accomplished little and left the American home towns continually exposed to amphibious attack (*above*). With England bled white by the Napoleonic wars, and with America weakened by sectional dissension, neither side had the strength to sustain an effective invasion. Though both sides tried again and again, the war settled early into a pattern of scattered skirmishes which virtually guaranteed that the outcome would be inconclusive.

THE U.S.S. "CONSTITUTION," renowned as "Old Ironsides," rakes the crippled *Guerrière* in a famous engagement off Nova Scotia on August 19, 1812. Its last mast shot away after 30 min-utes of point-blank broadsides, the *Guerrière* surrendered. To Americans, whose navy entered the war with fewer than 20 ships, the defeat of one of England's 600 vessels was a major victory.

A victory that named a hero

On November 6, 1811, about 800 U.S. troops camped for the night near an Indian village on the Tippecanoe River. General William Henry Harrison had been authorized to attack the village after his parleys with the great Shawnee Tecumseh had failed to settle land disputes or to stop sporadic killings. But

Tecumseh's absence, which had prompted Harrison to risk the expedition, encouraged hotheaded tribesmen to strike first.

Just before dawn, some 450 braves stormed the camp. They were driven off in a fierce battle *(above)*. Although the soldiers lost 61 killed and 127 wounded, far more than the Indians, Harrison claimed a resounding triumph, and British arms left behind by the Indians increased the clamor for war on England. Harrison would be elected President in 1840 on the slogan "Tippecanoe and Tyler too," but the 1811 triumph helped drive the Indians into a brief alliance with England.

TECUMSEH FALLS during the battle of the Thames, mortally wounded by a mounted American reputed to be Richard Mentor Johnson, later a Vice President. The great Indian leader had fought despite the incompetence and broken promises of his British allies. But after he died, his followers melted away, leaving the U.S. with the upper hand in the border war.

In a daring stratagem, 14 American warships under Captain Thomas Macdonough engage a British squadron while riding at anchor off

Deadlock on the border, triumph on the lakes

AMERICANS in 1812 generally concurred with Thomas Jefferson's opinion that "the acquisition of Canada this year as far as the neighborhood of Quebec, will be a mere matter of marching." But the vast, sparsely settled borderlands presented enormous tactical difficulties. Moreover, green troops, as at Queenston (*right*), together with fainthearted commanders, made a shambles of the army's elegant three-pronged invasion plan. Not until late 1813 did America win its first important victories under leaders of genuine stature. Oliver Hazard Perry smashed the British fleet on Lake Erie (*next page*), permitting him to ferry about 4,000 men under William Henry Harrison into Ontario. On October 5 the self-styled victor of Tippecanoe clashed with his old adversary Tecumseh along the Thames River. When the chief of chiefs fell mortally wounded (*opposite*), England lost the battle and its Indian allies. And when the British launched an invasion in 1814, they were thwarted in the battle of Lake Champlain (*below*).

ATTACKING QUEENSTON, Americans cross the Niagara River, only to be crushed when panicky militia refuse to follow. By the artist's error, Americans are in red, redcoats in blue.

Plattsburg on September 11, 1814. British troops, at left, fighting to cross the Saranac River, withdrew soon after their fleet surrendered.

COMMANDER of a jerry-built squadron, 28-year-old Oliver Hazard Perry sits before his banner, inscribed "Don't give up the ship." That had been the dying order of Captain James Lawrence, after whom Perry's flagship was named, and in the battle of Lake Erie Perry helped make the phrase a battle cry of the U.S. Navy.

ELUDING gunfire on Lake Erie, Captain Perry, with his 12-year-old midshipman brother seated behind him, abandons the *Lawrence*, which wallows *(left)* with its bulwarks battered in and its deck slick with blood. Once aboard the *Niagara (right)*, Perry slashed through the British fleet and quickly forced its surrender.

115

SIR GEORGE COCKBURN, who joined the navy at nine, turns his back on burning Washington. Napoleon, whom he escorted to exile on St. Helena, called him "choleric and capricious."

An ignominious campaign around the nation's capital

IN 1814, in order to take American pressure off Canada, England increased its own pressure on the Middle Atlantic coast. To Admiral George Cockburn's fleet, which had turned Chesapeake Bay into a British lake, were added many more ships and General Robert Ross's seasoned infantry, released by the fall of Napoleon. Their logical objective was Baltimore, chief base of the pesky privateers. But first Cockburn and Ross routed a ragtag militia at Bladensburg and set Washington on fire to revenge the Americans' burning of York (now Toronto).

This side trip cost the British dearly, for by September 12, when their huge armada hove to off Baltimore, 10,000 Americans were in a rage over their capital's fate and were deploying to put up a stiff defense. The invaders struck simultaneously by land and sea. Before serious fighting began on shore, two young skirmishers recognized Ross and neatly shot him off his horse. With Ross's death "the army lost its mainspring," and two days later the fleet failed to reduce Fort McHenry *(opposite)* and force entry into Baltimore harbor. Thoroughly disheartened, the British returned to their ships, lay quietly offshore four weeks more, then sailed away to the south.

A British cartoon, showing President James Madison fretting about his dinner while Washington burns, calls him a tool of Napoleon.

AN ANTHEM IS BORN on September 14, 1814, as Francis Scott Key spies Old Glory flying above Baltimore's Fort McHenry. Inspired by the fort's all-night stand under terrific bombardment, he wrote the words to "The Star-Spangled Banner." Key had sailed out to the British fleet a week before to ask for a friend's release. Both were held until the battle had ended.

117

Peace without victory and a bloody epilogue

O N November 4, 1813, England offered to negotiate an end to the war in North America. But afterward its leading ministers stalled and made impossible demands, confident that British victories would force the U.S. to submit to a dictated peace. Decisive victories did not come. Instead, sharp reverses at Plattsburg and Baltimore damaged England's prestige in Europe and added to the discontent at home. Grudgingly the British government authorized realistic compromises to match America's. The final treaty, framed at Ghent, managed to restore prewar conditions without mentioning the causes of war. Before word of this cautious peace could reach America, the war's bloodiest battle was fought near New Orleans on January 8, 1815. With a wasteful courage that provided a fitting climax to years of futile conflict, Sir Edward Pakenham paraded his scarlet legions into impregnable American positions (below), to die in a "leaden torrent no man on earth could face."

THE PEACE is concluded as John Quincy Adams (*center*) and Lord Gambier exchange copies of the Treaty of Ghent on December 24, 1814. The American negotiators argued constantly but were aided by Britain's preoccupation with European affairs.

THE SLAUGHTER at New Orleans begins as the British, marching from right to left, are riddled by Americans dug in on the Rodriguez Canal. Jackson, near the U.S. flag, saw his right flank repel the redcoats along the Mississippi (*foreground*).

6. SLAVERY: THE GREAT DIVIDE

DURING the half century that preceded the Civil War no anguish more violently racked the American body politic than that caused by the passions aroused by slavery. The first high fever in what would prove to be an almost mortal illness for the federal union came with the Missouri Compromise debate that began in the House of Representatives in 1819 and kept the Congress in constant ferment for two years. It all started when Alabama applied for admission to the Union as a slave state—and Missouri surprised and angered the North by applying at the same time and requesting the same status. No one disputed that Alabama should come in as a slave state. Under the terms of a gentlemen's agreement in Congress the number of slave states in the Union was to be kept equal to the number of free states, and the admission of Illinois a year before had created an imbalance in the North's favor, which would be righted by Alabama. But Missouri would throw the balance the other way. So on February 13, 1819, Representative James Tallmadge of New York offered an amendment declaring that no more slaves could be brought into Missouri and that the children of those already there must be freed upon reaching the age of 25. North and South, the uproar began.

Contributing to the ensuing confusion, during the debate the House moved into new quarters in one of the two rectangular wings of the Capitol. It had been five years since the burning of the building by the British. During those years the members had met in such varied places as Blodgett's Hotel and in a

THE TRAGEDY OF SLAVERY is dramatized in a poignant English painting of the mid-1800s showing families of Negroes being broken up at a railroad station in Richmond.

James Tallmadge, whose antislavery amendment started the Missouri Compromise furor, served in Congress only two years. A leading New York lawyer, he was regarded by some as a poor politician—"one of nature's bad bargains," said an observer. Nevertheless he became lieutenant governor of New York.

Jesse Thomas, whose suggestion of a slavery boundary solved the Missouri problem, went to Congress first as a delegate from the Indiana Territory. Then he helped Illinois break away from Indiana and became a senator—from Illinois. Thomas nominated William Henry Harrison for President in 1840.

temporary building hastily erected by public-spirited citizens. The spacious new chamber was the talk of Washington. Tall marble columns supported the visitors' gallery, with great crimson drapes between to help deaden a persistent echo. Huge candlesticks stood on Speaker Henry Clay's desk, and a canopy of red silk hung above his chair. Some people sniffed that such luxury was out of place in a democratic legislature.

Many of the House members were new, too—86 of 186 representatives—and in that fact lay the rub. More than half of the newcomers were from the free states. In 1790 representation in both houses of Congress had been divided fairly equally between North and South, but by 1820, although the balance still held in the Senate, in the House free-state votes outnumbered those of slave states by 24. And if Missouri came in as another free state, even the Senate would be weighted against the South. This was what terrified the slave interests. Southerners felt that by presuming to set conditions for Missouri that no other state had ever been forced to meet, Congress would be assuming powers not specifically granted it by the Constitution. If this was carried one step further, Southerners feared, Congress might even claim the power of abolition; with Northern control, millions in slave property might be wiped out by a simple majority vote.

THE South was at bay, fear was an ugly undercurrent of the debate and the word "disunion" was spoken openly by the South for the first time. Southerners were concerned partly over the specific issue of Missouri, partly over the broader issues that lay beyond it. Slaves were the basis of Southern wealth. If slavery was barred from the new state, Southern slave traders would lose a valuable market and Southern economic interests would be disregarded when Missouri's vote was cast in Congress. Furthermore, if the North achieved superior voting power throughout Congress it could help itself to economic advantages at the expense of the plantation South.

A great divide was widening between the two sections: the North with its small farms and growing industries, the South changing year by year into the huge plantation economy which legend would erroneously identify with the entire region as "the Old South." The furious congressional debate between these two factions was a fearsome omen—"a title page," John Quincy Adams observed, "to a great tragic volume."

It was clear that some middle ground had to be found. Emotions on both sides grew stronger and stronger as arguments raged over the endless proposals and counterproposals. Finally a slavery settlement was worked out along lines suggested by Senator Jesse Thomas of Illinois. Thomas' amendment drew an imaginary line across the continent at 36° 30', with the further spread of slavery to be prohibited "forever" north of this line—except in Missouri. Under the compromise, to balance the admission of Missouri as a slave state, Maine was to enter the Union as a free one, thus maintaining the balance of power: 12 states on each side.

The compromise settled little. The North felt that it gave the South much the better of the bargain. It permitted slavery in Missouri, where the North had sworn to block it. Worse, it permitted the further spread of slavery south of the artificial line. And though most of the unsettled land south of the new slavery line belonged to Mexico, that was small consolation. It was widely believed at that time that most of the land north of it (the present wheat and corn belts) was useless prairie, "resembling the steppes of Tartary." Northern congressmen fought the compromise bitterly.

The bill passed the House by three votes—and then John Randolph made one last effort to scuttle it. Randolph, although he admitted slavery to be an evil, insisted that Congress had no right to limit the institution's spread. He clamored for reconsideration of the Thomas amendment. Shrewdly Speaker Clay ruled that the insistent Virginian would have to wait until other business had been transacted. But when Randolph arose again it was too late; Clay had seized the opportunity to sign the bill and send it secretly back to the Senate, which had already approved a similar bill. The Senate passed the new measure without debate.

The storm now broke over the Cabinet. President Monroe, hesitant and questioning, was convinced that the limitation of slavery, "if not in direct violation of the Constitution," was "repugnant to its principles." Monroe would have vetoed the measure outright had he not feared the possibility of civil war. Secretary of State John Quincy Adams, on the other hand, disliked the compromise not because it was unconstitutional but because, he said, it perpetuated the Constitution's "bargain between freedom and slavery," which he called "morally and politically vicious." But Adams supported the measure as the best that could be passed under the circumstances. Ultimately the President did sign the bill, establishing slavery for the first time in a state beyond the Mississippi River.

Indignation mounted among the Northerners. A meeting of New Yorkers termed slavery an evil damaging to the welfare of the entire nation. In Philadelphia a slate of antislavery presidential electors was framed, and DeWitt Clinton of New York was named to oppose Monroe, who until then had been the most popular Chief Executive since Washington. Somberly the aged Thomas Jefferson termed the settlement "a reprieve only."

And indeed it was. The compromise became law in March 1820. By fall the

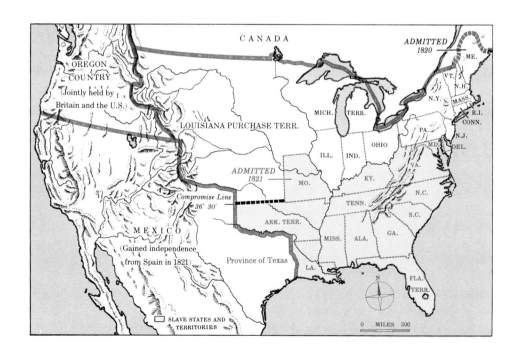

MISSOURI COMPROMISE:

THE U.S. SUNDERED

The controversial Missouri Compromise left the United States almost equally divided: 12 free states and 12 slave states (in brown) plus the free territory of Michigan and the slave territories of Florida and Arkansas. The amendment proposed by Senator Thomas, which made the Missouri Compromise possible after months of congressional debate, barred slavery north of 36° 30' in the Louisiana Purchase Territory—except for Missouri. By this provision Texas was admitted to the Union 25 years later as a slave state and Oregon became a free territory in 1848.

dispute had flared up again, hotter than before. In the intervening months Missouri had adopted a state constitution which excluded free Negroes from entering the new state. Northerners in Congress, infuriated by this provision, refused to approve the constitution, blocked Missouri statehood and started the fight all over again.

At this point Henry Clay, who had earlier resigned the speakership, moved into the center of the dispute. Clay's heart was heavy with foreboding. He was not a profound man. He was from a border state, and he neither saw nor cared to see the deeper moral and legal aspects of the slavery question. What he did see was that the country he loved, the Union he served, was in terrible danger. Nothing, he knew, could be worse than disunion and civil war. America was the hope of all the newborn and struggling republics across the world. Slavery, he had said, was a curse to master and slave alike, but the Union was what mattered.

It was Clay, finally, who found a solution. Let Missouri make clear, he suggested, that its constitution's offensive provision was not intended to abridge the freedom of American citizens—including, presumably, free Negroes—and only then let her be admitted to the Union.

The Northerners fought this second compromise fiercely; it was obviously intended to sidestep the issue instead of meeting it head on. But now Clay began to work on the waverers. To the Kentuckian politics was the art of the possible, of making government work. He knew that he could not change minds that were already made up. But he could and did cajole the uncertain. He was indefatigable now. "He uses no threats, or abuse," wrote Representative William Plumer Jr. of New Hampshire, "but all is mild, humble, and persuasive—he begs, entreats, adjures, supplicates & beseaches us to have mercy upon the people of Missouri." Nor was he above flattery. He kept telling the Northerners he was sure they had "too much justice, good sense, and good feeling" to vote wrong on Missouri. He found the votes, and the Clay compromise slipped through, 87 to 81.

Missouri became a state in August of 1821. But the echoes of the debate would not die out. It was the intensity of the reaction in the North that dismayed the rest of the country. It was clear now that before the Missouri issue arose, the thinking of Northern antislavery groups had been based on a grave misconception: that the status of slavery had long since been settled. It had not, and the question would arise again.

IN one sense the South was right in its contention that slavery was, from the first, part of the warp and woof of the Union. Many slaves could trace their families back in America for more generations than could some of the founding fathers. Until the Revolution, slavery had existed in all 13 states. It gradually disappeared in the North, where the climate, the economy and the popular conscience were against it, although Yankee skippers were by no means opposed to a profitable trade in slaves. But no effort was made to limit its spread by law until the Ordinance of 1787, which forbade slavery in the Northwest Territory. In New York and New Jersey, although plans for gradual emancipation were in effect, slavery still existed as late as 1827. At least once Congress had washed its hands of the entire question: in 1790 the House denied that emancipation was in its power.

Up to the 1790s there had been a Southern drift toward gradual emancipa-

Because their work was so physically demanding, sugar cane cutters were the South's most costly field hands. At one period their price rose so high in the New Orleans slave market that a Louisiana planter tried hiring Irish and German immigrants instead. This expedient backfired: in the middle of a sugar harvest the hired workers went on strike for double pay.

tion, but then it began to reverse itself. There were by that time an estimated 700,000 Negroes in slavery. "Thank God they are," declared one South Carolina congressman, and he called upon his colleagues to witness what had happened in Santo Domingo. In this Spanish and French possession, which later became the Dominican Republic, Negroes struggling for liberation had been merciless in their battles against French efforts to suppress the rebellion. Nothing terrified United States Southerners more than the specter of infiltration by such free Negroes whose example might inflame American slaves with revolutionary ideas of liberty, equality and fraternity. By 1800, the United States slave population had jumped to 900,000, but even these numbers could not meet the demand for slave labor, and kidnapers along the Mason and Dixon Line continued to pounce on freedmen above the border.

South Carolina, which had abolished the slave trade in 1787, actually reinstated it in 1803 because, as William Lowndes explained, the illegal trade went on anyway, without supervision or control. In 1808 the trade was abolished permanently by federal legislation. But by then slavery was so much a part of life in the South that all talk of emancipation had virtually disappeared. Thus, time and history were working changes in men's minds of which they themselves were all unaware until the cleavage widened into the painful schism of 1819.

Printed evidences of slave trading such as this raffle notice (above) and an auctioneer's business card were commonplace in the South. The slave traffic was such big business that one important company of traders, Franklin and Armfield, netted over half a million dollars for each of its partners, while a dealer in Memphis is said to have earned $96,000 in just one year.

THE facts of economics, too, were making irrevocable changes in the thinking of men. In the 1820s the South was still primarily a society of fairly small plantations. At that time it displayed more of the breezy characteristics of the frontier than the "aristocratic" society that legend depicts. Neither the Appalachian uplands nor the tobacco-growing valleys of Kentucky and Tennessee were suited for the big plantation type of agriculture, and depletion of the land in the older states had given rise to soil conservation programs and plans for the introduction of small industries.

Suddenly, at the end of this decade, the plantation system began to renew its youth. Better breeds of cotton had been developed. The cotton gin, invented in 1793 by Eli Whitney of Connecticut, efficiently combed the troublesome seed out of short-staple cotton and thus made possible a production of the crop greater than the South had ever known. And the demands of the Industrial Revolution both in England and New England were calling for cotton, more and more cotton.

Of equal importance, the Louisiana Purchase and the later theft of Indian lands in Georgia and Alabama opened vast new areas for plantation economies. The Louisiana Delta had proved ideal for growing sugar cane, and by the 1830s Louisiana would produce one half of the nation's sugar.

To raise these crops, slaves were moved inland by the thousands from the seaboard states. The new plantation South needed more slaves to insure its prosperity; the old slave-dealing South needed to spread slavery to insure itself against poverty. Interest in soil conservation dwindled as the new supply of rich lands opened up, and diversification of the economy was indefinitely postponed—a fact that would have fatal consequences for the South in 1861.

In 1790 the South had raised 1.5 million pounds of cotton. By 1810 it was raising 85 million, and by 1820 the total was 160 million. Slaves, once a burden on their masters, had now become a huge economic asset.

The full, rich blooming of the "Old South," the traditional South of the plantation, was a hothouse flowering that lasted a bare 20 years. Even for that brief period this Old South was less a fact than a dream, a Southern ideal based on the institution of slavery. The goal of the Southerners who had the dream was the Greek city-state, with the equality of the master class guaranteed by the fact that even the lowest of them were superior to the most able slaves. Even the slaves accepted a large part of this dream, taking a pitiful pride in the ancestry of their white owners, and basking in the reflected glory of a master who had wealth and social position.

Above all, slavery was a social system, for both whites and blacks. Assured that the color of their skin admitted them to membership in the superior caste, even the poorest whites were drawn to the support of what the South called its "peculiar institution" of slavery. Only a handful of Southerners owned the great houses with the white columns, or the supposedly happy slaves in the cabins, or the wines, saddles and Chippendale chairs from overseas, or the rich fields white with cotton. But this was the Southern ideal, the life to which every white man aspired.

Economically, a different system might have worked, but there came a time when slavery seemed the only possible way of regulating the relationship between the races. This is what Calhoun had in mind when he declared slavery to be "a good—a positive good." In no country, he said, was so much done for the laborer, or "more kind attention paid to him in sickness or infirmities of age." This was oratory. Slave death rates were higher than those of free men, and few lived long enough to be taken care of in age.

But the Southern way of life had its elements of beauty too, and it won a passionate loyalty from all its white citizens, rich and poor, whether they shared the ideal or the less pleasant reality. To be sure, in some places the glittering surface of plantation life masked drunkenness, evil and depravity. Yet the eminent Boston divine William Ellery Channing commented that for all their vices the Southerners of the aristocracy had greater virtues than the New Englanders. They had grace, gallantry, courage, charm and a warmth that won all who knew them. "Could I but take from the Virginians their sensuality and their slaves," Channing said, "I should think them the greatest people in the world."

Freed slaves lived in fear of being kidnaped by whites such as this gang of ruffians and then being sold back into slavery. The reward for such villainy was high and the danger was slight, despite protective laws, since Negroes were not allowed to serve as witnesses. One Philadelphian devised an unsavory variation: he married mulatto women, then sold them as slaves.

As for the slave, he too was the result of the society that held him in bondage. His life was bounded by a few square miles around his cabin, dominated by fears and mysteries he could not understand. His pleasures were few: some jigs and shuffles, spirituals and folk tales that blended his terrors and trials with the darkness of a half-forgotten Africa, his rum and whiskey, and perhaps coffee and molasses at Christmastime.

In most places slaves were given a certain minimal protection from the law. The Alabama legal code of 1852, although granting the owner the right to a slave's "time, labor and services" and unquestioning obedience, also required that masters provide their slaves with food, clothing and care. Southerners also maintained that they could not afford to mistreat slaves—who were, after all, valuable property. "I always tell them it is the slaves who own me," one South Carolina woman complained. Day in and day out, she had to doctor them, train them, look after them. A Virginia agricultural magazine advised, "Your negroes will breed much faster when well clothed, fed and housed." And nothing worse could be said of a slave master than the quiet comment: "I have been told that he does not use his people well."

Still, life under slavery, even when not harsh, was not easy. Sometimes it was cruel. Under slavery (as under freedom for most of the century that followed) Southern Negroes could be tried only by their white superiors, not by their peers. They could offer no evidence against a white man. Furthermore, although stealing a slave was a serious crime, it was not a crime to kill him while punishing him.

Many slaves were grossly overworked, and the exhausted women often miscarried. Slaves were sometimes given only 15 minutes for lunch and forced to labor by the light of the moon. Even the old slaves washed clothes, cooked, gardened and cared for children. The smoke-blackened slave cabins were often badly built and sparsely furnished. While some slaves were free to raise their own vegetables and chickens for pin money, most were too weary to do so. "Hog and hominy" (the fatter the pork, the better) was their staple food for months at a time. As labor, slaves were profitable investments, for their keep seldom added up to more than $35 a year.

BRUTAL slave floggings were not so common as is sometimes believed, but they did occur. "Shrieks of anguish" sounded from house windows were not unusual, and William Lloyd Garrison once counted 37 bloody gashes on a human back that looked as though it had been raked with a currycomb. In field gangs the whip was always present and occasionally used. Punishment—or at least the threat of it—was at the very root of the slave system. It was applied deliberately, often in regret. "Never inflict punishment when in a passion," advised a Louisiana master, but another man was convinced that slaves would "not labor at all except to avoid punishment." Testifying to the latter view, the Northern writer Frederick Law Olmsted watched an entire field of Negro women raise their hoes and stop work the moment the overseer had passed, never lowering them until he turned toward them again.

Certainly slavery could not have long endured had owners been stripped of their power to punish. Most masters preferred the power of persuasion, of judiciously chosen bribes and rewards. Still, it was felt that there was some risk to treating slaves too well. The better the master, the more real the dream of freedom became.

All through the South a determined effort was made to paint a glowing picture of slave life for outside consumption. In this process a stereotype of the Negro was developing. "Sambo" was passing into folklore: the shuffling, childlike, happy-go-lucky, irresponsible figure of fun, who (no matter how old) remained a dependent "boy" all his life. At worst, the Southern attitude toward Negroes was identical to that shown toward other possessions. Newspaper advertisements referred to "breeding Negroes," and a master who reported the death of two slaves in the paper commented: "Neither a serious loss," then added as if with real regret: "One valuable mule has also died." At best, the story was different. The master could be a father to his slaves, and sometimes a loving and kind one; the slave children, one Southerner said, were "quite pets."

But the Southerners were well aware that the public opinion of the world was against them. However valiantly they tried to persuade themselves that the Negroes were happy and desired no other life, they knew better. They knew how the resentment of the Negro smoldered underneath—how a trusted

The North had to answer for terrible labor conditions of its own. Child laborers, like these youngsters sewing in a shoe factory, became an important factor in New England's growing manufacturing economy. In 1832 about one third of the nation's factory workers were children. They very often worked 12-hour days, six days a week, for as little as 11 cents a day.

female when punished might suddenly turn on her mistress, how more than one faithful body servant had waylaid his master with a club. They knew how thin was the crust upon which they walked. They could write, as did Governor James Hammond of South Carolina, that no human ties were closer than those of master and slave, then in the next breath burst out to the abolitionists: "Allow our slaves to read your writings, stimulating them to cut our throats! Can you believe us to be such unspeakable fools?"

It was argued that Negroes expected no better life—that many had, after all, been slaves in their native Africa. Not only was this a faulty rationale—the existence of slavery in a primitive land certainly did not excuse it in a civilized one—but it was a fallacious comparison. There was indeed slavery in Africa, but the family unit was recognized, there were courts and court trials, and labor was highly specialized.

Slavery had existed in South America even earlier than in North America, but with two significant differences. First, there was no color barrier; once freed, a Negro was accepted on equal terms with whites. Second, under both law and theology, the Negro slave in South America was a person and not a thing. Marriage was a sacred rite there even among slaves. Concubinage was condemned as adulterous. The Catholic Church strove to regularize unions between the races. The Latin American slave could be a husband and father, a merchant or artisan, a communicant of the Church. Freedom was always a strong possibility, and he could even dream of becoming a priest or a military officer. Never did his master have power of life and death over him. And it is certain that "Sambo" never developed in South America.

A mystical crusader for the freedom of her people, Sojourner Truth was born Isabella Baumfree about 1797 in New York State. A slave until freed by state law in 1827, she assumed her symbolic name in 1843, claiming divine guidance. Though she could neither read nor write, she became a famous and compelling orator at antislavery gatherings throughout the North.

IN the United States the Negro had to submit to a subtle process of degradation. The slaves' very religion was a painstakingly censored version of Christianity, planned to force the dependence of the slave upon his master. Religion was an outlet, not a discipline; marriage was a celebration, not a sacrament, and held no validity in law. The "family" was a mother and her children only; the children belonged to their master, not their father, who had neither rights to his offspring nor to his marriage bed. The "father of a slave is unknown to our law" was the ruling of a Southern jury. Slave children learned early that their parents had no authority and could offer them no safety or protection against the terrors of the world. It was the white master who held the power.

As the property of their masters, slave women often became the white men's mistresses. Lafayette in 1824-1825 observed with astonishment how much paler Virginia's black population had become since his first visit to America in 1777. A leading South Carolina family was known to have Negro ancestry but was, nonetheless, accepted as white. More than one white man brought a divorce suit against his wife for alleged relations with a slave. The women lacked this legal recourse. "My disgust is boiling over," wrote one plantation lady. "Like the patriarchs of old, our men live all in one house with their wives and their concubines; and the mulattoes one sees in every family partly resemble the white children." The idealized white Southern woman paid a high price for her unsullied purity. Often she saw her sons led astray by the easy availability of slave girls and her young children degraded, as Jefferson had observed, by learning from their parents of the awesome power they could exert over slaves.

But the change was coming. Northerners were convinced of it, many a Southerner suspected it and a few Negroes were already fighting for it. "Stand back, nigger, and let that lady on," roared a Washington streetcar conductor in the mid-1800s to an ex-slave, Sojourner Truth, as he flung her against the door. She threw back her head, and with her words announced the dawn of a new era for her race: "I am a lady, too."

Paradoxically, at the time of the great divide in the early 1800s some of the nation's most active organizations trying to deal with the Negro problem were in the South. Some were bona fide antislavery societies, as dedicated to the cause of Negro freedom as any groups in the North. Others were colonization societies, formed for the purpose of resettling American Negroes in Africa. Although in the North colonization became associated with the cause of emancipation, in the South the movement was something else entirely. Its purpose was to return to Africa only *free* American Negroes, thus—or so the colonizers hoped—removing from the scene the most active and troublesome agitators on behalf of freedom.

Colonization also was politically popular among the wage earners, North and South, who were affected by the economic competition of the free Negro. On the same basis it received support as late as 1862 from no less a leader than Abraham Lincoln, who urged Congress to supply funds for the purchase of Negro slaves for resettlement in Africa. If the Negroes could be deported, Lincoln said—and he personally urged a group of Negroes to permit themselves to be—it would do more than open the way to solution of the slave problem. When you reduce the supply of black labor, he said, "by precisely so much you increase the demand for, and wages of, white labor."

In fact, colonization was vigorously endorsed by influential Americans all over the country—but not by the Negroes themselves. In 1830, after 10 years of unrelenting campaigning, the country's foremost colonization society had resettled only 1,162 Negroes in Liberia. The Negroes of Philadelphia, claiming to be among America's first settlers, probably spoke for the majority when they asserted that "to thrust the free people of color into the wilds of Africa" would merely impose upon them another kind of slavery.

Slave, soldier and tyrant, Toussaint L'Ouverture led the rebellion which overthrew slavery in French Haiti and Santo Domingo. His bloody fight for freedom dismayed slaveholders and cheered antislavery factions everywhere; William Wordsworth composed a sonnet to him. But by 1801 he had become a cruel dictator. He was captured and died in a French dungeon in 1803.

ON New Year's Day, 1831, in Newburyport, Massachusetts, a slight, haggard man issued a newspaper and a promise and shattered the public peace for a generation to come. The paper was the *Liberator;* the promise was "I will be heard." The man was William Lloyd Garrison. His cause: the complete, immediate abolition of slavery in America.

In William Lloyd Garrison was the unyielding granite of the Puritan Fathers and some of the fanaticism of Salem. Garrison did not invent abolition; it had had its advocates for as long as slavery had existed. But no one did more than he to arouse public opinion in its favor—and against it as well. He had no knowledge of the enemy he fought and no interest whatever in the causes that had fastened slavery upon the country. But he never stopped fighting for its abolition. He burned the Constitution in public as "a covenant with death and an agreement with Hell" because it permitted slavery. He denounced the Union as "infamous and accursed" because it existed under a proslavery Constitution. He called America's churches "a brotherhood of thieves" because they did not espouse abolition. He was a goad, a gadfly, an unceasing irritant to the consciences of an apathetic citizenry. Scornfully he brushed aside all plans for gradual emancipation; slavery was a sin, and you could not wipe out sin piecemeal. "If slaves have a right to their freedom," he said, "it ought to be given to them, regardless of consequences."

For many years the abolitionists were almost as unpopular in the North as they were in the South. In 1835 a mob of rioters dragged Garrison through Boston at the end of a rope. He walked with head erect and eyes flashing, and when rescued he said quietly: "I am sure I could bring them to reason."

At about the same time an abolitionist editor in St. Louis named Elijah Lovejoy denounced the decision of an appropriately named Judge Lawless, who condoned lynchings as "beyond the reach of human law." Lovejoy's office was mobbed and his press was destroyed. He thereupon moved across the Mississippi to Alton, Illinois, where he continued his denunciations of slavery. Once again a mob sacked his office and this time Lovejoy was killed.

During the next few years, proslavery mobs howled down abolitionist meetings in New York, leveled an abolitionists' building in Philadelphia where rights of women and wrongs to Indians had also been discussed, set fire to a home for Negro orphans and stoned Negro churches. In their own congregations Northerners rarely heard slavery denounced. The famous Congregationalist Henry Ward Beecher, although opposed to slavery, considered it a minor problem compared with the "ferocious beast" of Roman Catholicism or the "modern infidelity" of Unitarianism.

WHO then were the abolitionists? Most of them were simple middle-class working people. Their selflessness was complete. Personally they had nothing to gain from abolitionism, and much to lose. They knew that the businessmen who were the community leaders opposed them fiercely. Northern business, which needed Southern markets for its prosperity, had a genuine fear of secession and civil war if the slave question was agitated.

Nothing deterred these crusaders for freedom. They traveled hundreds of miles to antislavery meetings. They distributed tracts and spirited runaway slaves out of the South by the hundreds. They were like waves eating away at rocks. Out of their agitation would come John Brown and "Bleeding Kansas," Abraham Lincoln and civil war. In addition to their own single-mindedness they had one great weapon: in the ranks of slavery's enemies were enlisted the acknowledged intellectual leaders of the time. There were Ralph Waldo Emerson and Henry Wadsworth Longfellow and Oliver Wendell Holmes; John Greenleaf Whittier, a poet-politician, fighting with all his Quaker passion; William Cullen Bryant, champion of "Free Soil . . . Free Men"; Henry Thoreau, the mystic, who said, "Let your life be a counter friction to stop the machine"; the clergymen William Ellery Channing and Theodore Parker; the orator Wendell Phillips, a Boston mayor's son whom a Virginia newspaper termed "an infernal machine set to music."

From the pens of such men came pamphlets calling for emancipation and insurrection which were sowed in the South where they aroused a passion of anger and fear among the white inhabitants. Charleston burned the pamphlets publicly, and President Jackson asked Congress to authorize postmasters to stop the distribution of "incendiary publications" or any other material that "tended to instigate slaves to insurrection."

The abolitionists supported the Underground Railroad, a system of Northern hideaways through which runaway slaves were passed to safety. The South

One of America's first boxers was the freed slave Tom Molineaux, who is seen in an English ring. Born in Virginia in 1784, Tom was given his freedom—plus $100— for whipping a neighboring plantation's best fighter. He worked his way to England and had considerable prestige there, though he failed in two close fights to beat the English champion, Tom Cribb.

fought the Underground Railroad with every weapon at its command. Maryland put a price of $12,000 in gold on the head of Harriet Tubman, the slave leader who had escaped to freedom north of the Mason-Dixon line but continually made trips back to bring out passengers on the Railroad.

Despite these antislavery efforts, the North had much to answer for in its attitude toward slavery. Southerners often compared conditions under slavery with conditions in the Northern mills. The comparison was valid only when the most fortunate Southern Negroes were matched with the least favored Northern millworkers—and even then the most abject millworker had the one thing Negroes wanted most: freedom. Yet those mills with their inhumane working conditions did exist, and many a Northerner supported the Southern view. "It is a well known fact," wrote one union leader, "that the blacks of the south enjoy more leisure, time, and liberty, and fare quite as well as the operatives in the northern and eastern manufactories."

There was, moreover, a double standard in the North. Northern workmen repeatedly demanded laws excluding Negroes from their trades. Many kindhearted Southerners who had freed their slaves saw them subjected to shocking brutalities in the cities of the North where they came into competition with free white labor. John Randolph fortunately did not live to learn of his freed slaves being driven off by Northern white violence from the Ohio farmlands he had provided for them. Great was the indignation in the North when Missouri prohibited the entry of any free Negroes into the state, yet New Jersey and Pennsylvania denied free Negroes the vote, and Illinois and Indiana imposed limitations on their immigration.

There was an utter lack of incentive for the free Negro. In no state could he serve on a jury or be elected to Congress or the state legislature. In most areas he could not ride in the same carriage or work in the same building with a white laborer. It was of no use for him to try to elevate himself, for good jobs were not open to the Negro. His segregation, social and economic, was complete. In Philadelphia, 17,000 were jammed into a dark and dirty slum area.

For writing abolitionist editorials, Elijah Lovejoy lost his press (above), his warehouse (below) and finally his life to an Alton, Illinois, mob in 1837. But his crusade was taken up by his brother Owen, who had seen the martyr die. Entering politics, Owen campaigned for Lincoln, was elected to Congress and introduced the amendment that finally abolished slavery.

EUROPEAN observers were shocked by what Alphonse de Lamartine called the "criminal irresponsibility" of the North. He asked indignantly, "To be treated everywhere as lepers. . . . To be ejected from theaters and public places. . . . To be consigned to special cars on the railways . . . as we would do in France in the case of unclean animals, is that equality?" Traveling through the United States in the 1830s, Alexis de Tocqueville noted that in the South the Negroes were less carefully kept apart from whites than they were in the North. The laws in the South were more harsh but the treatment was more kind. "The master is not afraid to raise his slave . . . because he knows that he can . . . reduce him in a moment to the dust." On the other hand, Tocqueville added, "The prejudice of race appears to be stronger in the states that have abolished slavery than in those where it still exists; and nowhere is it so intolerant as in those states where servitude has never been known." With the legal basis for separating the races gone, "slavery recedes but the prejudice to which it has given birth is immovable." Intermarriage in the North was legal but "infamous." In some places Negroes had the vote, but if they tried to exercise it "their lives are in danger." The schools generally would not accept the Negro, nor would the churches, nor even the cemeteries; "his bones are cast aside."

Goaded by the whip, chained Negroes in a coffle trudge along a Washington, D.C., street. A coffle was formed by shackling slaves with wrist and ankle irons while transporting them overland to market. The slaves even ate and slept in their chains. The Washington slave trade was abolished in 1850.

Plotting in secret, slave insurrectionist Nat Turner (standing) enlists recruits for his bloody 1831 uprising against Virginia whites. The fanatical Turner thought himself a prophet of the Lord and interpreted an eclipse of the sun in February 1831 as a sign of divine approval for his planned revolt.

In 1832 the classic white-steepled New England town of Canterbury, Connecticut, offered dramatic testimony as to how some Northerners, at least, felt about free Negroes. The headmistress of the Canterbury Female Boarding School was pretty 28-year-old Prudence Crandall, a descendant of Mayflower stock and a reader of William Lloyd Garrison's abolitionist newspaper. She admitted to her school that year a 17-year-old girl named Sarah Harris, who wanted to become a teacher. Sarah had attended the local public school and had been a star pupil. She also happened to be a Negro.

The wife of the Episcopal minister led the first demonstration against Sarah. When this failed, the daughters of some of the town's best families were withdrawn. At that point Prudence imprudently decided to convert the establishment into a boarding school for "young Colored Ladies and Misses." Twenty enrolled, but fear mounted in the town that real estate values would crash and that the local Negroes might move to establish their social and political equality with the whites.

At a town meeting, the traditional New England repository of free speech and democracy, the Reverend Samuel J. May, a noted New England abolitionist, showed up to put forward Miss Crandall's plan to move the school to the outskirts of town. He was not permitted to speak. Then a reign of terror began at the school itself. It was led by children, who paraded outside screaming and blowing horns. Shopkeepers and doctors refused to have anything to do with the school or its students. When Miss Crandall's father and brother tried to carry supplies to the building they were pelted with stones. Rocks crashed through the windows and the school's well was fouled. Then the Canterbury selectmen invoked the Vagrant Act, permitting fines or 10 lashes to be inflicted on any out-of-state resident who stayed on in the community after being warned to leave. Most of the Negro students were from out of state, and a 16-year-old girl volunteered for a lashing. Hastily, May posted bail.

The Connecticut legislature passed the "Black Law," prohibiting the establishment of any school for the boarding or instruction of colored students from outside the state. In Canterbury, church bells and cannon heralded the passage of the bill. When Prudence still refused to close the school she was jailed, but was bailed out the next day by May. In Boston, Garrison's paper, the *Liberator*, ran the headline GEORGIA OUTDONE. Meanwhile, the case moved on to the higher courts.

In 1834, three trials later, the school was still open, still fighting the entire community. But in the late summer of that year, the building was set on fire. Shortly afterward a large organized mob, brandishing clubs, completed the job of wrecking the schoolhouse. At that point Prudence Crandall's bridegroom of five days persuaded her to give up. In a letter the Reverend Samuel May wrote the epitaph to the affair. "I felt," he said, "ashamed of Canterbury, ashamed of Connecticut, ashamed of my country, ashamed of my color."

IN its violence and intensity the story of Prudence Crandall is perhaps an isolated case. But it is perfectly clear that at no time prior to the 1850s did the majority of Northern people care deeply about effective freedom for the Negro, or even about the abolition of slavery. The abolitionist movement was led, as John C. Calhoun was later to realize, by a highly vocal minority which brought pressure to bear upon Congress out of all proportion to its size. By the time of the Missouri Compromise, the South, having recognized the economic value of slavery, knew where it stood on the issue. The North did not. It was not until the antislavery movement became endowed with the moral fervor of a crusade that the North as a whole really became committed to doing something about the Negro.

A dismaying climax to the preliminary phase of the great schism over slavery came in Virginia, where Jefferson had compared the Missouri question to the ugly sound of a firebell in the night. "I tremble for my country when I reflect that God is just," he had said. His fear was that after "four generations of outrage" and so long a submission to the "boisterous passions" of their owners the slaves might rise up and take a frightful revenge.

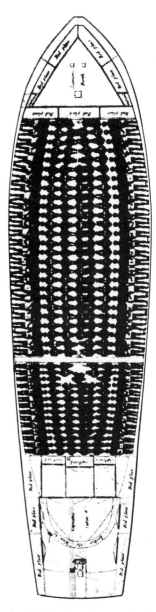

IN August 1831, five years after Jefferson died, there was such an insurrection in Southampton County, Virginia, under the hypnotic leadership of a slave named Nat Turner. At least 57 white men, women and children were murdered. Many Negroes—no one ever knew how many—were lynched in retaliation, and Nat Turner himself was executed. This uprising shocked the entire South. During the next three decades the dark memory of it hung on, so that the region never entirely exorcised a secret dread of a still larger and bloodier slave revolt. More than any other single factor, it was this insurrection which put an end to the Southern movement for either organized emancipation or emigration to Africa.

In January 1832, the Virginia legislature—which in 1821 had failed to pass an emancipation measure by a single vote—undertook the last major debate on slavery ever held on Southern soil. In the House of Delegates, Thomas Jefferson Randolph put forward his grandfather's plan for gradual emancipation, advocated in *Notes on Virginia.* Under Randolph's bill all slaves born on or after July 4, 1840, would become state property upon maturity and would be sent to a colony abroad. If the other states followed suit then after a time slavery in the United States would simply disappear.

Young Randolph reminded his fellow delegates of the ugly practice in Virginia of breeding slaves like oxen for the market. How could an honorable man, a patriot, bear to see his beloved and ancient state "converted into one grand menagerie?" Chief Justice John Marshall's son Thomas said bluntly that slavery "retards improvement—roots out an industrious population—banishes the yeomanry of the country—deprives the spinner, the weaver, the smith, the shoemaker, the carpenter, of employment and support."

But at the end of this earnest debate the House of Delegates had found no real solution. It had agreed that there was a Negro problem—but it was at a loss how to proceed from that point. No legislator could face the thought of mass abolition with its prospect of a great free Negro population roaming at large in the state. The only concrete suggestion made in the debate was deportation, yet all knew that most freed Negroes who were offered a chance to go to Africa turned it down—America was their homeland now. A local newspaper, summing up the debate, concluded "that humanity and policy . . . demand the removal of the free and those who will become freed," but added lamely: "It is not expedient . . . to legislate on abolition."

Stacked like logs, slaves suffered unimaginable privation during the terrible voyages from Africa, as shown in these two loading diagrams. Some (below) were chained sitting up and others lying down to get the most slaves into the least space in their filthy quarters. One slave in every five died en route.

The question was never again seriously raised in any Southern legislature. From then on, the several states simply ignored the whole question, and their silence in effect stated that slavery was no longer a local matter. Instead, it would keep on rending the whole nation.

The flush times of King Cotton

I N 1793, when slavery was steadily being undermined by the moral scruples
and falling profits of Tidewater planters, that "peculiar institution" was
given a new lease on life by the invention of a Northern tinkerer named Eli
Whitney. Whitney's cotton gin, which increased from one pound to 50 the
amount of fiber a slave could separate from seed each day, set off an economic revolution in the South. Cotton exports jumped from 138,000 pounds in
1792 to 1,601,000 in 1794. More and more land was devoted to supplying the
insatiable demands of looms in Great Britain and New England; by the 1850s
the annual crop had reached five million bales, or well over one million tons.

Pyramiding profits spread magnificent mansions *(opposite)* and the planter's gracious way of life throughout the cotton belt. But cotton proved to be
a tyrannical king. It concentrated larger and larger landholdings and more
and more slaves in the hands of fewer and fewer planters. It crowded thousands
of slaveless small farmers into the wild back country. And by propagating
human bondage it sharpened and deepened regional differences. The sugar
economy of Louisiana gave further impetus to slavery. By 1860, slaves ac-
counted for more than one third of the South's population, and slavery's grip
on the region's economy was so strong that it would take a war to break it.

Field slaves, the backbone of the South's economy, work near two presses (rear) which baled cotton.

134

A ROMANTIC RELIC of the Old South, a white-columned
mansion, built in the early 1800s in Greek Revival style,
stands in dilapidated splendor not far from New Orleans.

First-generation aristocrats of the booming South

WITH the Tidewater lands worn out by overproduction, cotton culture spread west and south, into the interior of the coastal states, across southern Tennessee, through Alabama, Mississippi and Louisiana, into Texas. Many a Southerner risked all he owned to buy slaves and land, and then, as his plantation prospered, rose to a life of unabashed splendor. Gleaming white "great houses" arose to replace crude cabins, and nightly the sound of dance music rolled out over green lawns which were trackless wilderness 25 years before.

What these "first-generation aristocrats" lacked in the culture and pedigree of the Tidewater gentry, they made up for in vigor, directness and hearty warmth. They prided themselves on their hunting dogs and blooded horses, and their gambler's instinct, which had prompted them to emigrate in the first place, was expressed in heavy bets on contests of every sort. At their private race tracks (*right*), hundreds of horses and great tracts of land were wagered, and sometimes pens full of slaves stood ready to back up their owners' last-minute bets.

A SUGAR REFINERY on a plantation (red building at right) bolsters the South's cotton economy. As new techniques stimulated production, Louisiana had 1,500 sugar estates by 1805.

RACING FANS flock to Louisville's Oakland House, whose track (*background*) was one of 11 scattered across Kentucky. This 1839 race between two great champions drew a crowd of 10,000.

Waist deep in cotton, field hands turn out in force for the harvest in this print by Currier & Ives. Picking was done as early as August

GINNING COTTON, one slave cranks, grinding the seeds from the cotton between toothed cylinders, while his partner prepares the clear fiber, known as lint, for pressing into bales.

The perennial problem of the cotton harvest

THE raising of cotton posed a curious harvest problem. Although good land might yield a 500-pound bale per acre, the average field hand could pick only half as much cotton as he could cultivate. At harvesttime each year *(above)*, there was a forced muster of pickers; every available slave was sent to the fields. But planters found that one half to two thirds of all their slaves were either unavailable or were ineffective because of illness or malingering. Torn between curtailing planting and getting more slaves, planters developed a rule of thumb: the optimum production unit was 100 slaves for every 1,000 acres. In good years, efficient management might produce a net profit of $250 on the labors of each hand.

and as late as January, depending on local climate. Because the cotton bolls ripened unevenly, a field had to be picked at least three times.

CHUTING BALES down a bluff *(above)*, workmen prepare to load cotton *(right)* on a riverboat. Planters hired whites for certain dangerous chute work rather than risk valuable slaves.

BUSTLING SLAVES in New Orleans' Jackson Square prepare to load their masters' sugar casks and cotton bales aboard steamboats. Behind them stand an equestrian statue of General Andrew Jackson, which was raised in 1856, and the spired Cathedral of Saint Louis (*at far right in the picture opposite*).

In placid Savannah, at the corner of Bay Street (foreground) and Bull Street, townsfolk pass a newspaper office and two general stores with

Thriving river ports and a languishing Tidewater

WITH the population of the South dispersed on back-country farms and self-sufficient riverside plantations, Southern towns were slow to grow into cities. In 1820, the South had only seven communities with more than 8,000 inhabitants, and just two of these, Charleston and New Orleans, were in the cotton belt. In 1850, there were still no more than 12 cities that exceeded Nashville's 10,000. To be sure, the continuing drift of cotton culture to the Southwest and the growth of major plantations transformed New Orleans into a sprawling metropolis (*right*) of over 100,000 by 1850, and small towns along the Mississippi were swollen with a big floating population of merchants, boatmen and speculators. But the growth of the cotton belt, in trade as well as population, came largely at the expense of the Tidewater. By the 1830s, the old coastal communities were in a decline. "Like most of our Southern townships and depots," one visitor said of Savannah (*below*), "it remains stationary and has an air of utter languishment."

BUSY LEVEE, docking place for $100 million in annual trade, lines four miles of New Orleans' Mississippi riverfront. In the Old South, every town of 2,500 had access to navigable waters.

merchandise displayed on railings. Beyond Johnson Square (center) and its monument to Nathanael Greene lie the residential outskirts.

Brisk trade in human property

At a Richmond slave sale an auctioneer (*left*) takes bids for a slave woman while traders lounge about inspecting Negroes still to be sold. This was a scene typical of the Southern slave sales in all respects save one. In most Southern cities the auction would have taken place at curbside or on the courthouse

steps. Only the people of Richmond quailed at public slave markets and found it more seemly to confine the trade to back-street auction rooms. Throughout the South, trading in Negroes was big business. As cotton grew more important the Richmond price of a prime field hand rose from $300 in 1795 to $1,200 in 1860. In New Orleans it was $1,800. Women slaves cost about 25 per cent less, except for "fancy girls" who might bring $2,500 or more. Trade was brisk. By 1860 there were 200 slave traders in New Orleans alone trying to meet the demands of the cotton states for Negroes to work on their plantations.

7. THE END OF A HECTIC ERA

THERE was an aching lump in the throats of the older men and women among the thousands who on March 4, 1817, watched James Monroe take the oath as fifth President. For this "last of the Revolutionary farmers," in his old-fashioned knee breeches, tall, rawboned, with mild blue eyes and rocklike features, was strongly reminiscent of the beloved Father of his Country. Like Washington, Monroe was matter-of-fact rather than brilliant, with an inner calm and solidity of character that inspired great confidence. His Secretary of State, John Quincy Adams, never profuse in his compliments, described Monroe as a man whose mind was "unwearied in the pursuit of truth and right, patient of inquiry, patient of contradiction . . . sound in its ultimate judgment and firm in its final conclusions." Jefferson declared he was "so honest that if you should turn his soul inside out there would not be a spot on it." During his two terms the country virtually had the benefit of three Presidents, for on his major decisions Monroe customarily sought the advice of his two predecessor Virginians, Madison and Jefferson.

But no Executive had had more experience of his own. To call the roll of Monroe's achievements was like reading the history of the young republic. Of frontier stock, he had grown up in a plain frame house with bare rafters and a huge open hearth. Described by Washington as "a brave, active and sensible officer" in the Revolution, he was wounded at Trenton. He had been governor of Virginia and had sat in Congress as a senator. He had been United States

LAST OF THE VIRGINIA DYNASTY to attain the White House, James Monroe observes the world with confidence in a Gilbert Stuart painting made soon after he became President.

minister to France and to England, and later Secretary of State and of War.

To a capital city long charmed by Dolley Madison, Elizabeth Monroe now brought glamor of a different kind. She imported a French chef for the White House. Since the mansion's furniture had been burned by the British in 1814, she redecorated, drawing upon her private furnishings and buying the rest: clocks and bric-a-brac, a piano from France, crystal chandeliers, a Bellangé pier table, silk and brocade drapes. Everyone turned out for the first reception, at which Elizabeth held court on a raised platform. But she was in such poor health that she declined to return any social calls, thus antagonizing official society and setting a precedent that has remained unbroken since.

Despite her own elegance, Mrs. Monroe's drawing-room entertainments attracted a strangely varied social set. Washington was still a swampy wasteland. Through this morass waded the guest list of the presidential receptions: senators and secretaries, farmers and foreign ministers, "judges, auctioneers and nothingarians," reported a newspaper, "all with their wives and some with their gawky offspring. . . ." Some wore fashionable shoes; some dragged mud across the carpets; some dipped snuff or chewed tobacco.

It was as if the Western frontier were invading the East and bringing along Western democracy. Soon the census of 1820 would tally about 4.5 million Americans in the old coastal North, three million (including slaves) in the South—and more than two million beyond the Alleghenies. The West had no tradition of local ways and local rights, but it was manifesting the spirit of leveling, equality, nationalism. While the ideas of Western democracy were traveling east, the people of the East were traveling west.

Elizabeth Monroe grew up in New York society and won a reputation for hauteur which she never completely lost. But she won hearts in Paris, where her husband was U.S. minister in 1790-1796. She was known as "la belle Américaine." So great was her popularity, it is said, that on entering a theater once she was greeted with a rendition of "Yankee Doodle."

THEIR first need was roads. Work had begun as far back as 1775, when Daniel Boone and his men had started the Wilderness Road that now connected Virginia and Kentucky, and all had "a fine supper" of bear meat to celebrate the occasion. The first mass route to the West was not Boone's but the Cumberland Road, or "National Pike" *(see Volume 2, page 126)*. This highway, begun in 1811, ran from mountainous Cumberland, Maryland, to Columbus in the Northwest Territory and, by the mid-1800s, westward to Vandalia, Illinois. It extended almost 600 miles—an 80-foot-wide clearing with a 20-foot strip of macadamized paving running down the center. Here lumbered the Western mail coaches; here moved droves of cattle coming east to market. Often, it was as crowded as the main street of a small town.

The "National Pike" was only one of several main arteries to the West. Others included the Lancaster Turnpike from Philadelphia into western Pennsylvania, and the Genesee Road from Albany across New York State, a route picked up by many New Englanders after they reached the Hudson. In the mid-1820s Americans were braving Indian attacks on the Santa Fe Trail to swap cheap cotton and cutlery for Mexican livestock and silver in the still-foreign regions of New Mexico. In 1825, Missouri's influential Senator Thomas Hart Benton managed to get a bill through Congress to build a road into the area from western Missouri, 650 miles across the southwest plains.

The great American trek beyond the Appalachians had started. In 1811, a single month saw 236 wagons move out of Robbstown, Pennsylvania, on the western highway to Pittsburgh. A family of seven was seen walking from New Jersey to Ohio, pushing their household goods in a wheelbarrow. Two thousand westbound families pushed through Gate No. 2 on the Dauphin Turnpike in Pennsylvania between March and December of 1817. "Old America seems to be breaking up and moving westward," commented a traveler, watching the white tops of the covered wagons.

For many migrants, highways marked only the beginning of the journey. The Cumberland Road connected with the Ohio River at Wheeling. Here one could embark on a great river barge or on one of the slender, elegant keelboats built for shallow waters, or on a Kentucky flat, little more than a raft with board sides. The river had a life of its own, and rivermen were a separate breed, rough-talking and hard-drinking. And something new was thundering at the docks, something marvelous and mechanical and far faster than vessels propelled by wind or man: the steamboat. Completion of the Erie Canal in 1825 was one more link between West and East. Travel from New York to Buffalo was cut from 20 days to six; the cost of moving a ton of freight dropped from $100 to five dollars.

THE West was beginning to fill up. Houses of brick and frame were rising where log cabins had stood. Candles were burning in the place of sputtering saucers of lard with a strip of white cloth as a wick. In 1810, there were seven families in Mount Pleasant, Ohio. In 1815, there were 90—plus seven stores, a meetinghouse, a school, a factory and three taverns.

What brought this mighty migration? Land at two dollars an acre was a compelling cause, but there were two even more important reasons: a depression and wholesale dumping of English manufactured goods. The country had been almost bankrupt at the end of the War of 1812. Worthless paper money (called "fog money") issued by state banks was everywhere. This problem had its roots in the actions of the Jeffersonians, who, a few years previously, had not only refused to renew the charter of the first Bank of the United States, but had proposed no alternative solution for controlling credit. Without the National Bank, paper money could be issued by almost anyone—and was. In 1816 a second National Bank was established through the efforts of Calhoun and Clay. But the officials of the bank were guilty of frightful mismanagement in first overexpanding and then contracting credit.

Ever since the War of 1812 ended, the great manufacturing centers of Britain had flooded the American market with cheap goods—cloth, pottery, iron products and other items. Hundreds of American factories, hurt by the competition, slowed down or shut down. Thousands of millworkers in the North and East were thrown out of work. By 1819 a combination of factors—the overexpansion of industry, loss of foreign markets, collapse of the Western land boom, failure of many banks—had set off a national panic.

Now came a cry that the nation must use only American-made products. War and embargo had called American industry into being and the infant industries could not be left to die. A protective tariff was pushed through in 1816 to keep coarse English cotton goods off the American market.

At about this time Clay began evolving what he was later to call the "American System": effective tariffs against foreign goods plus a continuing federal policy of internal improvements—roads, canals, etc.—to build up domestic strength. It was a bold plan, but it brought sarcastic rejoinders from Webster, whose ship-merchant constituents opposed helping American industry at the expense of United States shipping. What was so "American" about protection anyhow, he asked, inasmuch as America had never even attempted to adopt it?

The Executive Mansion was first painted white in 1817 to hide the scars of its burning by the British. But it had been known before that as the White House—partly because of its gleaming sandstone exterior and partly (so legend has it) because George Washington called it that after his wife's plantation in Virginia. This early view shows it after it had been painted.

But Clay pressed the fight. He was not the first to think of internal improvements. Jefferson in 1807 had proposed a large-scale program of federal aid for roads and canals. Yet it was Clay, with his political intuition, who could sense the wish and will of the American people, who felt the immensity of the continent, who knew that expansion was inevitable and desirable. An incurable optimist, he had a sense of his country's destiny and a vision that looked far beyond his own time. His system embraced two continents. He foresaw the entire Western Hemisphere presenting a united front under the lead of the United States—a "rallying point of human wisdom against all the despotism of the Old World." But before he could build a continental alliance, he must have a nation behind him. For almost 50 years he was to bend his energies to the task of building this essential foundation.

At first Clay was aided by the eloquent Calhoun, who as yet saw no threat to the South, as he later would, in the tariffs that would raise prices on goods Southerners bought from Europe. What primarily interested Calhoun at the outset was the young West. "We are great, and rapidly—I was about to say fearfully—growing," Calhoun told the House. He felt real fear. Since there was danger in this very vastness, it was essential that the remote regions be joined indissolubly to the rest of the nation. "The more strongly we are bound together—the more inseparable are our destinies," he said. Internal improvements could not only develop national markets but could also make the whole country far less dependent on other lands.

Others disagreed with this happy dream. Clay and Calhoun spoke for the middle-class aspirations of the new towns and the new states, too poor to develop their own roads and waterways and eager for federal aid. But was such aid constitutional? Madison thought not. He proposed using federal money for internal improvements only after it was sanctioned by a constitutional amendment. Calhoun argued that the program was already justified under the Constitution's "general welfare" clause, and he convinced Congress he was right. But after a bill was passed providing a permanent fund for roads and canals, Madison vetoed it on March 3, 1817—his last presidential act. Monroe, during his two terms, took much the same attitude as Madison.

Chief Justice John Marshall, here shown in silhouette, brilliantly led the Supreme Court for 35 years. Although his wife's ill health kept the Marshalls from joining in the capital's social life, he was a convivial and witty man. He once defined judicial distinction as "the ability to look a lawyer straight in the eyes for two hours and not hear a damned word he says."

THOUGH internal improvements were put off indefinitely, the federal authority was extended in other respects. In a series of memorable decisions, the Supreme Court, led by John Marshall, was adding new dimensions to the Constitution. The case of *McCulloch vs. Maryland* involved the new United States Bank, denounced as the creature of the "money power," blamed for the depression of 1819 and popularly known as "The Monster." When Maryland tried to tax the bank out of existence, its Baltimore cashier, James McCulloch, refused to pay. The state sued, and Marshall delivered the court's unanimous opinion. It was entirely constitutional for Congress to charter a bank, he said. "Let the end be legitimate . . . and all means which are appropriate, which are plainly adapted to that end, which are not prohibited, but consist with the letter and spirit of the Constitution, are constitutional." But it was *not* constitutional, Marshall ruled, for the state to tax the bank. It was an agent of the national government, and Maryland could not limit the nation's activity by use of the taxing power since "the power to tax involves the power to destroy."

In *McCulloch vs. Maryland,* and in other decisions, the court was firmly establishing the doctrine of judicial review it had enunciated earlier. Henceforth, the Constitution would increasingly be what the judges said it was. Daniel Webster represented his alma mater in the Dartmouth College case, and Marshall again delivered the court's opinion: a private corporation's charter was a contract protected under the Constitution from change by a state legislature. In 1821, in *Cohens vs. Virginia*, the court gave individual citizens convicted in the state courts the right of appeal to the federal judiciary. In *Gibbons vs. Ogden* in 1824, the court freed interstate commerce—and, in consequence, the railroads, planes and trucks of the future—from restrictive state legislation. Year by year Marshall was strengthening the powers of the central government and chipping away at the rights of the states.

Although Monroe's first years in office were marked by domestic tranquility, foreign relations were a constant concern throughout his two terms. The first source of difficulty was Florida, still held by Spain. This region, which Jefferson had tried to buy and Jackson had invaded on his way to New Orleans, remained a particular trouble spot. During the war the British had made a treaty with the Seminole Indians there and had built a fort. Now the Indians were raiding across the border and runaway slaves were using the fort as a refuge and as a base from which to plunder Georgia. General Jackson became the border commander late in 1817. With typical vigor he wrote a friend in Washington that, unless ordered otherwise, he would seize Florida, which could then be held as an indemnity for outrages against American property. Hearing nothing from Monroe and taking silence as consent, Jackson swooped down on Florida, captured several towns, executed two Englishmen for inciting the Indians to fight Americans, forced the Spanish governor to flee and hauled down the Spanish flag.

Spain was powerless to do more than protest. The British, although angry over the killing of British citizens, took no action. Jackson was widely denounced in Washington, but both Monroe and Secretary of State Adams agreed that the general had acted under his broad orders to "terminate the conflict." Adams declared that Spain must either maintain order in Florida or turn the region over to America. Conveniently, discussions with the Spanish were already going on in Washington to settle a number of border questions. Long negotiations got under way. At last a treaty was drawn up (but not finally ratified until 1821) in which the two nations agreed that: (1) Florida would belong to the United States, (2) the United States would pay up to five million dollars of the damages due its own citizens as a result of past raids from Florida and would also renounce all its claims on Texas, and (3) Spain would give up all claims it ever had on other territory included in the Louisiana Purchase.

Another source of friction with Spain was its South American colonies. They had been struggling for liberation, and American citizens had aided the insurgents by selling them ships and other contraband. The United States government had been unable to halt this traffic. By 1818 Spanish possessions in the Western Hemisphere had been so successful in freeing themselves that Henry Clay proposed that the United States recognize them. Monroe refused to do this until every formality of the Florida treaty was completed, so Spain would have no excuse to back out of that commitment. But by 1822, Mexico, Peru, Chile and Colombia had all declared their independence from Spain. Monroe urged Congress to recognize the new nations. Congress quickly did so.

The Latin Americans' drive for freedom was abhorrent to the conservative

Between 1814 and 1816, American imports from Britain jumped over 1,000 per cent. This woodcut, picturing a general store crammed with foreign goods, was used to campaign for a protective tariff. "Others may prefer the cloths of Leeds and London," declared tariff advocate Henry Clay, "but give me those of Humphreysville." That was a town in Connecticut.

monarchs of Europe, who saw grave danger to their security in the revolutions of the New World colonies. In 1818, Ferdinand VII of Spain thought he could capitalize on this fear to recover his lost dominions. Alexander I of Russia, Louis XVIII of France, Frederick William III of Prussia, Francis I of Austria and others, whose Holy Alliance of European monarchs was the pre-eminent force for reaction, were urged by the Spanish king to join him in forcefully ending the colonial uprisings. By 1823 a real fear arose in Washington that the Holy Alliance would try to return Latin America to Spain by force. France later acted so threateningly that the United States formally warned that it would tolerate no interference with the former Spanish possessions.

THERE was also another reason for fear. In September 1821, Czar Alexander claimed for Russia the entire Pacific coast from the Bering Straits to the 51st parallel—that is, the Alaskan-Canadian coastline almost to the present United States border—and ordered all foreign ships to avoid the area. Russians had already penetrated far south of that point. For years they had been operating a foundry at Fort Ross, only 70 miles north of San Francisco, producing excellent iron for plows, and for bells that still ring in California.

Monroe was fortunate that in this period of world upheaval he had Adams as Secretary of State. The son of the second President was a world citizen who since boyhood had spent nearly 20 years overseas. He had gone on some of his father's foreign missions during the Revolutionary era. President Washington had named him minister to Portugal, and President Adams had sent him on a special mission to Berlin.

More to the point, the Secretary of State had considerable firsthand experience with what was possibly the most mysterious world power of them all. He had known Russia since being sent there, as a lad of 14, to be secretary to the American minister. In 1809 he had returned to Russia as American minister himself. He had marveled then at Russia's "queer double-windows," and even more at the twisted talk. It took him a while to learn that when a Russian official assumed an extreme stand at the beginning of a discussion it was only to allow more opportunity for compromise at the end.

In July 1823, Adams was ready to deal with the Russians in their own coin. He announced "that we should contest the right of Russia to *any* territorial establishment on this continent, and that we should assume distinctly the principle that the American continents are no longer subjects for any new European colonial establishments."

This foreshadowed the Monroe Doctrine. The final impetus to that policy came when Britain's Foreign Secretary George Canning proposed that the United States and Britain act together to prevent any European interference with the former colonies of Spain. Jefferson backed this proposal, declaring the question of European interference to be "the most momentous . . . since the Declaration of Independence. That made us a nation; this sets our compass. . . ." But Monroe hesitated at the thought of any joint move with the British, mindful of Washington's admonition never to become entangled in "the toils of European ambition." It was Adams who suggested an effective middle course: America must act unilaterally. "It would be more candid," Adams said, "as well as more dignified, to avow our principles explicitly to Russia and France, than to come in as a cock-boat in the wake of the British man-of-war."

In the end Adams' course was adopted. The Monroe Doctrine—a name it

At a meeting of two South American heroes, Venezuelan Simón Bolivar (right) greets Argentinian José de San Martín. Both fought with Spain—thus posing foreign relations problems for the U.S.—but they later had a falling out. Bolivar was an unwilling administrator. "My destiny lies in camp or in barracks," he said. "For me, an office desk is a place of punishment."

was given a generation later—was made part of Monroe's message to Congress on December 2, 1823. Pointing out that the political systems of the Americas differed basically from those of Europe, the statement asserted that the Western Hemisphere was not open to further European colonization and that Europe would never again be permitted to threaten the independence of any American power. The United States would neither interfere with existing colonies in North or South America, nor concern itself with Europe's internal affairs or European wars that did not affect the New World.

It was a bold, defiant move, and its full influence would become clear only with passing decades. From the start, it was a declaration not only of hemispheric independence but of isolationism. The young republic was snapping its last political links with Europe. From now on, the nation would look inward, not out, secure behind its continental frontiers.

With this policy firmly proclaimed, Adams turned to negotiations with Russia. On April 17, 1824, the two nations signed a treaty setting their boundary in the Northwest at the line of 54° 40', the present southern border of Alaska. Although Russia retained Alaska and its toe hold on the continent, the director of the Russian iron foundry in California vainly protested to Moscow the new line, pointing out that Russia had previously "assumed the right to annex . . . the whole continent up to the Rocky Mountains. . . ." No such assumption was ever again to be tolerated.

D ESPITE President Monroe's doctrine, the first real test of Pan-American activity was unfortunate and abortive. Simón Bolívar, "The Liberator" of South America, had freed a vast area from Spanish rule—all of the present territory of Colombia, Venezuela, Ecuador, Panama, Peru and Bolivia. He had long dreamed of a United States of South America. In 1824 he asked the new South American nations to send delegates to Panama to discuss the possibility of a confederacy. In November 1825, the United States was invited to observe. All this fitted in with the brave plans of Henry Clay—Europe had its continental system, the Americas should have a counterpart. But a number of congressmen, particularly from the South, scorned the idea that the South American nations could ever federate as the United States had, or that the United States should encourage them to do so. Many of our subsequent troubles with Latin America stem from the arguments that ensued.

Behind the closed doors of both houses of Congress the debate raged, James K. Polk of Tennessee maintained that American participation in the Panama conference would involve us in entangling alliances. Robert Hayne of South Carolina voiced the fears of the South over the participation in the conference of certain countries controlled by Negroes—Haiti, for example. He expressed outrage at talk that Bolívar was planning to free Cuba, only 90 miles from Florida. This, Hayne cried, probably would mean the freeing of its slaves and an end of the slave trade, and must be prevented at all costs. Missouri's Benton joined in, asserting that "the peace of eleven States . . . will never permit black consuls and ambassadors" to enter the United States and inflame "their fellow blacks."

In the end, after all the talking was done with, two United States delegates were tardily dispatched as observers to the Panama conference. One man died before he arrived. The other was still en route when the conference adjourned.

Although Monroe's personal popularity during his first term had brought

PRUSSIA
FREDERICK WILLIAM III

RUSSIA
ALEXANDER I

AUSTRIA
FRANCIS I

SPAIN
FERDINAND VII

In 1815 these four European monarchs formed the Holy Alliance, dedicated to doing good works. But the same year Frederick William, Alexander and Francis joined Britain in setting up the warlike Quadruple Alliance—and Americans, confusing one group with the other, toasted: "The Holy Alliance and the Devil. May the friends of liberty check their career."

glowing references to his administration as an "era of good feelings," his second term was a time of quite bad feelings. True, the President was still well liked, and party politics had virtually disappeared—almost everyone professed to be a Republican. But sectionalism was on the increase. And with everybody in the same party, factional disputes began to break out. Almost from the start of Monroe's presidency, there were more contenders for the still-distant 1824 election than had ever yet been seen.

Monroe's own popularity had stemmed from his first inaugural address which showed that he, although a Republican, had accepted such key nationalist principles of the dying Federalist party as governmental backing for industry and a fair-sized army and navy. Now, new regional issues were arising, especially in the West. One centered around Monroe's 1822 veto of a bill that would have raised funds to repair the Cumberland Road by means of a toll. Another sprang from the insistence of the federal courts on payment of debts in hard cash despite various state laws intended to grant relief to people hard pressed by the depression of 1819. Westerners, who depended heavily on the Cumberland Road and who also comprised the greatest part of the nation's debtor group, were furious.

William Crawford was long driven by an ambition to be President, but was the victim of grim irony. In 1816 he might have had the nomination instead of Monroe, but refused it, sure that his turn would come later. Then with the prize almost won in 1823, a paralyzing stroke ended his chances for good.

THESE sectional matters, plus the ambitious jockeyings of the presidential hopefuls, began to create fresh political alignments. After Calhoun, then Secretary of War, announced his presidential candidacy in December 1821, members of Congress and others who were backing the candidacy of William H. Crawford, the Secretary of the Treasury, attempted to cut Calhoun's military budget and to block his military appointments.

Monroe tried to stay neutral in the struggle over his successor, but scarcely anyone else even tried. Jefferson favored Crawford, who had an excellent record as senator, cabinet officer and minister to France. Henry Clay had a lustrous reputation and strong backing in the West. John Quincy Adams was by all odds the best-qualified candidate. Calhoun, "the young men's candidate," wanted the office with all the intensity of his intense being. And finally, there was Andrew Jackson, "the hero of New Orleans."

The contest soon narrowed. In September 1823, Crawford, the only candidate with real backing in all sections, suffered a crippling stroke. Clay had to share his support in the West with Jackson of Tennessee. Jackson's backers were seeking broad geographical support, in the South making the most of his Southern birth, in the West emphasizing his identification with Tennessee, and hailing him among Northerners as a staunch advocate of high tariffs. Calhoun saw wisdom early and withdrew to become a vice-presidential candidate on both the Adams and Jackson tickets.

Thomas Hart Benton, champion of hard money, was brilliant but vain. A Westerner, he feuded constantly with Southerner John Calhoun. But when asked if he would hate his foe after Calhoun died, Benton answered, "No sir. When God Almighty lays His hand upon a man, sir, I take mine off, sir."

As the election neared, it became apparent that Jackson was the man to beat. Thomas Jefferson grew alarmed. He recalled that as a young senator, Jackson had many times been so choked up with rage he could not speak, and so now warned Webster that Jackson was totally unfit to be President.

Nevertheless, as the votes slowly trickled in after election day, Jackson was clearly ahead—he had 99 electoral votes to 84 for Adams. But Crawford and Clay had received enough votes between them to deprive either Jackson or Adams of the majority needed to win. The final choice would have to be made in the House of Representatives. And there, Adams' backing of Clay's American System, their many other points of agreement and, not least, Clay's own differences with Jackson were enough to tip the scale. Adams won in the House by a narrow margin provided by Clay's supporters.

This victory handed to a runner-up was a significant event, for it aroused Americans everywhere and marked a turning point in United States elections. "The people" had never been thought of before as a political force. In this representative republic which was not yet a democracy, the electors had been intended to exercise their personal choice, and the President had always been picked from a small group of the elite known to be qualified. After the Jackson-Adams contest, things would never be permitted to happen that way again. Unpleasant rumors that Clay and Adams had made a deal were beginning to simmer when Adams and Jackson met at a presidential reception. The scene was dramatic: Jackson, with his towering figure, deep-set eyes and firm mouth; Adams, undersized, bald, with arrogant features and prominent sideburns. For a moment they faced each other, then Jackson graciously offered his hand. But Adams—"stiff, rigid, cold as a statue"—responded curtly. He knew very well that he was taking office under a cloud.

In his inaugural address, Adams asked the indulgence of the people, aware, he said, that he was "less possessed of your confidence . . . than any of my predecessors." He pledged the faithful performance of his duty, and his upright and pure intentions.

But his appointment of Henry Clay as Secretary of State—a man he himself had once termed "essentially a gamester"—aroused a storm. "Bargain and corruption" was the outcry. Adams had known Clay well ever since they had served together on the Peace Commission at Ghent, and he had a deep respect both for Clay's awareness of the world beyond America's frontiers and for his demonstrated capacity to sacrifice local interests in a national cause. But it did look as though Adams had paid Clay off for his election. John Randolph of Roanoke alleged this so savagely that Clay—although notoriously unused to firearms—called for a duel. On the dueling ground Clay fired wildly and missed, whereupon Randolph gallantly spared Clay's life by emptying his own pistol into the air.

Riding a velocipede—first known as a "draisine" after its German inventor, Baron von Drais—a daring dandy demonstrates a fad that was all the rage during Monroe's Administration. Much esteemed by sporty types, the machine lacked both pedals and chain; the rider pushed himself along with his feet.

THE Adams administration was foredoomed. This was a tragedy, because Adams and Clay were dedicated and brilliant public servants. Adams took a far broader view of the nation's powers under the Constitution than either Madison or Monroe had. In his first annual message, he urged Congress to finance canals, roads, an observatory, a national university and much fuller exploration of the country's territory and resources, and to pass detailed legislation that would encourage both culture and commerce.

President Adams' energy was prodigious. He arose around 5. In summer he swam in the Potomac, and in winter he took long walks, returning to the White House in time to watch the sun rise. He then made a fire, read from the Bible and after breakfast received visitors and worked at his desk. He kept busy at such occupations until 5 p.m. Evenings the President spent writing in his diary or reading public papers.

He dreamed of a nation whose resources would be carefully controlled for the public good. The vast natural treasures of the West would be held in trust by the government and developed slowly, the proceeds to go toward internal improvements. Then, as real estate values climbed, the lands would be sold at good prices and the profits used as Jefferson might have used them: to further education and science and to create a trained elite to lead the republic. But Adams' dreams were largely ignored by the elected representatives of the people, who saw the public lands as something to grab and exploit. His planned economy was at complete odds with popular democracy.

SUDDENLY the 50th anniversary of independence was at hand. The Federal period, like the long dynasty of Virginia Presidents, was over. The end of the era—the end of the beginning—was symbolized in the ebbing lives of two men widely separated by philosophy and geography, once friends, then opponents, now friends once more. The elder statesman in New England was in correspondence with the elder statesman in Virginia.

John Adams, father of the President, was living out his days at the family homestead in Quincy, Massachusetts. He was 91, "the noble image of a serene old age." His favorite companions were his grandchildren, and they spent hours daily reading to the old Puritan—surprisingly enough, from the romantic works of Scott and Byron.

For Jefferson, at 83, a lifelong dream was being realized. "All my wishes," he had once said, "end where I hope my days will end, at Monticello." The house he called Monticello was not as bright and shiny as it became in its later restoration. Like its master, it was aging and shabby. It was crowded with children, showed signs of hard use and the ravages of debt. He had had to sell most of his library and to petition the Virginia legislature for a lottery to dispose of his property and give him relief from the debts incurred while in public service. But essentially he was happy.

Daniel Webster returned from a visit with a beguiling description of Jefferson's day: up at dawn, a quick look at his thermometer and an entry in the meteorological diary, writing letters till 9, then breakfast in his bedroom. "From that time till dinner he is in his library, excepting that in fair weather he rides on horseback from seven to fourteen miles. Dines at four, returns to his drawing-room at six, when coffee is brought in, and passes the evening till nine in conversation."

He longed to live until the 4th of July, 1826, the 50th anniversary of his Declaration. In June he fell ill but was still able to pen a few last words: "the mass of mankind has not been born with saddles on their backs nor a favored few booted and spurred, ready to ride them." He likened himself to "an old watch with a pinion worn out here and a wheel there."

In Massachusetts, Adams too felt his life slowly draining away. The town fathers asked him for a toast for the Fourth. He gave it: "Independence Forever," and declined to add a word more.

At Monticello, midnight passed and darkness faded into dawn. Jefferson roused himself from unconsciousness. "This is the Fourth?" he asked. His friend Nicholas Trist nodded. "Just as I wished," Jefferson said, and sank back. Shortly after noon he died. Adams lived a few hours more. For one to have died on the 4th would have been remarkable; for the two to go was so notable that their nation could never forget.

THE 1828 campaign for the presidency was under way almost before the Adams administration had begun. The nation's one party split in two. The Adams-Clay group became the National Republicans, later to be known as the Whigs, while the Jacksonians emerged as the Democratic Republicans,

This macabre political cartoon, addressed to the voter, was captioned "Jackson is to be President and you will be hanged." It was published during the vicious campaign of 1828 and referred to various stiff disciplinary measures taken by Jackson when he was a general—particularly the execution by hanging of six army deserters during the War of 1812.

later to be known as the Democrats. The Adams supporters had a program, but the Jackson men had something more useful: a grievance. They were resolved, they cried, that "the sovereign will of the people" was not to be set aside again as it had been in 1824. For the Jacksonians the contest of democracy versus aristocracy had begun.

President Adams was in trouble from the start. Vice President Calhoun, once an exponent of Clay's American System, had become, instead, an exponent of states' rights. He now found much to challenge in Adams' sweeping nationalist policies. As the Vice President then had the power to appoint Senate committees, Calhoun could do great damage to the President's program. Adams immeasurably added to his own difficulties by refusing to remove competent civil servants in favor of his political friends. A great many of these officeholders had originally been appointed by powerful enemies of Adams, so his high-minded effort to be nonpolitical was politically disastrous. Without the weapon of patronage, he was unable to build an effective party machine to back him—and the men he refused to replace with his own supporters often used all their influence against his policies and his re-election.

Rachel Jackson, who died after discovering her husband had been attacked through her, had wanted only peace and dreaded going to the White House. "I had rather be a door keeper in the house of God than to live in that palace," she said. Jackson had inscribed on her gravestone: "A being so gentle, so virtuous, slander might wound but could not dishonour."

THE savagery of that four-year-long political contest has rarely been equaled in the history of presidential campaigns. Jackson was charged with being a murderer, a slave trader, a conspirator with Aaron Burr, a gambler, a brawler, a cockfighter and an adulterer—and some of the charges came close enough to hurt. The Jacksonians struck back furiously, describing Adams as a monarchist, an aristocrat, who had all his life lived off the public treasury, and who had written a scurrilous poem—and not even this could humanize him. On such "issues" the campaign turned, though there was also the sharpest struggle yet between agricultural interests who wanted the lowest possible tariffs, and industrial interests who wanted the exact opposite.

Despite the viciousness of the attack against him, Jackson was elected by a wide margin—and then came the final harsh irony. His wife Rachel found a pamphlet and saw for the first time the campaign of filth that he had kept hidden from her. Now she could read of herself as a strumpet and her long marriage as adulterous. Jackson was Rachel's second husband. She had married him only after both thought her divorce from her first husband was final. When they later learned of their mistake, they remarried as soon as the divorce did take effect. The brutality of the political attack was a greater shock than Rachel could endure. She died a few days afterward. At her funeral Jackson wept. This was the price he paid for his victory.

The rowdiness of the Jackson inaugural is legendary. Most of the damage was done at the White House reception that followed the oath-taking: people clambering on the furniture in muddy boots, china and glassware smashed to the floor, waiters knocked off their feet. But the inauguration itself was dominated by the dignity of the tall, stooped new President.

The noisy crowd was there—a ship's cable was stretched across the wide flight of steps to hold the throng back, but it was quickly torn away—yet there was a silent moment as the President-elect mounted the east portico of the Capitol. He took his place opposite Chief Justice John Marshall, who administered the oath. His white hair blowing, Andrew Jackson then bowed to the people—and the people responded. In a flash, all hats came off, and shouting "rent the air and seemed to shake the very ground."

Cramped passengers make the 260-mile New York–Boston journey by stage. This picture is from an 1815 poster advertising a 39-hour trip.

The rapid pace of transportation

No country ever faced problems of transportation more staggering than those that confronted the United States during the 60 years after Washington's inauguration. By the mid-1800s the nation extended some 3,000 miles westward to the Pacific—an enormous, almost trackless expanse that soon began to fill up with people. The U.S. population, in those years between 1790 and 1850, increased more than 500 per cent, and great numbers of these new Americans moved west. Once there they became both producers and consumers, and an urgent need arose for means of conveying to the East the materials they wanted to sell, and for returning to the West the things they needed. The existing transportation system was woefully inadequate. There were a few important wagon roads, but transport by wagon was prohibitively slow and expensive. All other travel was by small boat, dog sled, on horseback or afoot.

In this dilemma, Americans turned to one of their greatest natural resources —the inland waterways. There was an abundance of navigable rivers and lakes, and where none existed men dug canals. At first the canals were short, serving mainly to circumvent waterfalls or rapids. But as the demands grew, the canals grew with them, getting ever longer and more elaborate.

The irony was that for all their success, the proud canals were threatened with obsolescence even before they began operating. The steam engine had been perfected in England in the mid-18th Century. By 1807 steam was pushing great vessels against the river currents and by the 1820s it was pulling railway cars along tracks. By 1853, plans had already been drawn for a railroad across the continent—just 49 years after the Lewis and Clark expedition had started on its grueling overland journey through the raw wilderness to Oregon.

TRAVEL-MINDED AMERICANS get news of the California gold rush in a New York post office. Wall notices tell of transportation opportunities to the West Coast. The trip was a hard one.

Travelers could reach the coast only by an arduous overland trip or sea voyage. For though the U.S. in 1849 had 9,000 miles of railroads, a coast-to-coast system was still years away.

Erie Canal workers excavate a deep cut. Though dug in a rough country known for bad weather, the canal progressed about a mile a week.

A big, bold ditch for commerce with the West

I T would be difficult to imagine a current-day project that would match in audacity the Erie Canal enterprise of the early 1800s. Even so farsighted a man as Thomas Jefferson declared that "talk of making a canal of three-hundred-and-fifty miles through the wilderness —it is little short of madness." Much of the country between Albany and Buffalo, through which the canal was to be dug, was thinly settled and rugged.

Nevertheless, the canal's backers persevered. The job took eight years and cost over seven million dollars; in all, 82 locks were built over a distance of 362 miles. The canal was an immediate and tremendous success. The cost of shipping freight across New York State dropped to only one twentieth what it had been, and the time in transit was cut by two thirds. Even though it offered bargain rates, the Erie Canal carried such a volume of traffic that it repaid its initial cost within 12 years.

MIXING THE WATERS, Governor DeWitt Clinton pours into the Atlantic Ocean a keg of Lake Erie water at ceremonies in New York Bay marking the opening of the Erie Canal on November 4, 1825. Clinton had been one of the canal's foremost advocates.

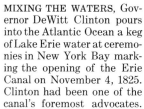

ENTERING THE LOCKS, traffic passes through the Erie near Albany. Besides carrying freight, the canal provided two types of passenger service: slow boats (2 mph) charged one and a half cents a mile; the faster "packets" (4 mph) charged five cents.

159

Amid lively controversy, the coming of steam

HOBBLED by primitive transportation, the expanding young republic should have welcomed the steam engine, which made possible conveyances that could be truly self-propelled rather than dependent on wind, current or animal muscle. But initially most Americans were cool toward the idea. The steam engine as developed in England was considered a source of stationary power, primarily for industrial use. It took imagination to see these snorting machines as a source of locomotion.

But amid this skepticism, there were a few visionaries who recognized the potentialities. As early as 1786 John Fitch was operating a steamboat on the Delaware River, but his enterprise failed. It was principally Robert Fulton who finally solved the problems of successful steamboating. Fulton had first experimented with steam

vessels in France, where one of his early designs sank because the engine was so heavy. His faith unshaken, he returned to the U.S. in 1806, his associate Robert Livingston having arranged for a monopoly to operate steamboats in New York State. Still the old prejudices remained, and Fulton's *Clermont* was ridiculed as "Fulton's Folly"—until it proved itself on the Hudson in 1807. In a few years, there was regular steamboat service as far west as the Mississippi.

Some of the same skepticism also attended the introduction of steam railroading; there were actually contests that pitted horse against locomotive to test which was better. But once steam had entered the race, it was only a matter of time before the horse—and the sailing vessel—vanished from the mass transportation scene.

EXPLAINING THE STEAM ENGINE, an 1848 British diagram of a locomotive demonstrates how a roaring blaze in the firebox could be converted into power to turn the vehicle's wheels.

FATHER OF THE STEAMBOAT, Robert Fulton is shown in this 1806 painting *(opposite)* with another nautical triumph—in Britain, his submarine *Nautilus* scores a hit on an old ship.

The remarkable vessel that sailed upstream

AT the time of the steamboat's arrival, the state of water travel in America was scarcely advanced over that of the ancient Phoenicians. Virtually all traffic proceeded one way—downstream. Only rarely was a keelboat forced back upstream by means of sails or towlines or by setting-poles that were driven into the bottom. Traveling in this fashion, 30 hard-working boatmen might take up to three months to make the 975-mile trip from New Orleans to Cairo, Illinois. As for flatboats, they could travel only with the current; when they arrived at New Orleans they were sold for the wood they contained. Their crewmen made their way home as best they could, sometimes walking the entire distance.

The steamboats changed all that. At first their speed against the Mississippi's slow-moving current was little more than three miles per hour, but by 1817 they were more efficient. That year a regular steamboat service was established that covered the 1,352 miles between New Orleans and Louisville in 25 days, one quarter the time that had been required by a score of sweating bargemen.

Fulton's "Paragon" plies the Hudson in 1808, a year after the "Clermont's" success. The "Paragon" was sumptuously appointed, with a

PASSING FLATBOATS on the Ohio, a steamboat churns by Cave-in-Rock in Illinois in 1835. Flatboats continued to appear on the river even after steam came into use, but their number dwindled rapidly. In 1846 more than 2,000 flatboats sailed down the river to New Orleans. But by the 1860s they had all but disappeared.

paneled dining room. But passengers were so unaccustomed to such rich surroundings that they had to be warned not to sleep in their shoes.

Meeting a steamboat, a train on New Jersey's busy Camden and Amboy Railroad picks up passengers who have just debarked from the

RACING A HORSE, the primitive Tom Thumb engine pulls ahead in its famous 1830 contest on the Baltimore & Ohio. Despite its initial success, the little steam locomotive broke down and lost the race. Delighted horse fanciers jeered at the "tea-kettle on a truck." Nevertheless, the owners of the B&O were convinced; after the race they switched over to steam.

vessel in the background. Early rail coaches displayed a marked similarity to the horse-drawn stagecoaches from which they were derived.

Horse versus iron horse—the survival of the fittest

RAILROADING in the United States lagged more than two decades behind the commercial development of steamboats. The simple concept of a railroad train—a string of cars drawn by a locomotive—first had to win acceptance over the notion of railroad tracks as merely a smoother roadway over which horses could pull vehicles. The Baltimore & Ohio operated on a horse-drawn basis for nearly four years. However, after 1830 the steam engine came into ascendancy; by 1840 some 409 chartered railroads owned almost 3,000 miles of track that served the major cities from New England to Georgia. Canals still flourished, but the iron horse had proved itself and the era of water travel was beginning to wane.

PRIMITIVE RAILROADING is shown in an early engraving. Passengers, some of whom sat in a carriage atop a flatcar, were protected against explosion by cotton bales behind the engine.

165

Key to a coming era of expansion

A thriving port, St. Louis in 1832 is jammed with river traffic. A ferry *(left)* unloads on the Illinois side of the river. Though rail linkage with the East was two decades away, the Mississippi was the great thoroughfare for travel in the West. During this period, St. Louis grew to be a bustling transportation center, with connections radiating out toward New York and Santa Fe by stagecoach and up the Missouri toward the Rockies and the wild frontier. The groundwork had been laid for a great movement to the West that would occupy much of the nation for the next quarter century.

CHRONOLOGY   A timetable of American and world events: 1789-1829

WORLD EVENTS	EXPANSION and EXPLORATION	POLITICS	MILITARY and FOREIGN AFFAIRS	ECONOMICS and SCIENCE	THOUGHT and CULTURE
1789 Age of European Revolution begins	1789-90 Friction between Indians and American settlers on Northwest frontier becomes critical	1789 Organization of federal government at New York; Washington inaugurated		1789 First tariff legislation	1789 Establishment of University of North Carolina; first state university to begin instruction
1791 British Parliament passes act organizing Canadian government	1790 Organization of the Southwest Territory which was to become Tennessee	1790 House sets site of new national capital on the Potomac		1790 Hamilton's "Report on the Public Credit"	1789 Jedidiah Morse's *American Geography* published
1791-92 Legislative Assembly rules France	1791 Vermont statehood	1791 Creation of city of Washington, D.C.		1790 Samuel Slater establishes his textile mill at Pawtucket	1789-1800 "Republican" or Roman Revival period
1792 French Republic proclaimed. National Convention rules	1792 Kentucky statehood	1791 Bill of Rights (first 10 constitutional amendments) adopted	1791 General St. Clair routed near the Wabash	1790 Philadelphia-Lancaster turnpike begun	1790 John Carroll consecrated Bishop of Baltimore, first Roman Catholic episcopate in the U.S.
1792-97 War by First Coalition of European powers against France	1792 Robert Gray discovers the Columbia River	1792 Presidential Succession Act	1791 Britain appoints first minister to the U.S.	1790 First U.S. census reports 3,929,000 inhabitants	1790 Duncan Phyfe opens furniture shop in New York
1793 Reign of terror in France		1792 Washington and Adams re-elected for second term	1793 Citizen Genêt Affair	1791 First Bank of the United States chartered	1791 Massachusetts Historical Society; first historical association in U.S.
1793 France wars on Britain		1793 Supreme Court decides *Chisholm vs. Georgia*	1793 Washington's Neutrality Proclamation	1791 Hamilton proposes protective tariffs and agricultural bounties	1794 Charles Willson Peale's Philadelphia Museum; first independent museum in the U.S.
1794 Kosciusko leads Polish revolt against Russia		1793 Impact of French Revolution upon American native political parties becomes clear	1794 Congress authorizes construction of six warships; foundation of U.S. Navy	1792 Mint Act establishes decimal system of coinage	1794 James Hewitt's *Tammany,* early American opera
1794-1804 Haitians overthrow French rule		1794 Whiskey Rebellion	1794 Neutrality Act	1793 Eli Whitney invents cotton gin	1794 Chestnut St. Theatre opens in Philadelphia
1795-99 Directory governs France	1796 Land Act provides for survey of public lands and their sale at public auction	1795 Naturalization Act	1794 Battle of Fallen Timbers	1793 Jefferson devises mold-board plow	1795 Gilbert Stuart's "Vaughan" portrait of George Washington
1797-1840 Frederick William III, King of Prussia	1796 Tennessee statehood	1795 Provisions of Jay Treaty made public. Attack upon treaty by Republicans	1795 Treaty of San Lorenzo settles boundary and navigation issues with Spain	1793 Philadelphia yellow fever epidemic inspires improvements in sanitation and water supply	1799 Hannah Adams' *A Summary History of New England:* the author was probably the first American woman to earn a living by writing
1796 Thomas Malthus' *Essay on the Principle of Population*	1798 Organization of the Mississippi Territory	1796 In *Ware vs. Hylton,* Supreme Court declares treaties supreme over state laws	1797 XYZ Affair	1794 Arrival of Joseph Priestley stimulates interest in study of chemistry	1799-1800 Religious revivals in New York and Kentucky
1798-99 War of the Second Coalition against France		Sept. 17, 1796 Washington's Farewell Address	1798 Commercial intercourse with France suspended	1797 Newbold patents iron plow	
1799 Napoleon named First Consul		Dec. 1796 John Adams elected President	1798 Creation of Department of the Navy	1797-1809 U.S. ships make voyages to Japanese ports carrying goods for Dutch merchants	
		1798 Ratification of 11th Amendment	1798-1800 Undeclared war with France on high seas	1798 Eli Whitney develops system of interchangeable parts that presages mass production	
		1798 Alien and Sedition Acts	1799 *Constellation* defeats *L'Insurgente*	1799 Nathaniel Bowditch publishes *Practical Navigator,* pioneering work in navigation	
		1798-99 Kentucky and Virginia Resolutions			
		1799 General Post Office established			
		1799 Death of Washington			

1800   Jeffersonian Years

WORLD EVENTS	EXPANSION and EXPLORATION	POLITICS	MILITARY and FOREIGN AFFAIRS	ECONOMICS and SCIENCE	THOUGHT and CULTURE
1800 Louisiana secretly transferred to France		1800 National capital transferred to Washington	1800 By treaty of Morfontaine, U.S. ends defensive alliance with France	1800 Census shows 5,308,000 inhabitants	1800 Parson Weems' *Life of Washington*
1802 British and French make peace		1800 Presidential election; Adams vs. Jefferson	1801-05 Tripolitan War	1800 Cowpox vaccination introduced into U.S. by Dr. Benjamin Waterhouse	1800 Library of Congress founded
1802 French subdue rebellion in Santo Domingo		1801 Adams defeated for presidency; deadlock between Burr and Jefferson broken by Hamilton	1802 U.S. Military Academy opened	1801-14 Albert Gallatin Secretary of the Treasury; carries out Republican policy of financial retrenchment	1801-09 Washington Allston, Romantic painter, studies in Europe
1803 Britain and France at war	1803 Louisiana Purchase	1801 "Midnight judges" appointed			
1804 Napoleon, Emperor of France	1803 Ohio statehood	1803 Supreme Court decision in *Marbury vs. Madison*		1803-07 Renewal of European wars brings prosperity to U.S.	1803 First authenticated American piano built by Benjamin Crehorne
1805 British defeat French at Trafalgar	1804-06 Lewis and Clark expedition	1803 South Carolina reinstates slave trade	1804 Stephen Decatur recaptures and destroys the *Philadelphia*	1805 Robert Fulton builds first marine torpedo	1805 Mercy Otis Warren's *History of the...American Revolution*
1806 Britain blockades French coast	1805 Michigan and Louisiana Territories formed	1804 First regular caucus of congressmen to choose presidential candidates	1805 Treaty of Peace with Tripoli		1806 Webster's *Compendious Dictionary of the English Language* published
1806 Napoleon imposes Continental System of blockade	1806 Pike's expedition to Colorado	1804 Burr kills Hamilton in a duel	1806 First Non-Importation Act	1807 Fulton's *Clermont* makes maiden voyage	1806 Pennsylvania's Academy of Fine Arts opens
1807 British abolish slave trade		1804 Jefferson is re-elected		1807-08 U.S. exports drop almost 80 per cent in these two years	
		1805-06 Aaron Burr's negotiations with foreign powers			

1810 Prelude to War

Europe and the World

1807 ...Britain and France blockade each other's ports

1808 Bonaparte's Bayonne Decree

1809 Metternich chief minister of Austria

1810 Spain's American colonies refuse to acknowledge Joseph Bonaparte as king

1810 Napoleon reputedly revokes Milan and Berlin decrees

1812 Castlereagh suspends restrictions on U.S. shipping

1812 Napoleon invades Russia

1814 Napoleon exiled to Elba

1814 Congress of Vienna confirms Louis XVIII of France and Ferdinand VII of Spain

1815 Battle of Waterloo; Napoleon exiled to St. Helena

1815 Formation of Holy Alliance

1815 Quadruple Alliance formed

States and Territories

1809 Organization of Territory of Illinois

1809 Death of Meriwether Lewis

1810 West Florida annexed by Executive proclamation

1811 First steamboat on western waters, at Pittsburgh

1811-18 Cumberland Road to Wheeling

1812 Louisiana statehood

1813-14 War with Creek Indians

1816 Indiana statehood

1817 Regular steamboat service on the Mississippi

1817 Formation of Alabama Territory

1817 Mississippi statehood

1818 Illinois statehood

1819 Arkansas organized as a territory

1819 Alabama statehood

Politics and Law

1807 Arrest and trial of Aaron Burr

1808 Congress forbids importation of slaves

1808 James Madison elected President

1810 Supreme Court, in *Fletcher vs. Peck*, declares a state law unconstitutional

1811 Motion to renew charter of Bank of U.S. defeated

1812 Madison re-elected President

1814 Hartford Convention

1816 James Monroe elected President

1816-30 Liberalization of state voting requirements

1818 Henry Clay proposes U.S. recognition of Latin American republics

1819 Missouri statehood bill introduced into Congress; Tallmadge amendment

1819 Supreme Court decides *McCulloch vs. Maryland* and Dartmouth College cases

Foreign Affairs

1807 *Chesapeake-Leopard* Affair

July 1807 British warships ordered from U.S. territorial waters

1807 Embargo Act

1809 Non-Intercourse Act reopens trade with all powers except England and France

1810 Macon's Bill No. 2 empowers President to reopen U.S. trade with England and France

Nov. 1810 President Madison reopens commerce with France

1811 Battle of Tippecanoe

1811 U.S. renews Non-Intercourse provisions against Britain

June 1812 Declaration of war

August 1812 *Constitution* beats *Guerrière*

1812 General Hull invades Canada

1813 Defeat of the *Chesapeake*

Sept. 1813 Battle of Lake Erie

Oct. 1813 Battle of the Thames

Nov. 1813 Castlereagh proposes direct negotiations for peace

1814 Washington, D.C., burned

Sept. 1814 Battle of Lake Champlain

Dec. 1814 Treaty of Ghent

Jan. 8, 1815 Battle of New Orleans

1815 War with Algiers

1817 Rush-Bagot Agreement; mutual demilitarization of Great Lakes

1818 U.S.-Canadian boundary to Rockies fixed; joint occupation of Oregon Territory

Economics

1808 American Fur Company founded by John Jacob Astor

1808 John Stevens' *Phoenix*; first American steam vessel to sail on the ocean

1808-09 Economic depression

1810 Census shows 7,239,000 inhabitants

1810-20 Southern cotton crop expands from 85,000,000 to 160,000,000 pounds per year

1812 Benjamin Rush's *Diseases of the Mind* published; pioneering work in study of psychiatry

1812-14 Wartime boom in almost all areas of commerce

1814 First steam vessel of war, designed by Robert Fulton

1814 Waltham, Massachusetts, mill combines all processes of cotton manufacture in one establishment

1815 British East Indies opened to American shipping with no discriminatory duties

1815-16 British manufactures flood American market

1816 First U.S. tariff designed specifically for protection

1816 Charter granted for second Bank of the United States

1816 First U.S. savings bank

1817-25 Construction of Erie Canal

1818 First regular transatlantic packet service

1818 First steamboat on Great Lakes

1819 First major banking crisis in U.S.

Arts and Culture

1808 Methodist Church adopts a constitution

1809 Washington Irving's *A History of New York . . . by Diedrich Knickerbocker* published

1810 Organization of first regular orchestra in U.S., Boston Philharmonic Society

1811 *Niles' Weekly Register* founded

1814 Francis Scott Key writes lyrics of "Star-Spangled Banner"

1815 *North American Review* begins publication; first important American review

1815-20 Religious revivals resume in New York and New England

1815-60 "New England Renaissance" in letters

1817 Organization of American Colonization Society

1817 William Cullen Bryant's "Thanatopsis"

1819 William Ellery Channing founds the Unitarian Church in Massachusetts

1820 Growth of the Nation

Europe and the World

1820 Revolution in Spain

1820 Congress of Troppau considers suppression of revolutionary tendencies

1820-30 George IV, King of England

1822 Congress of Verona discusses suppression of Greek and Spanish insurrections

1823 French restore Spanish monarchy

1824-30 Charles X, King of France

1825 First steam locomotive passenger service in England

States and Territories

1820 Maine statehood

1820 Moses Austin given Spanish charter to settle 300 families in Texas

1820 First U.S. missionaries in Hawaii

1821 Missouri statehood

1821 U.S. takes possession of Florida

1825 U.S. adopts policy for transfer of eastern Indians across the Mississippi

Politics and Law

1820 Missouri Compromise

1820 Congress declares foreign slave trade is piracy

1820 Monroe re-elected President

1821 *Cohens vs. Virginia* restates paramount position of Supreme Court over state courts

1824 Supreme Court in *Gibbons vs. Ogden* widens congressional authority over states

1824-25 Disputed presidential election; House declares J. Q. Adams victor

1825 Emergence of new parties: Democratic Republicans and National Republicans

1827 In *Martin vs. Mott*, Supreme Court upholds President's right to call out state militias

1828 Andrew Jackson defeats J. Q. Adams for presidency

1828 Doctrine of nullification

1829 Jackson's inauguration symbolizes triumph of common man

Foreign Affairs

1822 Congress provides for regular diplomatic relations with Latin American republics

1823 Monroe Doctrine proclaimed

1824 Treaty with Russia ends Northwest boundary dispute

1826 Panama Congress, beginning of Pan-American movement

Economics

1820 Census shows 9,638,000 inhabitants, with more than 2,000,000 west of Alleghenies

1823 Nicholas Biddle, President of Bank of the United States

1824 Henry Clay first uses "American System"

1824 Increased tariff protection

1825 Feverish canal building

1825 Opening of Erie Canal

1827-38 Tide of great Irish and German migrations to U.S.

1828 Tariff of Abominations

1828 Construction of Baltimore and Ohio Railroad starts: first passenger railroad in U.S.

1828 First trade fair

Arts and Culture

1820 James Fenimore Cooper's first novel, *Precaution*, published

1820-60 Greek Revival dominates U.S. architecture

1821-22 American Colonization Society purchases land in Africa and establishes Republic of Liberia

1824 Robert Dale Owen founds New Harmony, Indiana

1824-50 Peak of evangelistic fervor and revivalism in New York, Massachusetts and Pennsylvania

1826 National Academy of the Arts of Design organized

1827-38 Publication of John James Audubon's *Birds of America*

1828 Nathaniel Hawthorne's first novel, *Fanshawe*

1828 First labor paper in U.S., *Mechanics' Free Press* of Philadelphia

1829 William Lloyd Garrison's *Genius of Universal Emancipation*; advocates immediate emancipation of Negro slaves

FOR FURTHER READING

*These books were selected for their interest and authority in the preparation
of this volume, and for their usefulness to readers seeking additional information on specific points.
An asterisk (*) marks works available in both hard-cover and paperback editions.*

GENERAL READING

Bailey, Thomas A., *A Diplomatic History of the American People*. Appleton-Century-Crofts, 1958.

Carman, Harry J., Harold C. Syrett and Bernard W. Wishy, *A History of the American People* (Vol. I). Alfred A. Knopf, 1960.

*Hofstadter, Richard, *The American Political Tradition*. Alfred A. Knopf, 1948.

Hofstadter, Richard, William Miller and Daniel Aaron, *The American Republic* (Vol. I). Prentice-Hall, 1959.

McMaster, John Bach, *A History of the People of the United States, from the Revolution to the Civil War* (8 vols.). Appleton-Century, 1883-1913.

Morison, Samuel Eliot, and Henry Steele Commager, *The Growth of the American Republic* (Vol. I). Oxford University Press, 1962.

*Parrington, Vernon L., *Main Currents in American Thought*. Harcourt, Brace & World, 1939.

Warren, Charles, *The Supreme Court in United States History* (Vol. I). Little, Brown, 1960.

THE EARLY REPUBLIC (CHAPTERS 1, 2, 3)

Albion, Robert G., *The Rise of New York Port, 1815-1860*. Shoe String, 1961.

Baldwin, Leland D., *Whiskey Rebels*. University of Pittsburgh Press, 1939.

Beveridge, Albert J., *The Life of John Marshall* (Vols. III & IV). Houghton Mifflin, 1939.

Bowers, Claude G., *Jefferson in Power*. Houghton Mifflin, 1936.

Bridenbaugh, Carl and Jessica H., *Rebels and Gentlemen*. Reynal & Hitchcock, 1942.

Chinard, Gilbert, *Honest John Adams*. Little, Brown, 1933.

Dauer, Manning J., *The Adams Federalists*. Johns Hopkins, 1953.

Freeman, Douglas Southall, *George Washington* (7 vols., Vol. VII by Carroll, John A., and Mary W. Ashworth). Scribner's, 1948-1957.

*Kurtz, Stephen G., *The Presidency of John Adams*. University of Pennsylvania Press, 1957.

Malone, Dumas, *Jefferson and the Ordeal of Liberty*. Little, Brown, 1962.

Miller, John C., *Alexander Hamilton: Portrait in Paradox*. Harper & Row, 1959. *The Federalist Era, 1789-1801*. Harper & Row, 1960.

*Morison, Samuel Eliot, *The Maritime History of Massachusetts, 1783-1860*. Houghton Mifflin, 1921.

*Peterson, Merrill D., *The Jefferson Image in the American Mind*. Oxford University Press, 1960.

Phillips, James Duncan, *Salem in the Eighteenth Century*. Houghton Mifflin, 1937. *Salem and the Indies*. Houghton Mifflin, 1947.

Schachner, Nathan, *Thomas Jefferson*. Thomas Yoseloff, 1957.

Smith, Page, *John Adams* (2 vols.). Doubleday, 1962.

Stephenson, N. W. and W. H. Dunn, *George Washington* (2 vols.). Oxford University Press, 1940.

Tatum, George B., *Penn's Great Town*. University of Pennsylvania Press, 1961.

White, Leonard, *The Federalists: A Study in Administrative History*. Macmillan, 1948.

Whitney, Janet, *Abigail Adams*. Atlantic-Little, Brown, 1947.

Writers' Program, New York, *A Maritime History of New York*. Doubleday, 1941.

EXPLORING THE WILDERNESS ·(CHAPTER 4)

Abernethy, Thomas P., *The Burr Conspiracy*. Oxford University Press, 1954.

*Bakeless, John, *Lewis and Clark, Partners in Discovery*. William Morrow, 1947.

De Voto, Bernard, *Across the Wide Missouri*. Houghton Mifflin, 1947.

The Course of Empire. Houghton Mifflin, 1952. *The Journals of Lewis and Clark*. Houghton Mifflin, 1953.

*Schachner, Nathan, *Aaron Burr*. Frederick A. Stokes, 1937. *Alexander Hamilton*. Thomas Yoseloff, 1957.

THE SECOND WAR WITH BRITAIN (CHAPTER 5)

Adams, Henry, *History of the United States* (Vols. V-IX). Scribner's, 1890.

Beirne, Francis F., *The War of 1812*. E. P. Dutton, 1949.

Brant, Irving, *James Madison* (Vol. VI). Bobbs-Merrill, 1961.

Burt, A. L., *The United States, Great Britain, and British North America to 1820*. Russell & Russell, 1961.

Clark, Allen C., *Life and Letters of Dolly Madison*. W. F. Roberts, 1914.

*Coit, Margaret L., *John C. Calhoun*. Houghton Mifflin, 1950.

Engelman, Fred L., *The Peace of Christmas Eve*. Harcourt, Brace & World, 1962.

Forester, C. S., *The Age of Fighting Sail*. Doubleday, 1956.

Fuess, Claude M., *Daniel Webster* (2 vols.). Little, Brown, 1930.

Furman, Bess, *White House Profile*. Bobbs-Merrill, 1951.

*James, Marquis, *Andrew Jackson, The Border Captain*. Bobbs-Merrill, 1933.

Johnson, Gerald W., *Andrew Jackson*. Minton, Balch, 1927.

Kirk, Russell, *Randolph of Roanoke*. University of Chicago Press, 1951.

Mayo, Bernard, *Henry Clay, Spokesman of the New West*. Houghton Mifflin, 1937.

Perkins, Bradford, *The First Rapprochement: England and the United States, 1795-1805*. University of Pennsylvania Press, 1955. *Prologue to War: England and the United States, 1805-1812*. University of California Press, 1961.

Tucker, Glenn, *Poltroons and Patriots*. Bobbs-Merrill, 1954.

Van Deusen, Glyndon G., *The Life of Henry Clay*. Little, Brown, 1937.

Wiltse, Charles M., *John C. Calhoun* (Vol. I). Bobbs-Merrill, 1944.

DOMESTIC AND FOREIGN PROBLEMS (CHAPTERS 6, 7)

Bemis, Samuel Flagg, *John Quincy Adams and the Foundations of American Foreign Policy*. Alfred A. Knopf, 1949. *John Quincy Adams and the Union*. Alfred A. Knopf, 1956.

Cresson, William P., *James Monroe*. University of North Carolina Press, 1946.

Dangerfield, George, *The Era of Good Feelings*. Harcourt, Brace & World, 1952.

Dodd, William E., *The Cotton Kingdom*. Yale University Press, 1919.

Dunbar, Seymour, *History of Travel in America*. Tudor, 1937.

Eaton, Clement, *The Growth of Southern Civilization, 1790-1860*. Harper & Row, 1961.

Elkins, Stanley M., *Slavery: A Problem in American Institutional and Intellectual Life*. University of Chicago Press, 1959.

Filler, Louis, *The Crusade Against Slavery, 1830-1860*. Harper & Row, 1960.

Hurd, Charles, *The White House: A Biography*. Harper & Row, 1940.

Kirkland, Edward Chase, *Men, Cities, and Transportation* (Vol. I). Harvard University Press, 1948.

Litwack, Leon, *North of Slavery*. University of Chicago Press, 1961.

Olmsted, Frederick Law, *The Cotton Kingdom*, ed. by Arthur M. Schlesinger. Alfred A. Knopf, 1953.

Payne, Robert, *Canal Builders*. Macmillan, 1959.

Perkins, Dexter, *A History of the Monroe Doctrine*. Little, Brown, 1955.

Phillips, Ulrich B., *American Negro Slavery*. Peter Smith, 1952.

Stampp, Kenneth, *The Peculiar Institution*. Alfred A. Knopf, 1956.

*Stover, John F., *American Railroads*. University of Chicago Press, 1961.

Sydnor, Charles, *The Development of Southern Sectionalism, 1819-1848*. Louisiana State University Press, 1948.

Taylor, George, *The Transportation Revolution*. Holt, Rinehart & Winston, 1951.

ACKNOWLEDGMENTS

The editors of this book are particularly indebted to the following persons and institutions for their assistance: Eric L. McKitrick, Associate Professor, Columbia University; Dr. James J. Heslin and Paul Bride, New-York Historical Society; Albert K. Baragwanath and Henrietta Beal, Museum of the City of New York; Lillian Green, Metropolitan Museum of Art; Lewis Stark, New York Public Library; William Davidson and Elizabeth Clare, Knoedler Galleries; George Schriever, Kennedy Galleries Inc.; Dorothea Shipley, Old Print Shop, Inc.; Carl Stange, Library of Congress; R. N. Williams II, Historical Society of Pennsylvania; James A. Bear and Pearl L. Tilman, Thomas Jefferson Memorial Foundation; Richard B. Harrington, Anne S. K. Brown Military Collection; Dean A. Fales Jr. and Huldah M. Smith, Essex Institute; M. V. Brewington, Peabody Museum; Alonzo Lansford; Joseph B. Zywicki, Chicago Historical Society; and Judy Higgins.

The author, for her part, wishes to thank three of her colleagues at Fairleigh Dickinson University—Professor and Mrs. John Dollar and Dr. Kenneth MacKenzie—for their many valuable criticisms and suggestions in the preparation of the manuscript of *The Growing Years*. She also extends her appreciation for the assistance given her by Clifford Beebee, Stephen F. Cohen, Albert E. Elwell, Alice Grundman, Kathleen Hoagland, Louise Kirscher, Olga Podtiaguine, Henry Poleti, and her parents, Mr. and Mrs. Archa W. Coit.

PICTURE CREDITS

The sources for the illustrations in this book are shown below. Credits for pictures from left to right are separated by semicolons, top to bottom by dashes. Sources have been abbreviated as follows: Bettmann—The Bettmann Archive; Brown—Brown Brothers; Culver—Culver Pictures; LC—Library of Congress; Metropolitan—The Metropolitan Museum of Art, New York, N.Y.; N-YHS—The New-York Historical Society, New York, N.Y.; NYPL—The New York Public Library; N.Y. State Hist. Assn.—New York State Historical Association, Cooperstown, N.Y.

Cover—Courtesy of the Boston Athenaeum, on loan to Museum of Fine Arts, Boston.

End papers drawn by Thomas Vroman.

CHAPTER 1: 6—Owned by Davenport West Jr., courtesy American Heritage Publishing Co., Inc. 8 through 11—Bettmann. 12—No credit—Brown. 13—Bettmann. 14, 15—Bettmann except bottom right, N.Y. State Hist. Assn. 16, 17—N.Y. State Hist. Assn.; Culver. 18—Courtesy of the Maryland Historical Society. 19—N.Y. State Hist. Assn.—NYPL. 20, 21—NYPL; courtesy of the Boston Athenaeum, on loan to Museum of Fine Arts, Boston. 22, 23—Herbert Orth, from the Collections of The Historical Society of Pennsylvania; Herbert Orth, courtesy Prints Div., NYPL. 24, 25—Eric Schaal, courtesy Metropolitan, Rogers Fund, 1942. 26, 27—Courtesy The Peale Museum, Baltimore, gift of Mrs. Harry White; Herbert Orth, courtesy of the Pennsylvania Academy of The Fine Arts. 28, 29—Herbert Orth, courtesy N.Y. State Hist. Assn.; Eric Schaal, NYPL—Herbert Orth; Herbert Orth, courtesy The Phelps Stokes Collection, Prints Div., NYPL. 30, 31—The Historical Society of Pennsylvania, courtesy American Heritage Publishing Co., Inc.

CHAPTER 2: 32—Leonard McCombe, Adams National Historic Site, Department of the Interior, National Park Service. 34—NYPL—from *Report of The Commission on The Renovation of The Executive Mansion.* 35—Culver. 36, 37—Bettmann. 38—The Library Co. of Philadelphia. 39—Culver. 40, 41—U.S. Department of Commerce, Geodetic Survey; Culver—LC; Herbert Orth. 42, 43—Colt's Patent Fire Arms Manufacturing Co., Inc.; N. R. Farbman, owned by Philip S. Dalton, San Francisco, Calif. 44, 45—Eric Schaal, Essex Institute, Salem, Mass., except top right, courtesy of Peabody Museum of Salem and American Heritage Publishing Co., Inc. 46, 47—Eric Schaal, courtesy of Peabody Museum of Salem except bottom left, Eric Schaal, courtesy Mrs. James B. Drinker. 48, 49—Eric Schaal, courtesy N-YHS; courtesy Museum of The City of New York. 50—Courtesy Argosy Gallery, New York, N.Y., and American Heritage Publishing Co., Inc. 51—Prints Div., NYPL—courtesy the Worcester Art Museum. 52, 53—Museum of The City of New York.

CHAPTER 3: 54—Eric Schaal, courtesy Peabody Institute of the city of Baltimore. 56—Courtesy The Huntington Library, San Marino, Calif. 57—Bettmann. 58, 59—N.Y. State Hist. Assn.; NYPL—Bettmann. 61—Culver. 62, 63—Bettmann; Culver. 64—LC; courtesy The Historical Society of Pennsylvania. 65 through 75—Eric Schaal, courtesy the Thomas Jefferson Memorial Foundation, Inc. (bottom page 72, china courtesy Tiffany & Co.).

CHAPTER 4: 76—Robert S. Crandall, courtesy Bowdoin College Museum of Art, Walker Art Building, Brunswick, Maine. 78, 79—Culver; NYPL. 80, 81—After a print in the *Analectic Mag.* (1815), vii, 329, engraved by Strickland from a drawing by St. Memin; Bettmann. 82, 83—Culver; Bettmann—Herbert Orth, courtesy of Yale University Library. 84, 85—Culver except top right, Ralph Morse. 86, 87—Henry B. Beville, courtesy LC; Herbert Orth, courtesy Yale University Art Gallery, Mabel Brady Garvan Collection. 88, 89—Courtesy Montana Historical Society; De Venny-Wood Studio, courtesy Missouri Historical Society, St. Louis—Herbert Orth,

courtesy of Yale University Library. 90, 91—Eliot Elisofon, courtesy Gilcrease Institute, Tulsa, Okla., except bottom left, Herbert Orth, courtesy of Yale University Library. 92, 93—The Knoedler Galleries, New York, courtesy American Heritage Publishing Co., Inc.; Fernand Bourges, The Knoedler Galleries, New York—Herbert Orth, courtesy of Yale University Library. 94, 95—Henry H. Baskerville, The Knoedler Galleries, New York.

CHAPTER 5: 96—The portrait of William Henry Harrison, by Rembrandt Peale, is published with the consent of its present owner, Eli Lilly of Indianapolis. 98, 99—Bettmann except right, Herbert Orth, detail from kerchief in N-YHS. 101—Top Culver. 102—Bettmann. 104, 105—The Library Co. of Philadelphia—Bettmann; Francis Miller. 106, 107—Culver; Bettmann. 108, 109—Courtesy of the Maryland Historical Society; courtesy U. S. Naval Academy Museum and American Heritage Publishing Co., Inc. 110, 111—Courtesy American Heritage Publishing Co., Inc. 112, 113—Henry B. Beville, courtesy Prints and Photographs Div., LC; Walter A. Curtin, The Royal Ontario Museum, Toronto, Canada—Harry Shaw Newman. The Old Print Shop, Inc., N.Y.C., courtesy American Heritage Publishing Co., Inc. 114, 115—Collection of Irving S. Olds, courtesy American Heritage Publishing Co., Inc. 116—Courtesy of Trustees of National Maritime Museum, Greenwich, England and American Heritage Publishing Co., Inc.—Anne S. K. Brown Military Collection. 117—The Star Spangled Banner Flag House Association, Inc., Baltimore 2, Md. 118, 119—Herbert Orth, courtesy Smithsonian Institution—Yale University Art Gallery, Mabel Brady Garvan Collection, courtesy American Heritage Publishing Co., Inc.

CHAPTER 6: 120—Courtesy Chicago Historical Society. 122—N-YHS—Bettmann. 124, 125—Culver; N-YHS. 126, 127—Bettmann. 128, 129—NYPL, Schomburg Collection. 130—Bettmann. 131—NYPL. 132—Courtesy LC—Culver. 133—NYPL. 134—Kennedy Galleries, New York; Bradley Smith. 136, 137—From the original in The Louisiana State Museum, New Orleans, La., courtesy American Heritage Publishing Co., Inc.; The J. B. Speed Art Museum. 138, 139—Courtesy Museum of The City of New York—courtesy American Heritage Publishing Co., Inc.; Harry Shaw Newman, The Old Print Shop, Inc.; New York, N.Y. 140, 141—Courtesy of Boston Public Library; Fernand Bourges, Preston Player Collection, Knox College Library—courtesy Georgia Historical Society, Savannah. 142, 143—Eric Schaal, Kennedy Galleries, New York.

CHAPTER 7: 144—Courtesy Metropolitan, bequest of Seth Low, 1929. 146, 147—Bettmann; NYPL. 148, 149, 150—Bettmann. 151—Bettmann except bottom Culver. 152—Bettmann—N.Y. State Hist. Assn. 153—Bettmann. 154, 155—Culver; Bettmann. 156, 157—Courtesy American Antiquarian Society, Worcester, Mass.; Fernand Bourges, courtesy Suffolk Museum at Stony Brook, L. I., Melville Collection. 158, 159—Eric Schaal, NYPL; Culver—Eric Schaal, N-YHS. 160, 161—Walter A. Curtin, courtesy Radio Times Hulton Picture Library; N.Y. State Hist. Assn., courtesy American Heritage Publishing Co., Inc. 162, 163—Eric Schaal, NYPL—Eric Schaal, courtesy Metropolitan, Rogers Fund, 1942. 164, 165—Eric Schaal, Kennedy Galleries, New York—N-YHS. 166, 167—Fernand Bourges, courtesy Arthur Ziern.

Back cover—Bettmann.

INDEX

*This symbol in front of a page number indicates a photograph or painting of the subject mentioned.

Abolition movement, 123, 124, 129-133
Adams, Abigail, *14, 19, 33, 39
Adams, John: Vice President, 7, 11; President, 19, 34; characterization and career, 33-34; and Hamilton, 33, 40-41; Jefferson on, 34; political beliefs of, 34, 56-57; maintains peace with France, 34-36; resists plans for conquest of Spanish territories, 35, 83; attacks on, 36; and Alien and Sedition Acts, 36-37; Cabinet of, 40; defeated in 1800 elections, 41; appointment of "midnight judges," 60; death of, 71, 154; desk of, *32; home of, *34; quoted, 26, 81; mentioned, 9, 12, 150
Adams, John Quincy, 33; peace commissioner, 104, *119; and Missouri Compromise, 123; Secretary of State, 145, 149, 150; background and career, 150; initiator of Monroe Doctrine, 150; treaty with Russia, 151; presidential candidate (1824), 152; relations with Clay, 152-153; alleged deal with Clay, 153; President, 153, 155; domestic program of, 153-154; 1828 election campaign, 154-155; quoted, 122, 145
Agriculture. See Cotton; Sugar cane
Alabama, 62, 125, 136; Indian land cessions, 106; statehood, 121; legal protection of slaves, 126
Alaska, Russia in, 150, 151
Albany, N.Y., 146, 159
Alert, H.M.S., 101
Alexander I, Czar, 150, *151
Alexandria, Va., surrender of, 103
Algiers, and Barbary Coast wars, *map* 60, 62-63
Alien and Sedition Acts, 36-37, 38
Allen, Ethan, 37
Alton, Ill., proslavery mob, 130, *131
Amendments to the Constitution: Bill of Rights, 11; 11th, 38-39; 12th, 41
American Fur Company, 95
American Institute of New York, 52
American Liberty League, 58
American Philosophical Society, 23
"American System," 147-148, 152, 155
Ames, Fisher, 35
Anabaptists, *25
Architecture, Federal, *29, *44-45, 77, 82
Arkansas, slave territory, *map* 123
Arkwright, Richard, 51
Arts, 26
Assiniboin Indians, *90
Assumption bill, state debts, 13, 14
Astrea, the, 42
Attorney General, office of, 10

Bache, Benjamin Franklin, 36, 37
Baltimore, 50; British bombardment of, 104, 116, *117, 118
Baltimore & Ohio Railroad, *164, 165
Bangor, Me., surrender of, 103
Bank of the United States, 11, *29; first, 13-14; futile attempts for re-establishment, 104; second, 147, 148
Barbary Coast wars, *map* 60, *61, 62-63
Barron, Commodore Samuel, 60
Bayard, James H., 41
Beaver Dams, battle at, 102
Beecher, Henry Ward, 130
Benton, Thomas Hart, 146, 151, *152
Beverly, Mass., 63
Bill of Rights, 11, 37
Black Hawk, Chief, *90
Black Hawk War, 90
Blackfoot Indians, *90, 92
Bladensburg, Md., battle at, 103, 116
Blennerhassett, Harman, 84
Bodmer, Karl, 90
Bolívar, Simón, *150, 151
Boone, Daniel, 146
Boston, 8, 62, 63; port, 42, *43; and slavery issue, 130, 132
Boston Associates, 51
Boston *Weekly Messenger*, cartoon, *58
Bound servants, 8
British Columbia border issue, 105
British Royal Navy, in War of 1812, 100-105, 106, 108, *109, *112-115, 116
Brown, John, 130
Brown, Moses, 51
Bryan, William Jennings, 58
Bryant, William Cullen, 130
Buffalo, N.Y., 147, 159
Bulfinch, Charles, 29
Burr, Aaron, *41, 82; senator, 12; Vice President, 41, 61, 83; duel with Hamilton, 81-82, *85; plans for western empire, 83-84; trial of, 84-85; mentioned, 9, 155

Calhoun, John C., *98, 147, 152; "War Hawk," 98-99; and "American System," 148, 155; Vice President, 155; turns states' righter, 155; quoted, 102, 104, 126, 132, 148
Callender, James T., 37
Camden and Amboy Railroad, *164-165
Canada: desire for annexation of, 98, 100; attempts at invasion of, *map* 100-101, 102, *112, *113
Canadian-U.S. border issue, 105
Canals, 156, 165; Erie, 147, *158-159; federal aid for, 147, 148
Canning, George, 150
Canterbury, Conn., discrimination case, 132
Canton, China, 44, *46-47

Cape Cod, British raid on, 103
Carnes, Jonathan, 44
Champlain, Lake, battle of, *map* 101, 105, *112-113, 118
Channing, William Ellery, 126, 130
Charles, William, cartoon by, *104
Charleston, S.C., 15, 16, 130, 141
Chase, Samuel, *36, 37, 61-62
Cherokee Indians, 8, 84
Chesapeake, U.S.S., 98
Chesapeake Bay, British forces in, 103, 116
Child labor, 51, *127
Chile, independent, 149
China trade, 42, 44, *46-47, 80
Chisholm vs. Georgia, 38-39
Chrysler's Farm, battle at, *map* 100-101, 102
Church, Colonel John B., 85
Circuit courts, U.S., 11; Sedition Act trials, 37
Cities: Eastern, 8, *20-31, *43-45, *48-49; manufacturing, 42, *50-51; Western, *86, *166-167; Southern, *140-141
Civil rights, 11; and Sedition Act, 37
Claiborne, Governor William, 107
Clark, George Rogers, 59, 79
Clark, William, 69, 79-81, *82, 86, *88-89; journal of, *89
Clay, Henry, *101; background and career, 98; speaker, 98, 122, 123, 124; "War Hawk," 98-99, 107; peace commissioner, 104; saves Missouri Compromise, 124; "American System" of, 147-148, 152; envisages Pan-American alliance, 148, 149, 151; presidential candidate, 152; Secretary of State, 153; quoted, 99, 148
Clermont, S.S., 78, 160, 162
Clinton, DeWitt, 123, *159
Clinton, George, 16
Cockburn, Admiral Sir George, 104, *116
Cohens vs. Virginia, 149
Colleges and universities, 23
Colombia, independent, 149, 151
Colonization societies, 129
Colorado, exploration of, 85
Colt revolver, diagram of, *42
Columbia River, 79, 80-81
Columbus, Northwest Territory, 146
Commerce. See Trade
Confederation, 9, 11
Congress: first U.S., 7, 10; authorizes organization of executive branch, 10; establishment of procedures and precedents, 11; pay of members, 12; and debt-assumption bill, 13; and Jay Treaty, 18; voids French treaties, 35; interparty brawl, *37; voiding of laws of, by Supreme Court, 60-61; votes money for trading posts, 79; "War Hawks" in, 98-99; war vote of 1812, 99-100; and Missouri Compromise, 121-124;

recognition of independent South American nations, 149; and Panama conference, 151. See *also* Legislation
Connecticut, 8, 59; requirements for holding office, 56; at Hartford Convention, 107; discrimination case and "Black Law," 132
Constitution, U.S.S., 35
Constitution: provisions for executive departments, 10; presidential powers, 11-12; strict *vs.* loose construction, 13-14, 79; nullification issue, 38, 107; paramount law, 60; provision for convictions for treason, 85; and federal aid for internal improvements, 148; Supreme Court interpretations, 148-149. See *also* Amendments
Constitution, U.S.S., 100, 101, *109
Constitutional Convention, 9
Cooper, Thomas, 37
Cotton agriculture, 125, *134, *138-139; production figures, 125, 134; exports, 134; regions, 136
Cotton belt, 141
Cotton gin, 125, 134, *138
Cotton mills, *50-51
Courts. See Circuit courts; Judiciary; Supreme Court
Crandall, Prudence, 132
Crawford, William H., *152
Creek Indians, 105-106
Crockett, Davy, 79, 105
Cuba, 151
Culture, 8, 77-78; Philadelphia as center of, 20, 23, 24, 26
Cumberland, Md., 146
Cumberland Road, 146, 147, 152
Cumberland Valley, settling of, 8
Currency, 11, 42; "fog money," 147
Custis, George Washington Parke, 103

Dartmouth College case, 149
Dauphin Turnpike, 146-147
Davie, William R., 36
Dearborn, Major General Henry, 100
Debt, public. See Finance
Debts, private: owed to British subjects, 18; 1819 depression debts, 152
Decatur, Stephen, Jr., 60, *61, 63, 101, 104
Decatur, Stephen, Sr., 35
Delaware, 59
Delaware, U.S.S., 35
Delaware River, *22-23, 160
Democratic Republicans (later Democrats), 154-155
Derby, Elias, *45
Derna, Tripoli, attack on, *map* 60
Detroit, surrender of (1812), *map* 100, 102, *106
Discrimination: religious, 56; racial, 131-132

East Coast, in War of 1812, *map* 103; British blockade, 102, 103;

LIST OF MAPS FOUND IN THIS VOLUME

All maps by Rafael Palacios

The American navy on the Barbary Coast   60
The war in the North: victory on the lakes 100-101
War in the East: the battle of the coast   103
Missouri Compromise: the U.S. sundered   123

British raids, 103, 104, *108, 116
Eastport, Me., British landing at, 103
Eaton, William, 60
Economy: Northern, 42, 122; increase of commercial independence, 53; effect of trade restrictions and embargo, 63, 99; Southern plantation, 122, 125-126, 134, 141; 1819 depression, 147, 152; Adams' program, 153-154. *See also* Finance; Industry; Shipping; Trade
Elections, *57; 1802 and 1803 Republican gains, 59. *See also* Franchise; Presidential elections
Ellsworth, Oliver, 36
Emancipation: reversion of trend in South, 124-125, 133; in North, 124, 129; pamphlets, 130
Embargo Act, 57, 63, 97, 107
Emerson, Ralph Waldo, 130
English influences: lingering, 8; waning, 99
"Era of good feelings," 152
Erie, Lake, battle of, *map* 100, 101, 113, *114-115
Erie Canal, 147, *158-159
Essex, U.S.S., 100
Europe: of Napoleonic era, 62, 63, 99; Holy Alliance, 150
Excise taxes, 11, 16
Executive departments, 10

Fallen Timbers, battle of, 14
Fame, the, launching, *44-45
Faws, Abraham, 18
Federal aid, 58, 147-148, 153
Federalist, the, 59
Federalist party: emergence of, 18; Adams-Hamilton antagonism, 33, 40; hurt by Jay Treaty, 34; urges war with France, 35; and Alien and Sedition Acts, 36, 37; split, 36, 40-41; in 1800 elections, 39-41; election losses (1802-1804), 59-60; and Embargo Act, 63; and Louisiana Purchase, 79; demise of, 152
Ferdinand VII, King of Spain, 150, *151
Finance: Hamilton's program, 11; amount of national and state debts, 12; domestic-debt certificates, 12-13; debt-funding and assumption bill, 13, 14; Jefferson and Gallatin policies, 58, 147; federal aid for domestic improvements, 58, 147-148, 153; War of 1812, 104, 108; postwar problems, 147, 152. *See also* Currency; National Bank; Tariff; Taxation

Fitch, John, 8, 160
Flatboat, 147, 162, *163
Flathead Indians, *88-89
Florida: plans for conquest of, 35, 83, 98; Jefferson tries to buy, 62, 78, 149; seizure of, 149; slave territory, *map* 123
Florida treaty, 149
Floyd, Charles, 81
Foreign affairs: Washington's French policy and declaration of neutrality, 15-16; his Farewell Address warning, 19, 150; Adams' French policy, 34-36; Jefferson's peace policy, 62, 63; Barbary Coast wars, 62-63; trade sanctions against Britain and France, 63, 97; Monroe Doctrine, 150-151. *See also* Treaties; War of 1812
Fort Laramie, *93
Fort McHenry, attack on, 116, *117
Fort McKenzie, *90
Fort Mims Indian massacre, 105
Fort Pitt, 8
Fort Ross, Russian foundry at, 150, 151
Fort Wayne, 98
Fox Indians, 90
France: U.S. debt to, 12, 16; relations with, in wake of her Revolution, 15-16; at war with Britain, 17, 63; raids on American shipping, 34, 62, 63, 97; "XYZ Affair," 35; undeclared naval war against (1798-1800), 35; Treaty of Morfontaine (1800), 36; Louisiana ceded to by Spain, 62, 78; purchase of Louisiana from, 78; interference in South America, 150
Franchise, 56, 131
Francis I, Emperor of Austria, 150, *151
Franklin, Benjamin, 23, 36
Frederick William III, King of Prussia, 150, *151
Frémont, John C., 83
French Revolution, 15, 16
Frontier: way of life, 8, 77-78; pro-Republican, 39; prowar, 98. *See also* Indians; Settlers; West
Fulton, Robert, 78, 160, *161
Fur trade, 17, 79, 92, *93-95; British, 79, 80

Gallatin, Albert, 58, *59, 104
Gambier, Lord, *119
Garrison, William Lloyd, 127, 129-130, 132
Gass, Patrick, 81, 82
Genesee Road, 146
Genêt, Citizen Edmond, 15-16
George, Henry, 58

George III, King, 63
Georgia, 125; in *Chisholm vs. Georgia*, 38-39; Indian raids, 62, 149; Indian land cessions, 106
Gerry, Elbridge, 34-35, *58
"Gerrymander," cartoon, *58
Ghent, Treaty of, 105, 118, 119
Gibbons vs. Ogden, 149
Government, federal: executive departments (1789), 10; powers of, strict *vs.* loose construction dispute, 14; early threats to authority of, 16-17, 38; aid for internal improvements, 58, 147-148, 153; authority strengthened by Supreme Court, 148-149. *See also* Congress; Judiciary; President, office of
Government, local, *10
Gray, Robert, 79
Great Britain, 42, 125, 134, 149; at war with France, 17, 63; instigation of Indian attacks, 14, 17, 98, 111; harassment of U.S. shipping, 17, 18, 62, 63, 97; impressment of American seamen, 17, 18, 62, 97; Jay Treaty with, 17-18; effect of U.S. trade restrictions, 97; relations before War of 1812, 97-99; War of 1812, 100-119; initial peace terms, 104; Treaty of Ghent with, 105, 118, 119; imports to U.S., 147, *149; proposes joint stand against European interference, 150
Great Lakes, fight for control of, in War of 1812, *map* 100-101, 108, 113
Green River trappers' rendezvous, 94-95
Greene, Nathanael, 141
Griswold, Roger, *37
Gros Ventre Indians, *88
Grosvenor, Thomas P., 98
Grundy, Felix, 99
Guerrière, H.M.S., 100, *109

Haiti, 151; liberation, 129
Hamilton, Alexander, *13; background and characterization of, 10, 82; political philosophy of, 10-11, 15; *vs.* Jefferson, 10-11, 15, 18; Secretary of the Treasury, 10; fiscal program, 11; and payment of war debt, 12-13; and Bank of the United States, 13-14; loose constructionist, 14, 15; and Jay Treaty, 16, 18; and Whiskey Rebellion, 17; in Reynolds affair, 18-19; Federalist leader, 18, 40; and Adams, 33, 40-41; urges war with France, 35, 36, 40; urges conquest of Spanish territories, 35, 83; on nullification, 38; law practice, 40, 81; in Jefferson-Burr election tie, 41; duel and death of, 81-82, *85; quoted, 10, 13, 33, 36, 41, 57; mentioned, 9, 12, 29
Hamilton, Elizabeth, *14, 19, 82
Hamilton, Philip, 85
Hammond, James, 128
Hampton, Va., British raid on, 103
Hardy, Admiral Thomas, 103
Harris, Sarah, 132
Harrison, William Henry, *96; in battle of Tippecanoe, 98, 110-111;

in War of 1812, 102, 106, 113
Harrison Land Act (1800), 78
Hartford Convention, 107
Havre de Grace, Md., British raid on, 103, *108
Hayne, Robert, 151
Henry, Patrick, 9
Hoban, James, 18
Holmes, Oliver Wendell, 130
Holy Alliance, 150; members, *151
Hornet, U.S.S., 101
Horseshoe Bend, battle of, 105-106
House of Representatives, 11; and Jay Treaty, 18; Missouri Compromise debate, 121-123; chamber, 122; and emancipation question, 124
Houston, Sam, 105, 106
Hudson River, 49; steamboats on, 160, *162-163
Hull, General William, 100, 102, *106

Illinois, 146; settling of, 78; statehood, 121; limits entry of free Negroes, 131
"Implied powers," 14
Impressment of American seamen, 17, 18, 62, 97, 105
Independence, Mo., *86
Independence Hall, *23, *27
Indiana: Indian warfare, 14, 98, *110-111; settling of, 78; limits entry of free Negroes, 131
Indians: frontier warfare, 8, 14, 98, *110-111; incited by British, 14, 17, 92, 98, 111; in Georgia, 62, 149; trade with, 79, *93; Western Plains, *88, *90-91, *93; theft of lands of, 90, 125; in War of 1812, 102, 105-106, 111, *112, 113. *See also* separate tribes
Industrial Revolution, 125
Industry: at end of Revolution, 42; expansion of, 42, 51, 52-53; assembly-line production, 42; textile, *50-51, 125; products, 53; Southern, 125; working conditions, *127, 131; postwar plight and protective tariff, 147; government backing for, 152
Internal improvements: Gallatin-Jefferson policy, 58, 148; Clay's program, 147-148; Adams' support for, 153
Irving, Washington, 102
Isolationism, 151

Jackson, Andrew, 58, 84, *107; in War of 1812, 105-107, 119; statue, *140; seizure of Florida, 149; presidential candidate (1824), 152-153; 1828 election campaign, 154-155; cartoon, *154; President, 130, 155; quoted, 99
Jackson, Rachel, *155
Jarvis, John Wesley, 63
Java, H.M.S., 101, 102
Jay, John, 9, 11, 17-18
Jay Treaty (1794), 9, 17-18, 34; public demonstrations against, *16
Jefferson, Martha, 66, 69
Jefferson, Thomas, *12, *54, *64; envoy to France, 10, 62, 74; Secretary of State, 10, 15, 62; *vs.* Hamilton, 10-11, 15, 18; political philosophy of, 11, 15, 56-57; and

debt-assumption bill, 13; and National Bank bill, 13-14; strict constructionist, 14, 57; and Genêt episode, 16; White House design of, *18; leader of Republicans, 18; First Inaugural Address, 19, 55-56; on Adams, 34; presidential candidate in 1796, 34; Vice President, 34; and Sedition Act, 37-38; author of Kentucky Resolutions, 38; cartoons on, *38; elected President, 41; background, 56; characterization, 57-58; adaptable in methods for achieving goals, 57, 58, 79; appraisal of first term, 58, 59; cabinet of, 58-59; re-election, 59-60; war on judiciary, 60-62; peace policy, 62, 63; and Barbary States, 62, 63; Embargo Act, 57, 63, 97, 107; and Monticello, 64, 66, 68-75; interests and talents, 64, 69, 72, 73; gravestone design, *64; furniture designs, *70-71; correspondence, 71; and West, 78, 83; Louisiana Purchase, 78-79; and Lewis and Clark expedition, 79, 80, 81; Burr "conspiracy," 84-85; on Missouri Compromise, 123, 133; internal improvements program, 148; on European interference, 150; and 1824 elections, 152; death, 71, 154; quoted, 10, 13, 37-38, 56, 57, 113, 145, 159; mentioned, 9, 82, 86, 128, 145
Jefferson plow, *66
Jews, discrimination against, 56
Johnson, Richard Mentor, 112
Judicial review, power of, 60-61, 148-149
Judiciary: federal courts, 11; Adams' "midnight judges," 60; Jefferson's war on, 60-62. *See also* Circuit courts; Supreme Court
Judiciary Act (1789), 11, 60
Judiciary Act (1801), 60

Kentucky, 146; statehood, 7; Indian raids, 8; farming, 125; horse racing, *136-137
Kentucky Resolutions, 38, 107
Key, Francis Scott, 98, 104, *117
Knox, Henry, 7, 9, 10, *12
Krimmel, J. L., painting by, *30-31

Labor: of Northeast, pro-Republican, 39; shortage of skilled, 42; child, 51, *127; unemployment, 63, 147; slave, demand for, 125, 143; Negro competition to white, 129, 131; Northern mill conditions, 131
Lafayette, Marquis de, 9, 128
Lafitte, Jean, 106, *107
Lamartine, Alphonse de, 131
Lancaster Turnpike, 23, 146
Land: acquisition by settlers, 78, 147; taken from Indians, 90, 125; Adams' program for use of public, 153-154
Latrobe, Benjamin, 31
Law: Constitution paramount, 60; slavery provisions, 126, 127, 128. *See also* Legislation
Lawrence, Captain James, 115
Lawrence, U.S.S., 101, *114-115

Lee, Henry, 39
Legislation, federal: Bill of Rights, 11; Judiciary Act (1789), 11, 60; early fiscal, 11, 13; Alien and Sedition Acts, 36-37, 38; Judiciary Act (1801), 60; Embargo Act (1807), 63, 97; nonintercourse, 1809-1810, 97; protective tariff, 147
L'Enfant, Pierre, 39, *40
Leopard, H.M.S., 97
Lewis, Meriwether, 69, 79, *80, 81, 82, 85, 86, *88-89
Lewis and Clark expedition, 68-69, 79-80, *81, *82-83, 86, *88-89, 90
Liberator, abolitionist paper, 129, 132
Liberia, 129
Life, way of: Southern, 8, 126; in Northeast and East, 8, 77-78; of Western settlers, 8, 77-78; Philadelphia, *20, *24-25, *28
Lincoln, Abraham, 129, 130, 131
L'Insurgente, 35
Livingston, Robert, 59, *78, 160
Longfellow, Henry Wadsworth, 130
"Loose constructionists," 14, 79
Louis XVIII, King of France, 150
Louisiana: plans for conquest of, 35, 83; ceded to France by Spain, 62, 78; exploration of Territory, 79-81, 89; slavery borderline through Territory, *map* 123; sugar cane economy, *124, 125, 134, *136; cotton, 136; Spanish claims renounced, 149
Louisiana Purchase, 78-79, 86, 98, 125
L'Ouverture, Toussaint, *129
Lovejoy, Elijah, 130, 131
Lovejoy, Owen, 131
Lowell, Francis, 51
Lowell, Mass., cotton mills, *51
Lowndes, William, 125
Lundy's Lane, battle of, *map* 100, 102
Lyon, Matthew, *37
Lyon, Pat, *21

McCulloch vs. Maryland, 148
Macdonough, Captain Thomas, 105, 112
Macedonian, H.M.S., 99, 101
McHenry, James, *39, 40
Madison, Dolley, 98, *102, 103, 104, 107, 146
Madison, James, *76; in Congress, 11, 13; and National Bank bill, 13; author of Virginia Resolutions, 38; characterization of, 58-59; Secretary of State, 58, 59; in *Marbury vs. Madison*, 60-61; as President, 97, 98, 99; during attack on Washington, D.C., 103, 104; cartoons, *63, *116; and federal aid, 148, 153; quoted, 16, 78, 99; mentioned, 58, 98, 102, 145
Maine: British invasion of, 103; statehood, 122
Manhattan, *48-49
Manufacture. *See* Industry
Marbury vs. Madison, 60-61
Marshall, John, 55, 62, *148; envoy to France, 34-35; establishes power of judicial review for Supreme Court, 60-61, 148-

149; in Burr trial, 84-85; upholds federal law over states' rights, 148-149; mentioned, 36, 133, 155
Marshall, Thomas, 133
Maryland, 131; franchise, 56; British invasion of, 103, 116; in *McCulloch vs. Maryland*, 148
Mashuda, the, defeat of, *map* 60
Massachusetts, 8; franchise, 56; at Hartford Convention, 107
Maximilian, Prince, expedition of, *88, 90, *92-93
May, Samuel J., 132
Mexico, 122; Pike in, 85; independent, 149
Michigan: settling of, 78; free territory, *map* 123
"Midnight judges," 60
Militia: in Whiskey Rebellion, 17; in War of 1812, 102, 103, *113, 116
Mississippi, 62; plans for separate confederacy, 83; cotton, 136
Mississippi River: importance of, 78, 167; search for source of, 85; trade, *140-141; travel, 160, 162, *166-167
Missouri, 146; applies for statehood, 121; admitted as slave state, *map* 123, 124; state constitution, 124
Missouri Compromise, 122; *map* 123, 132; congressional debate, 121-123, 124
Missouri River: trading posts, 79; search for source of, 79-80; transportation, 167
Molineaux, Tom, *130
Money. *See* Currency; Finance
Monroe, Elizabeth, *146
Monroe, James, *144; envoy to France, 34, 78; Secretary of War, 106; and Missouri Compromise, 123; characterization of, 145; background and career, 145-146; and federal aid, 148, 153; and seizure of Florida, 149; popularity of, 151-152; "era of good feelings," 152; mentioned, 13, 18, 19
Monroe Doctrine, 150-151
Montana, exploration of, 81, 89
Monticello, 64, *65-75, 154
Morfontaine, Treaty of (1800), 36
Morgan, Daniel, 17
Morocco, and Barbary Coast wars, *map* 60, 62-63
Morris, Gouverneur, 39, *41
Mount Pleasant, Ohio, 147
Muhlenberg, Frederick A., *9, 11
Mulattoes, 128
Murray, William Vans, 36

Napoleon Bonaparte, 36, 63, 78, 97, 99, 103; mentioned, 59, 62, 84, 106, 116
Napoleonic Wars, 62, 63, 78, 97, 99, 108
Nashville, 141
National Anthem, 104, 105, 117
National Bank. *See* Bank of the United States
"National Pike," 146
National Republicans (Whigs), 154

Nationalism, rise of, 98
Naturalization Act (1798), 36, 38
Naval Chronicle, London, 102
Navy Department, 35
Negroes, free: franchise, 56, 131; states' limitations on entry of, 124, 131; kidnaping of, 125, *126; status in South America, 128; and colonization (deportation) efforts, 129, 133; competition to white labor, 129, 131; Northern discrimination, 131-132; Southern fear of, 133, 151
Nelson, Admiral Horatio, 103, 106
Netherlands, U.S. debt to, 12
Neutrality: 1793 declaration of, 16; Adams' policy, 34-36; Jefferson's policy, 62, 63; scorned by War Hawks, 99
New England: way of life, 8; town meetings, *10, 132; commerce and industry, 42, *44-45, 46, *50-51, 125, *127, 134; effect of trade restrictions, 63, 99, 107; opposes war with Britain, 98, 99; Hartford Convention, 107. *See also* Northeast
New Hampshire: franchise, 56; requirements for holding office, 56; at Hartford Convention, 107
New Jersey, 9; franchise, 56, *57, 131; requirements for holding office, 56; slavery in, 124
New Mexico, 146
New Orleans, 134, *140-141, 162; purchase, 78; battle of, 106-107, *118-119; slave trade, 124, 143
New York: absent in 1789 presidential election, 7; slavery in, 124, 128; transportation, 146, 147, 159, 160, 167
New York City, 16, 50, 103; first U.S. capital, 7, 20; rise as port, 42, *48-49; trade fairs in, *52-53; abolitionist vs. proslavery elements, 123, 130
New York *Evening Post*, *63
Newburyport, Mass., 62, 129
Niagara, U.S.S., 101, *114-115
Niagara River, attempted crossing of (1812), *map* 100, 102, *113
Nicholson, John, 61
North: and Missouri issue, 121-124, 132-133; economy compared to South, 122; and slavery problem, 123, 124, 129-131, 133; history of slavery in, 124; competition of free Negroes with white labor, 129, 131; fear of Southern secession, 130; labor conditions, *127, 131; racial segregation, 131-132. *See also* New England; Northeast
North Carolina: late ratification of Constitution, 7; franchise, 56
Northeast: pro-Republican city laborers, 39; growth of cities, 42, *44-45, *48-49; and Embargo Act, 63; and Louisiana Purchase, 79; population (1820), 146. *See also* New England
Northwest Ordinance, 78, 124
Northwest Passage, search for, 89
Northwest Territory, 146; holdover British posts in, 17; population growth, 77; settling of,

77-78; slavery prohibited in, 124
Notes on Virginia, Randolph, 133
Nullification doctrine: Kentucky and Virginia Resolutions, 38; Hartford Convention, 107

Ohio: settling of, 8, 78; Indian raids, 14; population in 1800, 77
Ohio River travel, 147, *163
"Old Ironsides," 100, *109
Olmsted, Frederick Law, 127
Oregon, 79, 86; Clark's claim, 81; U.S.-British joint occupancy, 105, *map* 123; free territory, 123
Oregon Trail, 95
Osgood, Samuel, 10

Pacific: search for overland water route to, 79, 80, 89; Russian claims, 150, 151
Paine, Thomas, 59
Pakenham, Major General Sir Edward, 106, 118
Panama Congress (1826), 151
Paragon, S.S., *162-163
Parker, Theodore, 130
Party system, political: emergence of, 18, 39; Washington warns against, 19; firmly established, 39-40. *See also* Democratic Republicans; Federalist party; Republican party; Whig party
Pawtucket, R.I., cotton mill, *50, 51
Peacock, H.M.S., 101
Peale, Charles Willson, 26, *27
Peale, Rembrandt, painting by, *54
Penn, William, 20, 22
Pennsylvania, 38, 146; Whiskey Rebellion, 16, *17; franchise, 131
Pennsylvania Academy of Fine Arts, 26
Pensacola, battle of, 106
Perry, Captain Oliver Hazard, 100, 101, 113, *114-115
Peru, independent, 149, 151
Philadelphia, 9, 16, *20-23, *28-31, 50, 146; second U.S. capital, 14, 20; yellow fever epidemics, 14-15, 25; population growth, 20, 30; cultural center, 20, 23, 24, 26; economic center, 20, 22, 49; life in, *20, *24-25, *28; expansion of, 23, 30; abolitionist *vs.* proslavery elements, 123, 129, 130; Negroes of, 129, 131
Philadelphia *Aurora*, 36
Phillips, Wendell, 130
Pickering, John, 61
Pickering, Timothy, 36, *39, 40
Pike, Zebulon, *83, 85
Pinckney, Charles Cotesworth, 34-35, 41, 60
Piracy, 62; Barbary Coast, *map* 60, *61, 62-63
Pittsburgh, 17
Plantation economy, Southern, 122, 125-126, 134, 141. *See also* Cotton; Sugar cane
Plattsburg, battle of, *map* 101, 105, *112-113, 118
Plumer, William, Jr., 124
Politics. *See* Party system
Polk, James K., 151
Population: in 1790, 8; Northwest

Territory, 77; slaves, 125, 134; cotton belt, 141; 1820 census, 146; increase 1790-1850, 156
Ports, *22, 42, *43-45, *48-49, *140-141, *166-167
Postmaster General, office of, 10
Preble, Commodore Edward, 60
President, U.S.S., *map* 103, 104
President, office of: prestige, 9; powers, 11-12; title, 12
Presidential elections: of 1789, 7; of 1796, 34; of 1800, 41; voting before and after 12th Amendment, 41; of 1804, 59-60; of 1824, 152-153; 1828 campaign, 154-155
Prince, John, 44
Privateers, American, in War of 1812, 102, 108, 116
Property tax, 38
Put-in-Bay, battle. *See* Erie, Lake

Quakers, 23, *25, 29
Queenston, battle of, *map* 100, 102, *113
Quincy, Josiah, Jr., 8, *104

Railroads, 156, 160, *164-165
Randolph, Edmund, 9, 10, *13
Randolph, John, 13, 59, *98, 153; plea for peace, 99; and slavery issue, 123, 131, 133
Randolph, Thomas Jefferson, 133
Redemptioners, 8
Religious discrimination, 56
Republican (later Democratic) party: emergence of, 18; opposes war with France, 35; and Sedition Act, 37-38; policies of, 39; in 1800 elections, 41; election successes from 1802 to 1804, 59-60; embraces Federalist methods and principles, 79, 152; factional disputes, 152; split of, 154-155
Residence Act, 20
Revere, Paul, 100
Reynolds, James, and Mrs., 19
Rhode Island: late ratification of Constitution, 7; paper money, 42; at Hartford Convention, 107
Richmond, 84; slave trade, *120, *142-143
Richmond *Examiner*, 37
Roads, 23, 77, 85, 146-147, 156; federal aid for, 147, 148
Rocky Mountains, 89, *92, 93
Rodgers, Commodore John, 60
Roman Catholics, discrimination against, 56
Roosevelt, Franklin D., 58
Ross, General Robert, 116
Russia: mediation attempt (1812), 104; North American claims of, 150; treaty with (1824), 151

Sacagawea, 80, *81, *88-89
St. Clair, General Arthur, 14, *15
St. Louis, 79, 81, 130, *166-167
Salem, Mass., 42, *44-45, 50, 62
San Martín, José de, *150
Santa Fe, 85, 167; Trail, 146
Santo Domingo, 125, 129
Sauk Indians, 90
Savannah, *140-141
Sciences, 26, 80
Scott, Winfield, 102

Secession threats: Northeast, over Embargo, 63; Northeast, over Louisiana Purchase, 79; Southern, over slave problem, 130
Sectionalism: pro-Republican elements, 39; war party against neutralists, 98-100, 108; in Republican party, 152; Western grievances, 152. *See also* New England; North; Northeast; Secession threats; Slavery; South
Sedition Act (1798), 37, 38; trials, 37, 61
Segregation, racial, 131-132
Seminole Indians, 149
Senate, 11, 12, 122; and Jay Treaty, 18; impeachment votes, 61-62
Sequoyah, *84
Settlers: Northwest Territory, 77-78; housing, 77, 147; cartoon of, *79; westward move of, 146-147. *See also* Frontier; West
Shawnee Indians, *110-111
Shipping, 42, *44-45, 147; British harassment of, 17, 62, 63, 97; French harassment of, 34, 62, 63, 97; transatlantic, 49; piracy, 62; Mediterranean, 62-63; number of American ships seized by European belligerents (1803-1812), 63; 1807 Embargo, 63. *See also* Waterways
Shoshoni Indians, 80, 81, 89
Sioux Indians, *90-91, *93
Slater, Samuel, 50, 51
Slave trade, *120, 124, 125, *132, *142-143, 151; notice, *125; transatlantic trip, shiploading diagram, *133
Slavery, 8, 121, 134; Missouri Compromise, 122, *map* 123; basis of plantation economy, 122, 125-126; Northern attitudes, 123, 124, 129-131, 133; as social institution, 126; universal public opinion of, 127; in South America, 128. *See also* Abolition movement; Emancipation; Slaves
Slaves, *120, *124, *134, *138-140; question of British compensation for removal of, 18; federal tax on, 38; population figures, 125, 134; demand for, 125, 143; legal status and provisions, 126, 127, 128; life of, 126-127; death rate, 126; attitude of owners, 127-128, 131; concubinage, 128; fight for freedom, 129, *132, 133; runaway, 130-131, 149; prices for, 143. *See also* Negroes, free; Slavery
Snake Indians, *90-91
Societies for the Encouragement of Domestic Manufactures, 53
South: way of life, 8, 126, *136-137; pro-Republican planters, 39; effect of restriction of British trade, 99; and Missouri issue, 121-122, 132-133; economy of, 122, 125-126, 134, 141; slavery background, 124-125; emancipation movement, 124-125, 129, 133; colonization (slave emigration) societies, 129, 133; fear of free Negroes, 133, 151; mansions,

*135; population, 141, 146. *See also* Slavery; Slaves
South America: Negroes in, 128; liberation of Spanish colonies, 149-150, 151; plan for confederation, 151
South Carolina, 58; franchise, 56; requirements for holding office, 56; slave trade, 125
Spain: U.S. debt to, 12; plans for conquest of American territories of, 35, 83; relations under Jefferson, and efforts to buy Florida from, 62, 78; Florida treaty with, 149; South American colonies of, 149-150, 151
Sports: cockfighting, 8, *11; boxing, *130; horse racing, 8, *136-137
Stagecoach, 146, *156, 167; similarity of early rail coaches to, *164-165
"Star-Spangled Banner," 104, 105, 117
State Department, organized, 10
States: in first presidential election, 7; ratify Bill of Rights, 11; Revolutionary War debts of, 12-13; in 1804 presidential elections, 59; way of admission of new, 79; Northeastern *vs.* new, 79; balance of free *vs.* slave, 121, 122, *map* 123; interstate commerce freed from state legislation, 149
States' rights: Jefferson's doctrine, 14, 38, 57, 58; nullification doctrine, 38, 107; assertion by 11th Amendment, 38-39; weakened by Supreme Court, 148-149
Steamboat, 8, 147, 156, 160, *162-167
Stonington, Conn., raid on, 103
Stony Creek, battle at, 102
"Strict constructionists," 14, 78, 85
Stuart, Gilbert, 9; paintings by, 103, *145
Sugar cane agriculture, *124, 125, 134; refinery, *136
Supreme Court of the U.S.: role at beginning, 11; and Whiskey Rebellion, 17; no jurisdiction in original suits of individuals against states, 39; power of judicial review; 60-61, 148-149; upholds federal law over states' rights, 148-149; right of appeal to, 149
Supreme Court decisions: *Chisholm vs. Georgia*, 38-39; *Marbury vs. Madison*, 60-61; *McCulloch vs. Maryland*, 148; *Dartmouth College vs. Woodward*, 149; *Cohens vs. Virginia*, 149; *Gibbons vs. Ogden*, 149

Talleyrand, 34-35, 40, *62
Tallmadge, James, 121, *122
Tariff: of 1790, 11; protective, 147, 148; struggle over, 155
Taxation: first tariff, 11; whiskey tax, 11, 16; property tax, 38; slave tax, 38; War of 1812, 104
Tecumseh, Chief, 98, 102, 110-111; death of, *112, 113
Tennessee, farming in, 125, 136

Tennessee *Gazette*, 77
Territorial organization: Northwest Territory, 78; Missouri Compromise, *map* 123
Texas: slave state, 123; cotton, 136; U.S. claims renounced, 149
Textile industry, *50-51, 125
Thames, battle of the, *map* 100, 102, *112, 113
Thomas, Jesse, *122, 123
Thoreau, Henry, 130
Tidewater region, 8, 134, 141; soil depletion, 125, 136
Tippecanoe, battle of, 98, *110-111
Tocqueville, Alexis de, 131
Trade, 42, 44; transatlantic, 17-18, 42, 46, *49; China, 42, 44, *46-47, 80; effect of Napoleonic Wars on, 62, 63, 97; Barbary Coast, 62-63; Embargo, 63, 107; with Indians, 79, *93; nonintercourse legislation, 97; Southern, 141; postwar British imports, 147, *149; interstate, Supreme Court ruling, 149. *See also* Cotton; Fur trade; Shipping; Slave trade; Tariff
Trade fair, New York, *52-53
Trading posts, frontier, 79
Transportation, 146-147, 156; prices, 147, 159. *See also* Canals; Flatboat; Railroads; Roads; Stagecoach; Steamboat; Waterways
Trappers, 86, *87, *92, 93, *94-95
Treasury, organized, 10, 18
Treaties: Jay (1794), 17-18; of Morfontaine (1800), 36; Louisiana Purchase, 78-79; of Ghent, 105, 118, 119; Florida, 149; with Russia (1824), 151
Tripoli, and Barbary Coast wars, *map* 60, *61, 62-63
Trist, Nicholas, 154
Truth, Sojourner, *128, 129
Tubman, Harriet, 131
Tunis, and Barbary Coast wars, *map* 60, 62-63
Turner, Nat, *132, 133

Underground Railroad, 130-131
Unemployment, 63, 147
United States, U.S.S., 99, 101
University of Pennsylvania, 23
U.S. Army: standing (1789), 8; enlarged by Federalists, 35; reduced by Jefferson, 58; strength in 1812, 100; performance in War of 1812, 102, 103, 113; Republican acceptance of need for larger, 152
U.S. Navy: in Barbary Coast wars, *map* 60, *61, 63; strength and quality of (1812), 100, 109; in War of 1812, 100-102, 105, *109, *112-115; Republican acceptance of need for larger, 152

Vandalia, Ill., 146
Van Rensselaer, Major General Stephen, 100, 102
Vermont: independent republic, 7; requirements for holding office, 56; at Hartford Convention, 107
Virginia, 56, 146; way of life, 8; and debt-assumption bill, 13; slave insurrection, and debate in legislature, *132, 133
Virginia "dynasty," 107, 154
Virginia Resolutions, 38, 107
Voyages and Travels of a Corps of Discovery, Gass, etchings from, *82-83

Wabash Valley Indian attacks, 14
Waltham, Mass., cotton mill, 51
War Department, 10
"War Hawks," 98-99
War of 1812: background, 97-99, 108; congressional vote, 99-100; U.S. strategy, 100; British planning, 100; attempted invasion of Canada, *map* 100-101, 102, *112, *113; naval encounters, *map* 100-101, 102, *map* 103, 105, *109, *112-115; Indians in, 102, 105-106, 111, *112, 113; American privateers, 102, 108,

116; blockade of U.S. ports, 102, 103; militia, 102, 103; *113, 116; British raids along East Coast, *map* 103, 104, *108, 116; finances, 104, 108; Russian mediation offer, 104; peace negotiations, 104-105, 118; failure of British invasion from Canada, 105, 113; peace treaty, 105, 118, 119; Jackson's Southern campaign, 105-107, *118-119; appraisal, 107, 108; casualties, 108; war theaters, 108; economic effects, 147
Washington, George: feelings on office of President, 7-8, 12; first inauguration and Address, *8, 10; characterization, 9; affection shown to, on tours, 9, 12; Cabinet of, 10, *12-13, 15, 40; various presidential acts, 11, 12; and National Bank bill, 13, 14; and Genêt episode, 15-16; and Whiskey Rebellion, 17; and Jay Treaty, 17-18; public disenchantment with, in wake of Jay Treaty, 18, 19, 36; retirement and Farewell Address, 19; warns against permanent alliances, 19, 150; nonpartisan, 19, 39; appraisal of Administration of, 19; designated commanding general against France, 35; death of, 39; mourning for, *29, 39; quoted, 19, 145; mentioned, 20, 26, 28, 34, 36, 62, 145, 147
Washington, Martha, 103
Washington, D.C.: move of government to, 14, 30, 39; original city plan, *map* 40; in 1811, 98; British burning of, 103-104, *116; slave trade, *132; in 1817, 146, *147
Washington *Federalist*, 41
Waterways: importance of Mississippi, 78; in cotton belt, 141; travel, 147, 156, *162-163, 165, *166-167. *See also* Canals; Flatboat; Steamboat
Wayne, General Anthony, 14, *15

Webster, Daniel, 107, 147, 149, 152, 154
Webster, Noah, 8, *19
Wellington, Duke of, 105, 106
West: settling of, 8, 77-78, 85, 93, 147; population growth, 77, 146; Lewis and Clark expedition, 79-81, *82-83, 86, *88-89, 90; Burr "conspiracy," 83-84; Pike's expeditions, 85; misconceptions of, 86, 89; Indians of, *88, *90-91, 92, *93; transportation, 146-147, 156, 167; sectionalism, 152. *See also* Frontier; Fur trade; Northwest Territory; Settlers; Territorial organization
West Indies, trade with, 42
West Point, 8
Wheeling, 147
Whig party, 154
Whiskey Rebellion (1794), 16, *17
Whiskey tax, 11, 16
White House: design competition, *18; Adams' blessing for, *34; under Adams, 39; under Jefferson, 59; burned by British, 104, 146; under Monroe, 146; in 1817, *147; origin of name, 147
Whitney, Eli, 125, 134
Whittier, John Greenleaf, 130
Wilderness Road, 146
Wilkinson, Major General James, 83-84, 85
Wilson, Woodrow, 58
Wisconsin, settling of, 78
Wolcott, Oliver, *39, 40
Women, vote in New Jersey, 56, *57
Wordsworth, William, 129
Wyoming, 94

XYZ Affair," 35

Yankees, 8
York (now Toronto), burned by Americans, 116

PRODUCTION STAFF FOR TIME INCORPORATED

Arthur R. Murphy Jr. (Vice President and Director of Production)
Robert E. Foy, James P. Menton and Caroline Ferri
Text photocomposed under the direction of Albert J. Dunn and Arthur J. Dunn

✕

Printed by The Safran Printing Company, Detroit, Michigan
Bound by Rand McNally & Company, Hammond, Indiana
Paper by The Mead Corporation, Dayton, Ohio